A Practical Guide
To Behavioral Research

Tools and Techniques

SECOND EDITION

Robert Sommer
and Barbara B. Sommer

New York   Oxford
Oxford University Press
1986

Oxford University Press

Oxford   New York   Toronto
Delhi   Bombay   Calcutta   Madras   Karachi
Petaling Jaya   Singapore   Hong Kong   Tokyo
Nairobi   Dar es Salaam   Cape Town
Melbourne   Auckland

and associated companies in
Beirut   Berlin   Ibadan   Nicosia

Published by Oxford University Press, Inc.
200 Madison Avenue, New York, New York 10016

Oxford is a registered trademark of Oxford University Press.

Library of Congress Cataloging-in-Publication Data
Sommer, Robert.
A practical guide to behavioral research.
Bibliography: p.   Includes indexes.
1. Social sciences—Research. 2. Social sciences—Methodology.
3. Psychology—Research. 4. Social sciences—Research—Data processing.
I. Sommer, Barbara Baker, 1938–   . II. Title.
H62.S724734   1986   150′.72   85-18874
ISBN 0-19-503977-7
ISBN 0-19-503978-5 (pbk.)

Printing (last digit): 9 8 7 6 5 4 3 2 1
Printed in the United States of America
on acid-free paper

Preface

This book emphasizes a hands-on, multimethod, and interdisciplinary approach to behavioral research. It was motivated by our experiences as college teachers. We were surprised to find students graduating in the social sciences and related fields who had never conducted an interview, made systematic observations of behavior, run an experiment, or performed a content analysis of written material. Most of the students knew about these techniques and could give good verbal definitions of them, but they had never used them. It was as if they had read about a microscope without ever having looked into one. Most behavioral research techniques can be tried out in a research methods course or on one's own. Experience in using a technique is invaluable for learning about it as well as its limitations.

The multimethod approach assumes that several methods are better than one in shedding light on an issue. Research is defined in its broadest sense to encompass laboratory and field experimentation, interviews and participant observation, and case studies, as well as other specialized information-gathering procedures. Examples come from many different fields. The assumption is made that research on complex issues requires an interdisciplinary approach. While individual researchers may operate within the bounds of a single field, they must understand the special contributions that people in other disciplines can make.

Five years have elapsed since we wrote the first edition of this book. The interval has been characterized by rapid advances in statistical analysis but less so in method. The basic techniques for collecting behavioral science data—observation, experimentation, interviews, and questionnaires—have not radically changed during the past 5 years. However, the advent of the computer age has brought complex experimental designs and survey procedures within reach of students. All this poses a danger to the beginning researcher. The cardinal rule in any data analysis is GIGO—garbage in, garbage out. There is nothing in the computer or any other statistical tool that will substitute for sound technique in collecting data.

The basic structure of the first edition has been left intact. The emphasis remains on a hands-on approach to research. There is a new chapter on calculators and computers, new material on mail surveys, video as a research tool, qualitative research, and analysis of variance. The format for technical articles has been revised in accord with the current style manual of the American Psychological Association. Chapter 20, "Writing the Report," has an added section on reports that do not follow journal style. These reports are useful for disseminating research results to potential

v

users of the information unlikely to read technical journals. Chapter 21, "After the Report," provides guidelines and techniques for other means of disseminating research findings. A glossary of key terms and definitions has been added at the end of the book.

The book is suitable for students in research methods courses and for nonstudents who wish for a clear guide to conducting behavioral studies. These techniques are too important to be left in the hands of a small group of specialists. The long-run interests of a democratic society will be served by the widest possible understanding and acceptance of behavioral research methods.

We are deeply indebted to those students who read and evaluated the manuscript and the first edition, whose comments helped remove ambiguous phrases, jargon, and the occasional error. Valuable comments were received from a number of colleagues, including David Kenny, Richard Rasor, David E. Anderson, and Alan Maxwell.

Carol Van Alstine provided valuable secretarial help. We are grateful to the literary executor of the late Sir Ronald A. Fisher, to Dr. Frank Yates, and to Longmans Group, Ltd., London, for permission to reprint several tables from their book *Statistical Tables for Biological, Agricultural, and Medical Research* (6th ed., 1974).

Davis, Calif.   R.S.
April 1985   B.B.S.

Contents

Appendix A

Appendix B

Appendix C

I
Introduction to Research

1 Multimethod Approach

What Is Behavioral Research?

Behavioral research is everybody's business. It is difficult to imagine an occupation in which systematic information about human behavior is not relevant. Forest rangers are increasingly concerned about vandalism, arson, and litter in wilderness areas. NASA wants to know how groups of astronauts will react during space flights to distant planets. Food processors are concerned about the public response to new products. The lives of all of us have been touched, directly or indirectly, by the procedures and results of behavioral research.

There is an important difference between thinking about human behavior and doing research. Research is careful, patient, and methodical inquiry done according to certain rules. It is not simply an exchange of views among friends, colleagues, or experts. Anyone whose job depends on information about what people do or want should know how to obtain that information in a valid and systematic manner. Specifically, they should know to interview, construct a questionnaire, observe natural behavior, and conduct an experiment.

Even professions whose primary concerns are with machines must take account of human behavior. What is the most efficient way to arrange letters on a typewriter keyboard? What is the best way to arrange the instrument dials in a jet aircraft to minimize risks of confusion and error? The answers to such questions will be based, to some degree, on the results of behavioral studies. However, not all questions are behavioral. A comparison of the gas consumption of two types of engines is an engineering problem. Yet at some point that question will have behavioral aspects, perhaps in terms of the noise level of the two engines. Behavioral research cannot answer nonbehavioral questions. Whether adultery is good or evil is a moral and not a behavioral question. The interpretation of a court decision is a legal question. Such questions have behavioral implications, but the researcher must realize what parts of them are behavioral and what parts are not.

This book emphasizes systematic methods for gathering information. Visual inspection of a shopping mall is better than nothing, but a systematic observational study over a period of time will yield information that is more accurate and believable, and probably more useful. The game warden who believes that fluorescent blue or yellow would be more suitable than orange for hunting jackets under conditions of poor visibility could question several hunters on the issue. A better approach would be to do an experiment to determine the appearance of each color under different degrees of illumination. The range of questions that can be examined using the methods of behavioral research is enormous. It is the task of the researcher to set priorities for the questions to be asked, as well as to identify the best methods to be used.

Why Do Behavioral Research?

The two most common reasons for doing behavioral studies are (1) to obtain answers to pressing questions and (2) to contribute to theories of human behavior. Providing answers to pressing questions is called *applied research*. It is motivated primarily by the need to solve an immediate problem. One type of applied research that is receiving increasing attention is *program evaluation*. This involves determining the effectiveness of a program. Some government agencies now require evaluation to accompany all new projects. This has created the need for researchers who can adapt themselves to the politically charged and hurried world of legislation, government budgets, and bureaucratic jargon. Program evaluation must be done quickly or else it is useless. There is a growing recognition that evaluation, when done properly, can help to guide legislative action.

Investigations designed to answer general long-range questions about human behavior are considered *basic research* and are motivated largely by the researcher's curiosity. In practice, the division between applied and basic studies is far from clear. Most behavioral research arises from a combination of attempts to answer specific questions and the researcher's curiosity. A third category of behavioral studies, which may include your own interests, is *instrumental research*. This includes studies done as training exercises as or as part of a job assignment. Many people doing behavioral research for industry, the military, or government agencies work on prob-

BOX 1-1. Four Types of Research Studies

Basic research: Seeks answers to long-range questions. Motivated primarily by curiosity.

Applied research: Seeks practical answers to immediate questions. Goal is to obtain usable information.

Instrumental research: Undertaken as an academic, vocational, or professional requirement. Goal is to demonstrate competence in research.

Action research: Combines the testing of theory with application.

lems chosen by others. Some students become intrigued with research done as part of a class project and continue work on it afterward.

Social psychologist Kurt Lewin (1946) pioneered *action research* as a means by which behavioral scientists could contribute simultaneously to theory and practice. Lewin and his associates used this approach in communities attempting to reduce racial prejudice. The programs to change attitudes became experiments to be evaluated and revised before they were implemented elsewhere. Action research involves the potential users of the information in doing the research. Lewin believed that this participation of the potential users of the information reduces the gulf between research and application. Other reasons for doing action research are to increase people's involvement in an issue or problem, to develop a constituency for change, to reduce the distance between researchers and the public, to base program changes on sound information (the fruits of research) rather than guesses, to test theories of human behavior in natural settings, and to provide feedback to researchers on the utility of their work.

Not every study needs to be earthshaking. Sometimes a small investigation that answers only a single question is all that is needed. Susan Cross (1960), an occupational therapist in a mental hospital, found that many craft materials were unsuitable for older people with poor eyesight and coordination. Cross did a brief survey among elderly women about the problems they had in knitting. Among other things, she found that dull colors made knitting more difficult. She recommended that bright colors were preferable to dull ones for the elderly. This advice was followed in future purchases of craft materials. Although it was not a profound recommendation, it more than justified the small amount of time and effort invested in the survey.

Knowledge Is Connected

An introduction to research techniques would be easier if the methods and disciplines could be kept separate. This is not realistic; there is often a thin, blurred line between one procedure and the next. Constructing a questionnaire will involve interviews. An interview study will be preceded by observations to find out the questions to be asked. Interviews are scored using a method known as content analysis. Academic disciplines cannot be kept separate either. A sociologist undertaking participant observation among teenage youth will have more in common with anthropologists than with other sociologists who analyze census records. The psychologist observing children in a nursery may feel more kinship with zoologists than with laboratory-based experimental psychologists. It is important for students interested in human behavior to learn a variety of techniques. This will not only help them choose the best methods for a project but will also be indispensible for understanding relevant studies from other disciplines. To understand why people act as they do, one cannot view their actions solely in psychological terms, economic terms, or historical terms. Knowledge will be more thorough and accurate when it includes ideas and findings from many different sources.

An interdisciplinary approach is essential for research on complex problems. A small study of only one aspect of a problem, such as the relationship between airplane engine types and the amount of noise, might involve only a mechanical engineer and an acoustical consultant, but a larger study on airport noise might include an engineer, architect, physician or public health worker, and a behavioral scientist. Team members must avoid the jargon of individual specialties and develop a shared language. Each single investigation must be integrated into the larger effort and timetable.

Practical Experience

Specific techniques can be learned from a book. You can read the definition of a questionnaire, how it differs from an interview, and its advantages and disadvantages. To acquire skill in using the questionnaire as a research tool requires something more—experience. The difficulty in writing clear questions may not be evident yet. Thus, when you construct your first questionnaire, you are likely to make all the mistakes you have read about. Nor is it obvious how boring it is to spend an hour watching children on the playground for more than one day. Sixty minutes never seemed so long. Another thing that may not be apparent yet is the intellectual thrill of putting together a mass of data you have collected that helps to clarify a complex problem. The emotional side of research, the joy and excitement, as well as the frustration and boredom, are best learned by *doing* research. Like other skills, specific research techniques are learned most readily by following accepted procedures. After some proficiency is acquired, the student can decide when to ignore the rules.

Validity and Reliability

A major feature of good research is its *validity*. There are two general types of validity. *Internal validity* refers to whether the instruments or procedures measure what they are supposed to measure. *External validity* refers to the generalizability of the findings. Do the results extend beyond the immediate setting or situation? Research in natural settings often provides higher external validity than does research from the laboratory.

In addition to being valid, research should also be *reliable*. Reliability refers to the repeatability or replicability of findings. Instruments and procedures should produce the same results when applied to similar people in similar situations, or to the same people on a second occasion. Reliability is an important contribution to validity. However, a study can be reliable, but not be valid. For example, we might propose strength of hand grip as a measure of intelligence. We can measure hand grip with a high degree of reliability, but that does not mean we have a valid measure of intelligence. The measure lacks internal validity.

Multimethod Approach

Each technique for gathering information has its shortcomings. Experimentation is limited by artificiality, observation by unreliability, interviews by interviewer bias, and so on. There is no ideal research technique in the behavioral sciences. All methods have good and bad features. The advantages may lie along one dimension, such as economy; the disadvantages along another, such as objectivity. The goal of the researcher is not to find the single best method. For most problems, several procedures will be better than one. Even though each has its limitations, these tend not to be the same limitations. The artificiality of the laboratory can be supplemented by observation, which is high on naturalness but low on reliability; the questionnaire, which can be given to many people quickly, can be supplemented by detailed interviews with a few people to probe more deeply into significant issues. This has been described as the method of *converging operations* (Webb, Campbell, Schwartz, & Sechrest, 1966). A number of different research techniques are applied, each with somewhat different limitations and yielding somewhat different data. Conflicts between the information from different sources will sometimes occur. In one case, the letters received by a director of a veterinary hospital consisted mostly of complaints. On the other hand, interviews with pet owners bringing their animals to this same hospital showed a high level of satisfaction (Sommer & Tyburczy, 1978). There was no basic contradiction between the two sources of information. People dissatisfied with the hospital wrote letters of complaint and went elsewhere, while satisfied customers continued to visit the hospital. Both the complaints and the interviews contributed to an understanding of how the hospital worked.

Deciding on Methods

There are dozens of methods available to the behavioral researcher. Not all of these will be equally useful. Four techniques—observation, experiment, questionnaire, and interview—account for more than nine-tenths of the articles in social science journals. Some rules of thumb for selecting among these methods are presented in Box 1-2. Observation is well suited for discovering what people do in public. For private behavior, the personal diary is more appropriate. The experiment is an immensely powerful tool for deciding between alternative explanations of a phenomenon. It is less useful, however, for studying natural behavior or opinions. With opin-

---

BOX 1-2. Choosing Among Research Techniques

Problem	Approach	Research technique	Chapter
To obtain reliable information under controlled conditions	Test people in a laboratory	Laboratory experiment, simulation	6, 7
To find out how people behave in public	Watch them	Natural observation	4
To find out how people behave in private	Ask them to keep diaries	Personal documents	12
To learn what people think	Ask them	Interview, questionnaire, attitude scale	8, 9, 10
To find out where people go	Chart their movements	Behavioral mapping, trace measures	5
To identify personality traits or assess mental abilities	Administer a standardized test	Psychological testing	15
To identify trends in verbal material	Systematic tabulation	Content analysis	11
To understand an unusual event	Detailed and lengthy investigation	Case study	13

---

ions and attitudes, the questionnaire and interview are very efficient. Standardized tests are used to assess mental abilities.

In making a decision about methods, the problem comes first. What questions must be answered? The next issue involves the time and resources available. There is no point in planning an elaborate survey if there is no one to carry it out, or to prepare an observational study of a prison whose warden will not permit observers inside the walls. You may have to settle for interviews with ex-prisoners and a reading of prison diaries. Conditions are generally less than ideal in behavioral research. The subject's time is limited, certain techniques are unfeasible because of the setting or ethical considerations, and the researcher's time and budget are finite.

Researchers interested in human stress often encounter ethical problems when they conduct laboratory studies. An alternative is to seek out situations such as a hospital emergency room where stress already exists. A university during final exams would be a good source of tense individuals. Air traffic controllers represent a group for whom stress is an occupational hazard. The multimethod approach provides the option of observing stress as it occurs as well as laboratory studies with animals or human beings. The research team using several linked procedures is not putting all of its eggs into a single basket. One method can be used first, followed by another, than a third method. Information developed at each stage guides in the selection of the next procedure.

A multimethod approach is also useful in dealing with the unforeseen circumstances that arise in field research. Beginning researchers are likely to be discouraged when they go out to a shopping center and there is no one around to interview because it is too cold, windy, or because it is just an inactive period. One solution is to use such occasions to practice other data-gathering techniques. If there are no customers in the shopping center, then this may be a good opportunity to interview store employees or examine wear on carpets or linoleum, cigarette burns, graffiti, or other residues that will provide clues to usage. The experienced researcher always has several methods in reserve for occasions when the primary method cannot be employed. Making good use of unforeseen circumstances will increase the likelihood of the accidental discovery of new relationships.

Summary

Basic research aims at answering long-range questions. Applied research tries to provide solutions for immediate problems. Instrumental research is undertaken as either a training exercise or a job assignment. Action research combines the testing of theory with application.

Good research design maximizes *validity*, both internal and external, as well as *reliability*. An interdisciplinary approach is essential for research on complex social issues. For most problems, several procedures will be better than one. Even though each method has its limitations, these tend not to be the same limitations. In choosing between alternative methods, the problem comes first. The next issues to be considered are the time and resources available.

Limitations: Several small studies may lack the depth of a single lengthy investigation. It will be difficult to interpret the results when different procedures turn up conflicting information. There may not be time and resources available for more than a single study to be undertaken.

References

Cross, D. S. (1960). Color preferences of older patients. *Canadian Journal of Occupational Therapy, 27,* 9–12.
Lewin, K. (1946). Action research and minority problems. *Journal of Social Issues, 2,* 34–36.
Sommer, R., & Tyburczy, J. (1978, March). Waiting rooms: A study in user perception. *California Veterinarian, 32,* 21–23.
Webb, E. J., Campbell, D. T. Schwartz, R. D., & Sechrest, L. (1966). *Unobtrusive measures: Nonreactive research in the social sciences.* Chicago: Rand McNally.

Further Reading

Babbie, E. (1983). *The practice of social research* (3rd ed.). Belmont, CA: Wadsworth.
Rosenthal, R., & Rosnow, R. L. 91975). *Primer of methods for the behavioral sciences.* New York: Wiley.
Sussman, G., & Evered, R. (1978). An assessment of the scientific merits of action research. *Administrative Science Quarterly, 23,* 582–603.
Webb, E. J., Campbell, D. T., Schwartz, R. D., Sechrest, L., & Grove, J. B. (1981). *Nonreactive measures in the social sciences* (2nd ed.). Boston: Houghton Mifflin.
Williamson, J. B., Karp, D. A., Dalphin, J. R., & Gray, P. S. (1982). *The research craft* (2nd ed.). Boston: Little Brown.

2 Ethics in Behavioral Research

Most universities and scientific institutes require researchers to fill out special forms before they can conduct research with human beings. These forms are sent to a Committee on Research with Human Subjects, which looks them over to decide if the project should be allowed to proceed. Occasionally this committee decides that more information is needed or that greater care should be taken to protect the welfare of the respondents—and, in extreme cases, that the research is too risky and should not be undertaken. These procedures are considered necessary to protect the rights and welfare of people serving as research subjects. An example of a research approval form is presented in Box 2-1.

The need for these procedures first became apparent in medical research, where people might be exposed to dangerous drugs or radioactive materials. For legal as well as ethical reasons, procedures were needed to ensure (1) that the research plan was reviewed by a committee of competent scientists, (2) the rights and welfare of the subjects were protected, and (3) the subjects were adequately informed of the risks and benefits involved. It was not long before federal granting agencies extended these requirements to behavioral research. Several studies had gained notoriety because of the unorthodox procedures and/or the risks to unknowing participants.

Need for Outside Review

Asking an outside group to make a formal assessment of the risks of a proposed study is always desirable. A researcher can become so involved in a

BOX 2-1. Example of a Completed Human Subjects Approval Form

1. Investigator(s): Kathryn Anthony.
2. Title of research: *Personal Space and Smoking.*
3. Name and address of supporting agency or sponsor, if any: No sponsor, no outside support.
4. Period of time: September 30, 1977–March 30, 1978.
5. If radioactive materials will be used *in vivo,* list: None.
6. If investigational drugs will be involved, list generic names: None.
7. Affiliation, location, number of human subjects: Approximately 75 student volunteers from introductory psychology classes, who will receive small amounts of extra credit for their participation.
8. Students will be asked individually to enter a room and discuss a topic with an experimenter who is already there. Sometimes the experimenter will be smoking a cigarette and other times not smoking. The distance the subject stands from the experimenter will be measured. Afterward the subjects will be asked their attitudes toward the experimenter during the session and toward smokers, asked whether or not they are smokers themselves, and informed of the purposes of the experiment.
9. Potential risks, discomfort, or inconvenience: None except for a brief exposure to cigarette smoke for one-half of the subjects.
10. How will the rights and welfare of the subject be protected against the above risks? The experimental room is well ventilated, and exposure to cigarette smoke will be brief.
11. Potential benefits of this investigation for the individual subject and for society: Knowledge of the distance people space themselves from smokers can help in developing regulations for smoking in public places, and also for designing waiting rooms, work areas, and public locations to minimize inconvenience to nonsmokers.
12. Attach an informed consent document. See attachment.

project that some ethical problems are overlooked. The researcher may not be aware of all the risks involved. Even experts can disagree about the likelihood or amount of risk to participants. Some research carries hazards for society or for the researcher. The issue is whether the potential benefits are worth the risk, and the people subjected to the risk are informed of its nature and magnitude. Full disclosure can pose special problems for the behavioral researcher. To tell people the full nature of a study *in advance* can alter their actions. A common solution is to withhold information during the session and debrief the participants afterward. Some researchers will tell people that they are taking part in a psychological experiment that will not involve pain or any physical danger, and ask them for permission not to tell them about the experiment until afterward in order to obtain unbiased responses. Immediately following the session, each participant is given a printed sheet describing the purposes and methods of the study, and the experimenter is present to answer any questions.

Confidentiality and Anonymity

Two methods used by researchers to protect participants in behavioral studies are confidentiality and anonymity. *Confidentiality* means that the respondent's identity is known to the investigator but protected from public exposure. The researcher keeps any identifying information out of published reports. Confidentiality is particularly important when people's statements or actions would cause them some embarrassment if they became known. It is best for the researcher to be on the safe side regarding confidentiality, since it is difficult to predict how people's answers might be interpreted or used by others. Instead of identifying organizations or cities by name, a general description, such as "a middle-sized industrial city in the Northeast" or a fictitious name such as Yankee City or Worktown, is used instead.

The best way to ensure that the people you have interviewed or observed will not be embarrassed by your data is to remove identifying information, such as names and addresses, as soon as the data are tabulated. Some researchers use a special code at the time of the interview so that no names or other identifying information are in the researcher's files. The exact methods used to protect your respondents will vary according to the situation, but it is important to realize that behavioral researchers do not have the special right to confidential communication that the courts grant to physicians, lawyers, and the clergy.

Anonymity means that the researcher does not know the identity of the participants in the study. The best protection for people in an observational study is anonymity. It makes more sense to observe people in a public park or courtyard without knowing their names than to ask each person to sign a written consent form. Anonymity is also a useful safeguard in questionnaire and public opinion research. Most questionnaire studies do not ask people to sign their names. Often this is emphasized by telling respondents *not* to sign their names.

The ethical dilemmas in behavioral research should not be exaggerated or overdramatized. Most surveys, observational studies, and laboratory experiments pose little or no risk to the participants. Students asked to learn lists of words could be told the exact nature of the procedure, what is going to be done with the results, and so on. People whose movements are charted throughout the day would be told of the potential inconvenience of having an observer following them around. The researcher may decide to reserve information about how the results are to be used (e.g., comparing the time younger and older people spend sleeping) until the observations are concluded, but this withholding does not increase the risks to the participants, who know exactly what the researcher will be doing.

Psychologists' Code of Ethics

Professional organizations in the social sciences have developed guidelines for the ethical conduct of research with human participants. The first version of the ethical code for members of the American Psychological Association was developed in 1953, and has been revised several times on the basis of the experiences of researchers. The code for psychologists shown in Box 2-2 is accompanied by more detailed descriptions of ethical conduct for each of the 10 principles.

In carrying out your own studies, be sure to find out the procedures within your own organization, agency, or school for protecting research subjects. If you are at a university or research institution, you will probably fill out a form, such as that described at the beginning of this chapter, that will be reviewed by an official committee. *This may involve a delay of several weeks before you can begin your research.* You should plan for this delay beforehand. Don't wait until the last minute to obtain approval from an ethics committee. Filling out these forms is a valuable learning experience. You will have to answer questions that you may not have considered: How much should be told to the participants beforehand? How can the confidentiality of the completed questionnaires be maintained? Will the researcher specify the name of the institution being observed? What if the observer should observe illegal behavior? Answering these questions is a good opportunity to foresee potential problems and develop ways of handling them before they arise.

Certain schools and agencies do not require these questionnaires to be filled out. The number of such institutions is becoming smaller each year as the need for formal review and careful monitoring of human research becomes more widespread. Research done as part of class projects may be exempt from some of the more cumbersome procedures, providing the instructor takes responsibility and there is no risk to the participants. Observational research in a public place that has no risk to the participants may not require signed consent; nor will mailed questionnaires, particularly if the replies are anonymous and the respondent's freedom not to participate is clearly indicated in the instructions. Even if your specific project does not require you to fill out the human subjects questionnaire, the responsibility for maintaining ethical standards remains. You will have to develop your own procedures for protecting participants from inconvenience or risk.

BOX 2-2. Ethical Principles of the APA

Preamble

Psychologists respect the dignity and worth of the individual and strive for the preservation and protection of fundamental human rights. They are committed to increasing knowledge of human behavior and of people's understanding of themselves and others and to the utilization of such knowledge for the promotion of human welfare. While pursuing these objectives, they make every effort to protect the welfare of those who seek their services and of the research participants that may be the object of study. They use their skills only for purposes consistent with these values and do not knowingly permit their misuse by others. While demanding for themselves freedom of inquiry and communication, psychologists accept the responsibility this freedom requires: competence, objectivity in the application of skills, and concern for the best interests of clients, colleagues, students, research participants, and society. In the pursuit of these ideals, psychologists subscribe to principles in the following areas: 1. Responsibility, 2. Competence, 3. Moral and Legal Standards, 4. Public Statements, 5. Confidentiality, 6. Welfare of the Consumer, 7. Professional Relationships, 8. Assessment Techniques, 9. Research with Human Participants, and 10. Care and Use of Animals.

Acceptance of membership in the American Psychological Association commits the member to adherence to these principles.

Psychologists cooperate with duly constituted committees of the American Psychological Association, in particular, the Committee on Scientific and Professional Ethics and Conduct, by responding to inquiries promptly and completely. Members also respond promptly and completely to inquiries from duly constituted state association ethics committees and professional standards review committees.

Principle 1: Responsibility

In providing services, psychologists maintain the highest standards of their profession. They accept responsibility for the consequences of their acts and make every effort to ensure that their services are used appropriately.

Principle 2: Competence

The maintenance of high standards of competence is a responsibility shared by all psychologists in the interest of the public and the profession as a whole. Psychologists recognize the boundaries of their competence and the limitations of their techniques. They only provide services and only use techniques for which they are qualified by training and experience. In those areas in which recognized standards do not yet exist, psychologists take whatever precautions are necessary to protect the welfare of their clients. They maintain knowledge of current scientific and professional information related to the services they render.

Principle 3: Moral and Legal Standards

Psychologists' moral and ethical standards of behavior are a personal matter to the same degree as they are for any other citizen, except as these may compromise the fulfillment of their professional responsibilities or reduce the public trust in psychology and psychologists. Regarding their own behavior, psychologists are sensitive to prevailing community standards and to the possible impact that conformity to or deviation from these standards may have upon the quality of their performance as psychologists. Psychologists are also aware of the possible impact of their public behavior upon the ability of colleagues to perform their professional duties.

Principle 4: Public Statements

Public statements, announcements of services, advertising, and promotional activities of psychologists serve the purpose of helping the public make informed judgments and choices. Psychologists represent accurately and objectively their professional qualifications, affiliations, and functions, as well as those of the institutions or organizations with which they or the statements may be associated. In public statements providing psychological information or professional opinions or providing information about the availability of psychological products, publications, and services, psychologists base their statements on scientifically acceptable psychological findings and techniques with full recognition of the limits and uncertainties of such evidence.

Principle 5: Confidentiality

Psychologists have a primary obligation to respect the confidentiality of information obtained from persons in the course of their work as psychologists. They reveal such information to others only with the consent of the person or the person's legal representative, except in those unusual circumstances in which not to do so would result in clear danger to the person or to others. Where appropriate, psychologists inform their clients of the legal limits of confidentiality.

Principle 6: Welfare of the Consumer

Psychologists respect the integrity and protect the welfare of the people and groups with whom they work. When conflicts of interest arise between clients and psychologists' employing institutions, psychologists clarify the nature and direction of their loyalties and responsibilities and keep all parties informed of their commitments. Psychologists fully inform consumers as to the purpose and nature of an evaluative, treatment, educational, or training procedure, and they freely acknowledge that clients, students, or participants in research have freedom of choice with regard to participation.

Principle 7: Professional Relationships

Psychologists act with due regard for the needs, special competencies, and obligations of their colleagues in psychology and other professions. They respect the prerogatives and obligations of the institutions or organizations with which these other colleagues are associated.

Principle 8: Assessment Techniques

In the development, publication, and utilization of psychological assessment techniques, psychologists make every effort to promote the welfare and best interests of the client. They guard against the misuse of assessment results. They respect the client's right to know the results, the interpretations made, and the bases for their conclusions and recommendations. Psychologists make every effort to maintain the security of tests and other assessment techniques within limits of legal mandates. They strive to ensure the appropriate use of assessment techniques by others.

Principle 9: Research with Human Participants

The decision to undertake research rests upon a considered judgment by the individual psychologist about how best to contribute to psychological science and human welfare. Having made the decision to conduct research, the psychologist considers alternative directions in which research energies and resources might be invested. On the basis of this consideration, the psychologist carries out the investigation with respect and concern for the dignity and welfare of the people who participate and with cognizance of federal and state regulations and professional standards governing the conduct of research with human participants.

Principle 10: Care and Use of Animals

An investigator of animal behavior strives to advance understanding of basic behavioral principles and/or to contribute to the improvement of human health and welfare. In seeking these ends, the investigator ensures the welfare of animals and treats them humanely. Laws and regulations notwithstanding, an animal's immediate protection depends upon the scientist's own conscience.

Anthropologists' and Sociologists' Code of Ethics

Anthropologists who conduct their research in other nations and cultures face special problems. They must be concerned about their relationship with host governments and local people. Their actions reflect on their own government. The statement of ethics adopted by the American Anthropological Association describes the anthropologist's responsibilities in six major areas:

1. To the subjects of the study, who are the anthropologists' paramount responsibility. Their welfare, dignity, and privacy come first.

2. The public is owed a commitment to honesty and openness, and a full discussion of the meaning and implication of the research.

3. To the profession of anthropology. Researchers should maintain a level of integrity and helpfulness in the field so that by their behavior and example they will not jeopardize future research there.

4. To students. The researcher must alert students to the ethical problems in research and discourage them from participating in projects employing questionable ethical standards.

5. To the sponsors. Researchers must be honest about their qualifi-

cations, capabilities, and goals, avoiding any promises that violate professional ethics. The sponsor must be aware of the researcher's commitment to full disclosure of sources of funds, personnel, and the dissemination of research results.

6. To one's own government and to host governments. Before beginning the study, the researcher must make sure that there will be no governmental interference that compromises the ethical standards of the research.

The American Sociological Association has a code of ethics that is similar in most respects to that of the psychologists and anthropologists but places more emphasis on the proper use of research findings. The code obliges the researcher to report all sources of financial support and any special relationship to the sponsor that might affect the interpretation of the findings.

Reactions to Your Report

Problems of handling your results are often as severe as protection of your respondents. What happens if you find out that someone is not doing the job properly or that employees are dissatisfied with their working conditions? Such conclusions have economic and political implications for others and for you. Don't expect to be regarded as a hero because you have identified problems. Many administrators do not want to hear about dissatisfaction among their employees. You are very likely to encounter immediate and heated resistance. This can take the form of a denial of the severity and extent of the difficulties, sarcastic comments about the impracticality of your recommendations, and the observation that your conclusions are trivial and hardly worth mentioning—What was the point of your study anyway? A critic will seize on some small item, such as a statistical error or misprint, to dismiss the entire report. Even when 98 percent of your findings and recommendations are complimentary, obvious, and harmless, some readers will condemn the entire report on the basis of the other 2 percent that they find objectionable. Don't let this discourage you. Getting people to change long-established procedures is a delicate, difficult, and time-consuming matter. You should try to anticipate the reactions that your report is likely to produce.

Some people will convert your report into an opportunity to criticize an individual or policy that they have disliked for years. These "friends" may severely damage your report. Try to keep the integrity of your findings above local squabbles. The best impression you can create is one of a reasonable and open-minded individual who is interested in what is happening and is not overly dependent on factions within the organization. The knowledge that you are connected with an outside agency that has a tra-

BOX 2-3. Conflict Over Release of Results

A scientist-physician and a public interest physician disagreed publicly over the issue of releasing research results. The scientist, Dr. Savitri Ramcharan, came to Washington, D.C., to present the preliminary findings of her study. These findings showed a link between oral contraceptives and increased rates of cervical cancer. However, Dr. Ramcharan believes it is still too early to become alarmed. She had not, in fact, notified the estimated 15,000 women in her sample of the preliminary results.

The public interest physician—Dr. Sidney Wolf, director of Ralph Nader's Health Research Group—disagreed. Wolf believed that the tentative findings are sufficiently important to alert women and physicians everywhere to the risks of taking the pill.

The basic conflict was over the release of preliminary research results. Should data be made public before the findings are conclusive? "It should always be made public," Dr. Wolf declared. "If the data are good—and hers are—they state that there is an increased amount of cancer among the group of women taking the pill, it is the worse form of paternalism to withhold this information." On the other hand, to release the preliminary results might jeopardize the study itself by provoking an exodus from the pill as well as causing undue alarm if the preliminary results do not hold up. ("A quarrel," 1978)

dition for impartial research can help convince others of your commitment to objective inquiry.

One solution to the problem of tentative results, which doesn't deal with the long-range implications, is for researchers to refrain from presenting results in any public forum until they are definitive. In practical terms, however, legislators and others making policy decisions want to have the best information available even if it is incomplete.

Summary

Most universities and research institutions have committees to review the ethical aspects of behavioral studies. Two major concerns are protecting the rights and welfare of human subjects and seeing that the subjects are adequately informed about the risks and benefits of their participation. Professional organizations of social scientists have developed guidelines for the ethical conduct of behavioral research.

Two methods used to protect participants in behavioral studies are confidentiality and anonymity. Confidentiality means that the respondent's identity, while known to the investigator, is protected from public exposure. Anonymity means that the researcher does not know the identity of the participants in the study.

Limitations: Ethical guidelines phrased in general terms are often difficult to apply in specific instances. It is also difficult to specify in advance all the ethical problems that might arise in the course of the study. Committees charged with protecting the rights and welfare of research subjects may be inflexible in interpreting rules and policies and thus discourage valuable and necessary research. On the other hand, committees may be unfamiliar with the risks in frontier areas of research and allow studies which expose people to unwarranted risks.

Reference

A quarrel over releasing pill data. (1978, May 23). *Sacramento Bee,* p. A4.

Further Reading

American Anthropological Association. (1973). *Professional ethics: statements and procedures.* Washington, D.C.: American Anthropological Association.

American Psychological Association. (1981). Ethical principles of psychologists (revised). *American Psychologist, 36,* 633–638.

American Sociological Association. (1984). *Code of ethics.* Washington, DC: Author.

Diener, E., & Crandall, R. (1978). *Ethics in social and behavioral research.* Chicago & London: University of Chicago Press.

Schuler, H. (1982). *Ethical problems in psychological research* (M. S. Woodruff & R. A. Wicklund, Trans.). New York: Academic Press.

3 How to Do a Literature Review

Science is an accumulative enterprise; each researcher builds on what has been done before. Finding out about previous work is called *reviewing the literature.* There is an excitement to following the thread of scientific inquiry—like reading a detective story in which the reader is asked, on the last page of the book, to join in the search for the crucial clue that will solve the mystery.

Networking

There is not one source of information on a topic, but many. A textbook in the area of your interest is a good place to start the search. The two places to look first are the table of contents in the front and the index in the back. Check any relevant sections and note down the names of pertinent references. If this is a one-time project, you can write these titles in a notebook. The notebook is better than cards, which are likely to become lost. If you intend to pursue the topic further, you can list relevant references on 3 × 5 cards and file them according to the author's last name.

A basic strategy of information gathering is called *networking.* A single source can supply certain bits of information *and* point you toward other relevant sources. Each source becomes a springboard to other sources. When all the names and titles that you encounter begin to look familiar, then you have come close to a good overview of the area. Your information on a topic will never be complete. Although it is desirable to learn as much as you can before the study, there will always be new bits of information coming in while the project is underway.

Using the Library

Set aside a specific time for visiting the library. Let us assume that your study concerns the use of parks and open spaces. Here are some of the steps in a beginning literature review:

1. Check the card catalog under subject headings. *Example:* Literature Review of Parks and Open Space. Try *parks, open space, recreation, landscape,* and *wilderness.* Check the names of specific parks. Briefly skim over the cards. Most of the titles will *not* be pertinent to your interests. Skip over these quickly to find the few that are. Copy down the call numbers, authors, and titles. Notice if the call numbers seem to cluster.

The most efficient guide to subject headings in the card catalog of a university or college library is the two-volume Library of Congress listing. These are very large volumes that are generally conspicuously placed in the card catalog area. These volumes will also provide other topic headings that might be relevant to your interest.

2. Check the library shelves around the call numbers that were mentioned most often in the card catalog. Librarians tend to place books on a topic close together. You are likely to find titles that were missed in the catalog search.

3. Visit the Reference Room to find out what is available. There may be specific reference works on parks and recreation. Look at copies of *Psychological Abstracts* and *Sociological Abstracts* under the heading of parks and recreation. Articles published during the current year will probably not have been abstracted yet.

If you have identified one or more key individuals who have done work on the topic, look under their names in one of the relevant Abstract volumes and in the *Social Science Citation Index.* The latter index covers most social science journals and is available both on computer and in bound volumes. For example, if you know that a key article on parks and recreation relevant to your own study was written by Mary B. Davidson and published in the 1980 volume of the journal, *Environment and Behavior,* consult the bound volume of the *Social Science Citation Index* covering articles published since 1980. Since the bound index covers 5-year intervals, this will be the 1981–85 volume. Under the author's name, you will find a list of researchers whose articles have cited her work, not only the article that interests you, but all her publications. This will also be an opportunity to locate additional articles published by Mary Davidson. There is no guarantee that these will deal with the topic that interests you, but it is likely that some of her other publications will be on the same topic. The index will indicate other researchers by name, journal, volume, page, and year. The abbreviated journal listings are defined in the index volume. In the example on page 23, PSYCHOS MED is *Psychosomatic Medicine,* J PERS SOC is *Journal of Personality and Social Psychology,* etc.

The most important information resource in the Reference Room is not

			VOL	PG	YR
DAVIDSON MB					
76 PSYCHOS MED	34	263			
GOLD R	J PERS SOC		34	99	76
NEIL ML	PSYCHOS MED		33	1014	78
80 ENV BEH	17	31			
MILLER B	YOUTH SOC		4	5	78
RUSH V	CAN J PSY		25	57	80

found on the shelves but is sitting at a desk waiting to assist you. The reference librarian is a trained professional whose job is to help people gain access to information. Don't just ask and run; explain your needs in detail. There are many ways in which a librarian can help.

Sourcebooks are available, often listed as "Guides to sources of information in education (psychology) (sociology) (political science, etc.)." These sourcebooks are probably indexed in the card catalog under the subject matter heading or may be found in the reference area of the library.

4. Next stop is the Periodical Room. It houses current issues of journals, magazines, and newspapers. There are scientific journals that cover virtually every field of knowledge imaginable. You will have noticed some of them cited in the reference books you examined. Current issues are likely to be found on open shelves in the Periodical Room. Earlier (noncurrent) issues may be housed separately by subject area in another part of the library. Start looking through the tables of contents of the journals that were mentioned most often. Remember that you are not looking for dozens of relevant articles but a few.

5. Government documents are probably not listed in the card catalog. They will be kept in a special documents section with its own librarian, who can locate the relevant reports. Some that are not in the library can be ordered from the Government Printing Office in Washington, D.C., or the state printing office for a nominal charge. Documents can also be borrowed from the other libraries or directly from a government agency.

6. If time and money are available, ask the reference librarian about a computer search. Supply the reference librarian with three or four *key terms*—words that describe the specific nature of your project. Often they are presented with minor headings.

Examples of key terms:
    Parks
        User behavior
    Recreation
        User behavior
        Parks

BOX 3-1. Steps in a Library Search

1. Check card catalog under subject heading. Write down call numbers of relevant books.
2. Browse through shelves containing relevant call numbers.
3. Check with reference librarian and consult abstracts, handbooks, and directories.
4. Consult key journals and periodicals, recent issues first.
5. Check government documents.
6. Consider value of a computer search.

By now you have probably reached the state of information overload. Make copies of the two or three articles that seem especially relevant to your interest, and take home a few of the key books for a longer perusal. It is difficult to both locate and read articles at the same time.

Direct Consultation

Find out the names of local individuals and agencies knowledgeable about the topic. They can supply information specifically about the situation in your community that may be included in any report. They can also be asked for the names of knowledgeable individuals.

The Parks Department is likely to have a public information officer who can answer many of your questions. Annual reports published by this agency, which will probably not be available in a university library, may provide valuable statistics. Parks Department staff may also be willing to help you directly in your research, either by making materials available, granting you permission to interview people in the park, or even providing direct financial assistance if your study happens to fit into a study of public parks. With other topics, it would be useful to contact private firms dealing with the issue.

It is gratifying to find how helpful outside people can be if they are approached in the right way. A further advantage of local consultation is the possibility of making valuable contacts. During conversations with local officials, students may learn about new programs and job opportunities.

Distant officials and authorities are more difficult to use as information sources. If you write to the author of a book on a topic, make your requests specific. Some famous persons are extraordinarily helpful with student inquiries. If you have a specific question that you think some distant authority can answer, don't hesitate to write a personal letter. Enclosing a stamped self-addressed envelope will increase the likelihood of a reply.

Summary

Reviewing the literature means finding out what previous research has been done on a topic. Networking involves locating sources and studies that point you toward other sources and studies. The library is almost always useful in locating information. In undertaking a library search, one should check the card catalog, browse through library shelves, check with the reference librarian, consult key journals, periodicals, and abstracts, check government documents, and consider the value of a computer search. There will also be situations in which direct consultation with known authorities will be helpful.

Limitations: It is easy to become overburdened with trivial and irrelevant studies during a library search. It is not easy to predict from a title how useful or relevant an article will be. Many books and periodicals will be unavailable locally and will require considerable time to find and obtain. Articles that are relevant may be so brief and lacking in detail as to be almost useless to the researcher who would like to repeat the study.

Further Reading

Doyle, J. M., & Grimes, G. H. (1976) *Reference resources: A systematic approach.* Metuchen, N.J.: The Scarecrow Press.

Greenwood, L. (1980). *How to search for information: A beginner's guide to the literature of psychology.* Lexington, KY: Willowood Press.

Kennedy, J. R., Jr. (1979). *Library research guide to education.* Ann Arbor, MI: Pierian Press.

Lester, J. (1984). *Writing research papers.* Glenview, IL: Scott Foresman.

McMillan, P., & Kennedy, J. (1981). *Library research guide to sociology.* Ann Arbor, MI: Pierian Press.

Morse, G. W. (1975). *Concise guide to library research* (2nd ed.). New York: Fleet Academic Editions.

Reed, J. G. (1983). *Library use: A handbook for psychology.* Washington, DC: American Psychological Association.

Woodbury, M. (1982). *A guide to sources of educational information* (rev. 2nd ed.). Arlington, VA: Information Resources Press.

II
Observational Methods

4 Observation

For a confirmed people watcher, observation is the ideal research method. However, there is more to observation than being a passive spectator. You have to decide beforehand where you are going to look, what you are going to look for (since you can't watch everything), and how to record what you see and hear.

Laud Humphreys was a graduate student in sociology at a midwestern university. He was struck by the frequency of police reports in the local newspaper describing arrests for homosexuality in public restrooms. Humphreys wondered why people would have sexual encounters in such public, drab, and smelly locations. Being a naturally curious person in need of a thesis topic, he visited public restrooms to find the answer.

His visits were fruitless. When he entered a restroom, he found nothing out of the ordinary. Men were present, to be sure, but they were doing what you might expect men in a public restroom to be doing. Humphreys expressed his puzzlement to a friend who was a homosexual. The friend laughed and told him that his approach was wrong. He wasn't acting the right way. His presence was inhibiting the behaviors he wanted to study. Public restrooms, he learned later, were called tearooms, and the homosexual participants were either trade or competition. Humphreys learned how he must act in order not to upset the delicate nonverbal negotiations taking place. He assumed the part of a watch queen, a voyeur who gets sexual satisfaction from observing other people's sexual acts. In this capacity, he was able to observe more than 50 homosexual encounters and write a book about his experiences, appropriately titled *Tearoom Trade* (Humphreys, 1970).

This topic lent itself to observation since most of the encounters were nonverbal. An unwritten rule of the tearoom is that no personal information is exchanged. Humphreys found that people came to the tearoom

29

because they wanted to remain anonymous. As a watch queen, Humphreys could observe the action as it occurred. However, his methods raised serious ethical problems. Is it proper for sociologists to observe people without identifying themselves as researchers? Yet if Humphreys had told the participants what he was doing, wouldn't this affect their actions? The answers to both these questions are probably yes. Humphreys was engaged in a highly questionable activity, but if he had explained this to participants, it would have changed their behavior. Fortunately, most observational studies aren't as difficult as the one Humphreys chose. You are probably not going to watch illegal activities by people who don't want to be identified. Observation is useful not only as a method in its own right but as an accompaniment to other procedures. Before beginning an interview study, it will be necessary to observe the situation first. You will want to know where to find people, how long they are going to be available, and possible distractions. Before beginning an experiment, you will want to know about the behavior in its natural state. Otherwise you run the risk of creating conditions in the laboratory that do not exist in the real world.

An advantage of observation is that it does not require conversation. You can observe pedestrians on a sidewalk 20 stories below or people who do not speak your language. Observation is the ideal method for studying commonplace nonverbal behaviors, such as gestures, postures, or seating arrangements, in which people may not be consciously aware of how they are acting.

Observation is economical in terms of money and equipment but expensive in terms of time. One invests long hours of waiting. This is well known to animal researchers, who spend weeks scouting the terrain and establishing observation posts before catching a glimpse of a rare bird or mammal. More than any other method, observation requires patience and luck. There is no certainty about who will appear and what will happen. It may rain or snow while you are there, be too hot or too cold, the setting too crowded or too empty. Also, without expensive equipment and apparatus, the observer's skills are severely tested. On the other hand, it is intensely satisfying to notice things that other people overlook. Generalization to the real world is easier when you have studied natural behavior. There are three types of observational procedures—casual observation, systematic observation, and participant observation.

Casual Observation

Casual observation is done without prearranged categories or a scoring system. It refers to eyeball inspection of what is happening. It is most useful at an early stage of research or as an accompaniment to some other procedure. For example, before one approaches hospital patients for interviews, it is desirable to spend some time watching behavior on the ward.

This will yield information that is indispensable for developing good questions. Casual observation is not a substitute for more systematic and detailed study, but occasionally it is the only method possible. A city planner visiting a housing project of India, for example, may have only a limited time to look around. This may mean a single tour in the company of a guide without the opportunity to talk to local residents. Keen powers of observation are required under these circumstances. Unless one knows what to look for, one might as well buy picture postcards or a tour book and save the time and trouble of a personal visit.

The vivid impressions of a first visit are worth recording. After several sessions, it is easy to become accustomed and desensitized to what is happening. First impressions are most useful when they are written down immediately. There can be no substitute for field notes kept on a day-by-day basis. These notes need not be typed or written in perfect grammar. A

Casual observation is an ideal technique for people watchers. Observing the people in a zoo can be as interesting and rewarding as watching the animals.

BOX 4-1. A Visit to the King Edward Hotel

The King Edward is slightly out of the way and this may have had some effect on the patronage, because on this particular Saturday evening there were very few people around. The major cause of the low amount of people was that this was the Saturday of the only holiday weekend in August and many people were out of town. One could also say that the King Edward depends on its daily rather than nightly group of patrons for the major portion of its customers. In the afternoon there were men in jackets and such; many white-and blue-collar workers and laborers but not the large numbers of transients such as would be found in bars closer to the main drag.

The TV was also on in the bar that evening. Every solitary in the bar was watching it, which undoubtedly has some bearing on the figures. Neither of the groups was watching it. No one was reading. There are two TV sets in the place, one facing toward the upper level of this two-level bar; however, there were no people sitting on the upper level. (There was no restriction against sitting on the upper level, it just wasn't done.) The fact that the TV was on may have had some effect on the seating pattern, more people sitting in the center where they could see the TV without distortion. The rear wall would be a considerable distance from the TV screen, and as the screen was not of a larger than normal size, the viewers in the center were quite close to the set that was located above the serving counter. Two solitaries who entered after a new program had gotten underway after 10 sat to the far side where they could neither see the screen nor be easily seen by me.

Sol A, a watcher, was an elderly man with his back to me, was watching intently, and sipping quite regularly, not looking to see the glass before he lifted it. He was, I would say, drinking unconsciously. I also noted he waited until the program changed before he got up to go to the lavatory.

Sol B was an elderly man in work clothes of a clean nature. He could perhaps be a night watchman, or something of that line. I noted he looked at the clock quite frequently in the 15 minutes or so he was there (I was there for about 5 minutes or so before beginning notations) and left at 9:35 before the program was over.

Group A was an almost nongroup group. There was very little conversation, and very little interest in anything beyond the table. "A" was dressed in sports clothes: checked cotton shirt, low-cut shoes. They weren't watching TV and left in the middle of a program.

B was in the large group. Conversation at this table ranged through the realm of sports with reference to the case before the courts of whether bridge is a game of chance or a game of skill, and whether Edmonton would have a good team in this year's football. The table was mixed—middle-aged and old, sports clothes and shabby, large glass and small. Five of them referred to family and children at one time or another, so this might be a boys'-night-out group of some sort. The extremely interesting aspect of this is that when three of the members of the group left there were only large-glass drinkers left. This could be coincidence or it might be significant. The three who left were all small-glass drinkers.

final report is best written after a long period of reflection, data gathering, and several drafts, but first impressions are most valuable when written while they are still fresh.

The notes in Box 4-1 were written by an observer following an hour-long session in a Canadian pub. The observer scribbled notes at the bottom of the observation sheet and typed them when he arrived home. In his notes, lone drinkers were referred to as Sols (solitaries). The notes were left in rough form because they were not primary data.

Systematic Observation

There are four major differences between observational research and just looking (Bickman, 1976).

1. It serves a specified research purpose.
2. It is planned systematically.
3. It is recorded systematically and related to more general propositions rather than simply being presented as a set of interesting curiosities.
4. It is subjected to checks and controls on validity and reliability.

Systematic observation employs a scoring system and prearranged categories which are applied consistently. This usually requires an observation checklist, on which information is recorded under the proper headings. Categories on the checklist should include those items of behavior that occur naturally in the situation and can be observed and recorded. Not everything that takes place is open to view. Casual observation is helpful for developing the categories to be used in systematic observation. In the study of drinking patterns in 15 bars in a New England city, Kessler and Gomberg (1974) found that they could record the following items on napkins or paper sheets without appearing conspicuous.

Number of drinks	Alone or in a group
Type of drink	Type of clothing
Number of sips per drink	Height estimate
Time to consume	Weight estimate
Total time in bar	Age estimate

The items were limited to what could be seen directly. What the patrons said to one another, their marital status, and their political attitudes lay beyond the range of an observational study. In establishing the reliability of the observational categories, two researchers went to a selected bar, sat either at a table or at the bar with instructions to independently observe the next patron entering the premises who sat in clear view of both observers. The patron was then observed throughout his or her stay in the bar. Agreement was high between the two observers using this procedure (almost 100 percent) except in the case of the age estimates.

A similar procedure was used at coffeehouses in college community. For each session, the observer entered the coffeehouse, purchased a beverage, and sat at a table that provided a good vantage point.The observer selected the next three lone individuals and three individuals in groups entering the premises who sat down within the observer's view. People were classified as lone or group patrons at the time they entered; if they were joined later, this was recorded separately on the observation sheet. Customers entering the coffeehouse to purchase takeout orders were not included in the sample.

The observer must choose a location from which behavior can be seen and recorded. This will be easier in some settings than in others. In the beer parlor, it was possible for the observer to station himself at a table and record activities on a loose sheet inserted in his newspaper. A city planning student studying behavior in a city park found a good view from a tall building overlooking the park (Ciolek, 1978). The choice of an observational post depends completely on local circumstances. There is no way to know in advance what will be the best vantage point. A videocamera can be useful in observational research. Interactions can be recorded at one time and transcribed later (see Chapter 14).

Participant Observation

The two observational methods described so far, casual and systematic observation, involve an outside observer coming in to watch what is happening. A different approach is called for when the observer becomes part of the events being studied. Known as *participant observation,* this approach was pioneered by the Chicago school of sociology. There are significant ethical and procedural problems in becoming an observer when one has a role in the setting. These problems are so serious that most investigators avoid this method entirely. There are, however, some situations in which participant observation can yield valuable information that could not have been obtained in any other way.

Criminologist George Kirkham took a year's leave from his university position to go through training in a police academy and work as a patrolman. Many of his fellow officers knew of his research interests, but the people on his beat looked on him as an ordinary policeman. Kirkham writes with great sensitivity about the changes in his own attitudes that occurred when he worked in a high-crime neighborhood. His records included events that occurred on his beat, his own attitudes and those of his fellow officers, and the responses of his family and friends to his new role.

> According to the accounts of my family, colleagues, and friends, I began to increasingly display attitudinal and behavioral elements that were entirely foreign to my previous personality—punitiveness, pervasive cynicism and mistrust of others, chronic irritability and free-floating hostility, racism, and a diffuse personal anxiety over the menace of crime and criminals that seemed at times to border on the obsessive. (Kirkham, 1975, p. 19)

In his role of policeman, he became a vociferous advocate of capital punishment even though, as a criminologist, he acknowledged its ineffectiveness as a deterrent. He also resented the courts' "coddling" of criminals. His inability to reconcile his conflicting perspectives began to seem like hypocrisy. He began to have doubts about who was the real George Kirkham. The answer, he acknowledged, lay in the situations in which he found himself. It was much easier to be detached and objective around a seminar table with a group of students than as a policeman in direct contact with violence.

Sharing the risks with his fellow officers gave Kirkham insights that he felt could not have been obtained through interviews or questionnaires. The hyperaggressiveness and braggadocio of his fellow officers began to make sense as a collective defense mechanism. Any show of weakness on the part of one patrolman threatened the entire force. Kirkham left his beat after a year's service and returned to a placid existence as a university professor. Unanswered questions impelled him to embark on an additional 6 month stint as a policeman in a small community with very little crime. The tension and hostility of the previous job were absent. He could come home and take off his badge and uniform with a "new and far deeper feeling of service and satisfaction" (Kirkham, 1975, p. 19).

A participant-observer has a defined and active role in what is happening, as distinct from being a spectator, bystander, or customer. This is not to imply that customers cannot make observations. The beer parlor study described earlier was done by observers posing as customers. This seems more properly classified as systematic observation rather than participant observation. Had the observer been a waiter or bartender who took the job specifically to record drinking patterns, then it would have been participant observation.

Sometimes researchers find themselves in a participant observation role through circumstance—for example, after an automobile accident or physical disability. Research through participant observation is a means of understanding the experience and also a way for them to use their professional training while they are immobilized.

Ethnography

The description and study of specific peoples and places is known as *ethnography*. At one time, ethnographers were concerned primarily with primitive societies. More recently they have turned their attention to the study of contemporary peoples in special settings, such as courtrooms, banks, and shopping malls. The observer looks, listens, asks questions, and records what is seen and heard. From all this emerges a picture of what is happening. This is not the picture of the artist who sketches a scene from a single perspective. It is more the approach of the detective who examines and puts together all sorts of evidence, including smudged fingerprints, bloodstains, torn clothing, and eyewitness accounts (Sanders, 1973). Although the terms *ethnography* and *participant observation* are often used interchangeably, ethnography, like other related terms used in the social sciences, such as qualitative sociology and field work, is more of an approach than a research method, because it combines several research techniques, including interviews, observations, and physical trace measures.

In both participant observation and ethnography, impressions are written down as field notes. These records are later summarized and discussed with colleagues or a research supervisor. Collecting field notes is often done by a single researcher, but the subsequent validation of observations and interpretations will be a shared enterprise.

How to Be a Good Observer

The first principle of good observation is to heed the Greek maxim "Know thyself." A skillful interpretation of your own responses provides valuable insights into what is happening in the situation and in you. Make it a practice to acknowledge and *name* your feelings: "I am beginning to become tense . . . I feel comfortable . . . something seems odd here." Try practice observations with a friend and share your feelings aloud. See if you can identify the internal cues for these feelings. Notice whether you hold your breath or stand differently when you are tense. Practice plus feedback will increase your sensitivity to such feelings.

Pay attention to nonverbal cues in the environment. These include people's posture, gestures, and privacy-seeking behaviors, such as turning away and gaze avoidance. When Robert Pace (1957) was observing a mental hospital ward, he found that patients acted disturbed when he sat out in the dayroom, and the nurses were bothered when he was inside the nurses' station. He gradually found himself forced back into a small area outside the nurses' station. Monitoring other people's reactions to his presence taught him which places were open and closed to him.

Flexibility is a required attribute for a participant observer or ethnographer. Methods will evolve during the course of the research, and procedures will be added, modified, or dropped. Unlike a laboratory study, new sources of information will appear during the course of the investigation and this will require new approaches or contacts. During field work, it will be impossible to keep track of everything that is happening at one time. Some selection among different variables or processes will be necessary along with constant monitoring of how they interact and measure in importance.

Systematic observation requires the researcher to take notes in a unobtrusive manner. The closer the recording procedure resembles normal activity in the setting, the better. One observer in a restaurant recorded observations on napkins; another in a classroom recorded participation in a notebook. Certain locations are more suitable than others for recording what is happening. Watching bicyclists at an intersection proved difficult when the observers stood on the street corner; cyclists became curious and altered their behavior. It was more effective to watch from inside a parked car. The researcher studying a playground might bring along a young child as a cover, to make the observer's presence more comprehensible. "Fitting in" is an art that develops through practice. The objective of the naturalist is to disturb nature as little as possible while studying it. Most of the time, it pays to have an observer who can blend into the setting. In laboratory research, it is often assumed that the physical appearance of the experimenter does not matter. Whether this assumption is true is an interesting question, but no one ever assumes it in a natural setting. Researchers who get their first introduction to observational procedures in a setting in which they do not fit will probably soon become discouraged. Elliott Liebow, who spent a year among streetcorner men in a black neighborhood in Washington, D. C. realized in the end that he would always be an outsider:

> This brute fact of color, as they understood it in their experience, and as I understood it in mine, irrevocably and absolutely relegated me to the status of outsider. . . . I used to play with the idea that maybe I wasn't as much of an outsider as I thought. Other events, and later readings of the field materials, have disabused me of this particular touch of vanity. (Liebow, 1966, p. 248)

George Schaller (1964) who studied gorillas in their natural habitat, describes the gradual process of becoming a good observer in the jungle:

> In civilization, one loses the aptitude for stillness, the habit of moving gently. It takes time to cease to be an outsider, an intruder, and be accepted once again by the creatures of the forest. The return to the wilderness is a gradual process, unconscious for the most part. Once the senses have been relieved of the incessant noise and other irrelevant stimuli that are a part of our civilization . . . the sights, sounds, and smells of the environment become meaningful again. Slowly the courage and confidence of man, previously nurtured by his belief in the safety of his civilized surroundings, slips away. Finally he stands there, a rather weak and humble creature who has come not to disturb and subdue but to nod to the forest in fellowship and to claim kinship to the gorilla and the Sunbird. (1964, p. 107)

In natural observation the researcher refrains from interfering in the ongoing activities. When a researcher decides to intervene—for example, by changing the furniture in a room or placing a red ball in a forest clearing—the procedure is known as a field experiment. The chief exception to the rule of noninterference occurs in participant observation, where the observer is part of the event being studied.

Increasing Reliability and Validity

In systematic observation it is desirable to employ at least two independent observers at an early stage of a study. Independent observers are two or more individuals who take notes separately and compare them afterward. Such comparisons may reveal ambiguities and overlaps in scoring categories. These comparisons should be made before the main body of observations is collected, not after. After you have finished making all your observations, if you learn then that some of the categories are not reliable, the value of the data will be diminished. When such problems can be identified beforehand, the scoring system may be improved to eliminate them, and then reliability checked a second time so that the observations can begin with confidence that the scoring system is reliable. Box 4-2 lists the steps for doing systematic observational research.

The use of independent observers may not be feasible in participant observation. Most studies using this method involve only a single researcher. The value of participant observation depends completely on the sensitivity, accuracy, and thoroughness of this one individual. The value of participant observation and ethnography depends most heavily on the researcher's powers of description and writing style. In systematic observation, the observer need only check on a printed sheet those items of behavior that occur.

The validity of field notes is increased through multiple contacts and

---

BOX 4-2. Steps for Systematic Observation Research

1. Specify the question(s) of interest (reason for doing the study).
2. Do casual observation, distinguishing between observation (the actual behaviors seen) and inference (interpretation, what you think it means).
3. Are the observational categories clearly described?
4. Design the measurement instruments (i.e., checklists, categories, coding systems, etc.).
5. Is the study designed so that it will be *valid,* (i.e., does it measure what it is supposed to measure and has some generalizability)?
6. Train observers in the use of the instruments.
7. *Do a pilot test.*
   a. Test the actual observation procedure.
   b. Check reliability of the two categories using at least two independent observers.
8. Revise procedure and instruments in light of the pilot test results. If substantial changes are made, run another pilot test.
9. Collect data.
10. Compile, analyze and interpret results.

sources. Material obtained from one source is checked against reports from other sources, although not in such a way as to violate confidentiality. Multiple points of entry to a group will also be useful for verifying impressions. One individual's point of view may not be shared by others. Differences in opinion can be fruitful in identifying problems with the procedure.

Qualitative notes also may be supplemented by interaction counts, photographs, or other more objective recording procedures within the context of a multimethod approach. This can be done on a teamwork basis with some individuals remaining in the role of participant observers while others are making more quantitative assessments. Each procedure complements and extends the other.

Stresses on the Observer

Those who observe behavior in natural settings can expect to endure physical discomfort and occasionally danger. It is not uncommon for zoologists studying animal behavior to stake out an area and spend weeks in fruitless waiting in a stuffy, hot, insect-ridden blind. Watching children play in the streets of Philadelphia during July and August may be no less uncomfortable and occasionally more dangerous.

Participant observation is *not* a widely used method in behavioral research. Of the techniques described in this book, it is the one that is most stressful for the investigator and has the most serious ethical problems. The decision to undertake participant observation should not be made lightly.

Undertaking field work among psychiatric patients living in the community, Estroff (1981) felt alone and isolated. There was no one with whom she could share the intimate facts of the daily observations and her own personal reactions and no one to whom she could express her occasional feelings of frustration, depression, or even elation about clients, staff, their interaction, or her own reactions to a roller coaster set of experiences.

Some uses of participant observation, although not all, have been severely criticized both inside and outside the research community. Ethical problems can be minimized when all of the following conditions are met: (1) the researcher is qualified for the role being occupied, (2) the observer does not drain resources and services intended for others, and (3) the observer informs colleagues, co-workers, and clients of the dual role to the extent that this is practicable. As a participant observer, one is privy to backstage behaviors. It is virtually *inevitable* that one will see illicit, unethical, and illegal acts. A participant observer working in a restaurant, for example, is likely to notice unsanitary conditions. One could put this more strongly and say that the observer *will see*, over a period of time, unsanitary conditions. There is probably no restaurant in the United States where

BOX 4-3. Pitfalls to Be Avoided in Observational Research

1. Reactive effects from being observed; a guinea pig effect in which awareness of being watched changes behavior.
   a. People becoming self-conscious and not behaving as they normally would.
   b. People attempting to accommodate the observer, doing what they believe the observer wants them to do.
   c. Influence of the observer's specific appearance or manner on peoples' actions.
   d. Changes in accommodation to the observer during the course of the study.
2. Investigator error
   a. Unclear and unreliable observational categories.
   b. Bias on the part of the observer.
   c. Changes in the observational procedures in the middle of the study.
3. Sampling error
   a. People being observed are not representative of the groups to which the results will be generalized.
   b. Inadequate time periods selected for observation.
   c. Sources of bias due to weather, day, location, etc.

this would not occur at least occasionally. How the observer deals with the situation is likely to be a source of severe personal stress. Should he or she "rat" on the other employees or keep quiet and risk exposing the public to a health risk? Ethical dilemmas are inevitable in participant observation.

There is also legal ambiguity about the status of field notes taken by researchers in the course of participant observation. The courts have not determined that such field notes are protected against subpoena. They might become part of the public record in court proceedings.

Box 4-3 lists sources of error to be avoided in observational research. The pitfalls apply to both quantitative and qualitative observations.

Limitations

Observation deals with behavior, not with attitudes or beliefs. Attitudes can be deduced from behavior only with caution. If you want to find out what people do, you can observe them. If you want to find out what they think, you should ask them directly. There are exceptions to both these rules, but in general, observation is a good method for studying natural behavior, while interviews and questionnaires are more appropriate for opinions and beliefs.

Reliability is always a problem in natural observation. The issue is most critical in participant observation, where there is only a single observer. In casual and systematic observation, the use of two independent observers is recommended during the early stages of the study. No matter how simple and straightforward the behavior being studied, it is still wise to check on reliability. If two independent observers cannot agree on what they see, the conclusions of the study are in doubt.

Summary

Observation is useful in behavioral research as a method in its own right and as an accompaniment to other procedures. It is economical in terms of money and equipment but expensive in terms of time.

Casual observation does not use prearranged categories or a scoring system. It is most useful at the beginning stages of research. Systematic observation employs detailed categories and a scoring system. When the observer becomes part of the events being studied, this is called participant observation.

Limitations: Since observation deals with behavior, it is difficult to deduce beliefs, attitudes, or opinions. Reliability is always a problem in natural observations. Participant observation typically creates serious ethical problems.

References

Bickman, L. (1976). Data collection I; observational methods. In C. Selltiz, L. S. Wrightsman, & S. W. Cook, *Research methods in social relations* (3rd ed.). New York: Holt, Rinehart and Winston.

Ciolek, T. M. (1978). Spatial behavior in pedestrian areas. *Ekistics, 268*, 120–122.

Estroff, S. E. (1981). *Making it crazy.* Berkeley, CA: University of California Press.

Humphreys, L. (1970). *Tearoom trade.* Chicago: Aldine.

Kessler, M., & Gomberg, C. (1974). Observations of barroom drinking; methodology and preliminary results. *Quarterly Journal of Studies on Alcohol, 35*, 1392–1396.

Kirkham, G. L. (1975, May). Doc cop. *Human Behavior, 19.*

Liebow, E. (1966). *Tally's corner.* Boston: Little, Brown.

Pace, R. E. (1957). Situational therapy. *Journal of Personality, 25*, 578–588.

Sanders, W. B. (1973). *The sociologist as detective.* New York: Praeger.

Schaller, G. B. (1964). *The year of the gorilla.* Chicago: University of Chicago Press.

Sommer, R. (1965). The isolated drinker in the Edmonton beverage room. *Quarterly Journal of Studies on Alcohol, 26*, 95–110.

Further Reading

Hartmann, D. P. (Ed.). (1982). *Using observers to study behavior.* San Francisco: Jossey-Bass.

Lofland, J., & Lofland, L. (1984). *Analyzing social settings: A guide to qualitative observation and analysis* (2nd ed.). Belmont, CA: Wadsworth.

Mellen, J., Hage, S., Pfeifer, S., & Carlson, D. (1983). *Research Methods for Studying Animal*

Behavior in a Zoo Setting. Videotape and text jointly produced by the Washington
    Park Zoo, Portland, Oregon, and the Minnesota Zoological Garden, Apple Valley, MN
    55124.
Shaffir, W. B., Stebbins, R. A., & Turowetz, A. (Eds.). (1980). *Fieldwork experience.* New
    York: St. Martin's Press.
Webb, E. J., Campbell, D. T., Schwartz, R. D., Sechrest, L., & Grove, J. B. (1981). *Nonreactive
    measures in the social sciences* (2nd ed.). Boston: Houghton Mifflin.
Weick, K. E. (1968). Systematic observational methods. In G. Lindzey & E. Aronson (Eds.),
    The handbook of social psychology. Reading, Mass.: Addison-Wesley.

5 Behavioral Mapping and Trace Measures

Behavioral Mapping

A special application of observational techniques, *behavioral mapping* is concerned specifically with people's behavior in their environments. In which settings do people spend their time, and how do these settings affect their behavior? Behavioral mapping involves an actual chart or plan of an area on which people's locations and activities are indicated. The mapping is done either at the time of the observation or later from records made in narrative form. This technique has practical relevance for urban design, transportation planning, geography, park management, and other fields concerned with people's locations and movements.

In a study of public housing in Cleveland, Ohio, researchers recruited tenants to serve as observers. The tenants were given special training so that they would record the kinds of behaviors observed in the project area, who was engaged in them, and how long the behaviors lasted. The observers identified 67 distinct behavior settings in and around the project. *A behavior setting* is a geographical location linked to customary patterns of behavior occurring over regular time periods. Examples of behavior settings include community meetings, laundry room activities, playground activities, and the use of the streets and sidewalks. In the number and range of behavior settings, the public housing project actually provided a more rich and varied environment than was available in nearby small towns or poor urban neighborhoods. However, most of these settings in the public housing project were outside the control of the tenants. The housing project consisted of alien, bureaucratic, and institutional spaces controlled by an impersonal management or by no one. It was this lack of control over space, rather than the number and variety of behavior settings, that differentiated the public housing project from other neighborhoods occupied by poor people. In addition to recommending specific architectural/environmental changes to improve the housing project, the research team also urged that more encouragement be given to local decision making and leadership (Bechtel, 1971).

A behavioral map, as indicated above, is a chart of people's locations in space. It is an empirical document that describes what behaviors actually occur rather than what was planned for the space (Ittelson, Proshansky, & Rivlin, 1970.) A neighborhood street may be more than a transit corridor. It may also be a place where people congregate, where children play, and in some areas, where drugs are traded.

In constructing a behavioral map, the observer can record only those items that are readily apparent, such as approximate age, sex, whether the person is alone or in a group, and what he or she is doing. There are various ways to record people's locations in space, including time-lapse photography, videotape, and prepared diagrams of an area filled out by an observer. Whatever method is used, the researcher must check its reliability and determine its effects upon the behavior of the respondents. Ittelson, Rivlin, and Proshansky (1976) found a high correspondence between their own observations of how hospital patients spent their time and the patient's own written estimates. It may also be possible to compare people's behavior when they know they are being watched and when they are unaware.

Behavioral maps can be place-centered or person-centered. A *place-centered* map shows how people arrange themselves within a particular location. A *person-centered* map shows people's movements and activities over a specified period of time. To construct a place-centered map, observers station themselves to watch the action in a particular location. They record on prepared diagrams the location and activities of the people in the area. A person-centered map begins with a designated number of individuals whose activities are charted throughout the day. Because the observations are very detailed, a person-centered map usually involves only a few individuals. One researcher who wanted to compare the residents of a convalescent home with participants in a day treatment center (nonresidential) selected eight people from each setting who were matched in age, health, educational level, and other characteristics and followed their activities throughout the day. She wanted to find out how much time the persons in each setting spent in social activities, how long they slept, whether they did craft work, and other details. On the basis of her observations, she was able to conclude that residents of the day treatment program were more active than were those in the convalescent home (Quan, 1978).

The choice of mapping procedure will depend on the researcher's goals. If the objective is to assess a particular location, such as the suitability of a room, building, or park, place-centered methods are preferable. If the goal is to learn about a group or individuals, such as the situation of elderly hospital patients, the observer will probably choose a person-centered approach.

Place-centered Maps

The first task is to draw a diagram showing all those architectural/environmental features that affect people's behavior. This should be based on your own measurements rather than the architect's blueprints, which are probably out of date and do not contain the portable features of the environment, such as chairs, tables, bulletin boards, wall clocks, and information signs. You can use existing floor plans or charts as a guide, but be sure to check the measurements yourself. The map can be drawn in ink and copied, or on stencil and mimeographed. Architectural features can be drawn

Behavioral maps. Place-centered maps were used to study space utilization in a university library. Students preferred to sit at the ends of the tables, since this minimized eye contact with others.

schematically or symbolically as circles, squares, and triangles. A stationery store will have Plexiglas stencils used by designers for tracing the outlines of chairs, tables, desks, and so on. You do not have to be a professional drafter to construct an outline map.

The next step is to list the behaviors to be recorded. Special scoring symbols are then used for each behavior. For example, Si—sitting, St—standing, Wa—walking, and so on. The list is compiled through casual observation of the setting. Categories should cover 80 to 90 percent of the behaviors found in the setting. Special symbols such as 01 and 02 can be used for "other behaviors," which are described in detail at the bottom of the map. The setting is then sampled at predetermined times and the behaviors recorded.

The research team in a mental hospital ward found that the categories listed in Table 5-1 included most of the behaviors they observed in the dayroom (Sommer & Ross, 1958).

When an unusual event occurred on the ward, such as a group sing led by the recreation therapist that took place about twice a month, this was scored in the "other" category and described at the bottom of the record sheet. Such events occurred so infrequently on the ward that the "other" category was not often used. The clearest finding from the observations was the minimal level of activity in the dayroom. Most of the occupants were sitting and doing nothing most of the time.

The reliability of the notation system should be checked. Some behaviors are difficult to categorize. On the hospital ward mentioned above, the researchers had a hard time distinguishing between patients sitting and

TABLE 5-1. Activity List for a Mental Hospital
                        Dayroom

Activity	Scoring symbol
Reading	R
Playing cards	C
Watching TV	TV
Listening to radio	Rad
Talking to other patient	T-P
Talking to nurse	T-N
Jigsaw puzzle, games	G
Sitting, doing nothing	S
Standing, doing nothing	St
Sleeping	Sp
In transit (walking)	W
Other (describe)	O_1, O_2

those watching television. Observers disagreed among themselves so often in making this determination that sitting (S) and watching television (TV) were combined into a single category. There is no point in including categories of behavior that cannot be reliably observed. Some of the more common methods for estimating scoring reliability are a percentage agreement score or a correlation coefficient (see Chapter 18). When observers disagree frequently as to the category in which a behavior belongs, further refinement of the scoring system and/or training of the observers is warranted.

The map should cover all the possible times when the area is being used. Some of the most interesting information from behavioral maps is recorded when "nothing is happening." One design team studying a school yard was struck by the number of times during the week when the yard was unoccupied. This led the designers to search for ways to increase community use of the school yard outside of school hours by including a picnic area, amphitheater, and other facilities in the renovation plan (Hester, 1975).

The observation sheet used by the research team is shown in Figure 5-1. The actual usage patterns of the school yard are shown in Figure 5-2.

Researchers in another school setting combined behavioral mapping of people's locations with furniture mapping, in which the location of furniture and equipment in each classroom was recorded throughout the school year. Using a floor plan of the room divided by a grid into 12 equal sections, the placement of desks and chairs was mapped biweekly. These records were useful in interpreting the behavioral maps that were recorded separately (Rivlin & Rothenberg, 1976).

In making your own observations, do not space the sessions too closely together on the same day. Otherwise, you are likely to see the same people doing the same things. To cover all the morning hours, 8 A.M. observations could be made on Monday, 9 A.M. sessions on Wednesday, 10 A.M. observations on Tuesday, and so on.

You will be pleasantly surprised how quickly place-centered observations can be done even for a comparatively large area. A place-centered map deals with instantaneous cross sections of behavior. Generally you will want to record what people are doing when you first see them. What they do afterward is *not* recorded. This will yield a series of behavioral maps at representative intervals throughout the day. Individual maps can later be combined into a single *composite map* showing location, density, and usage for all time periods (see Figure 5-1).

Person-centered Maps

Person-centered maps are especially useful in a comparative study of environments. Matching the subjects allows the researcher to interpret differences as being due to the settings rather than the characteristics of the sub-

	Pre-School		1-8 Grade		9-12 Grade		College		Adult	Elderly		Social Activity*	Setting for Interaction**
	F	M	F	M	F	M	F	M		F	M		
a. Walking													
b. Sitting													
c. Working													
d. Stop to talk													
e. Neighborhood meeting													
f. Active recreation													
g.													
h.													
i.													
j.													
k.													
l.													
m.													
n.													
o.													
p.													
q.													
r. Commercial													
s. Waiting for transportation													
t. Art													
u. Fantasy play													
v. Construction													
w. Role play													
x.													
y.													

*Record the Interaction Process associated with each activity and the number of people interacting in that manner. Use the key: P = Private, I = Impersonal, C1 = Cooperation, C2 = Competition, C3 = Conflict, A = Accommodation.
**Indicate the setting in which each activity takes place and the numbers of people, particularly in that setting.

FIG. 5-1. Observational sheet used in the behavioral mapping of a school yard.

FRED OLDS SCHOOL
INTENSITY OF ACTIVITY
TYPICAL WEEKDAY

Key to Intensity of Activity

Most
Intense

Least
Intense

FIG. 5-2. Composite map of interaction throughout the week, made by combining observational records over time.

jects. Judy Quan, in the study mentioned earlier, found that residents in the day treatment center were more active than residents of the convalescent home. Since she had matched these individuals beforehand on age, health, and other factors, it seemed logical to atttribute the difference to the two environments rather than the characteristics of the two groups of residents.

In constructing a person-centered map, the first task is to identify the sample and obtain their cooperation. At the outset, the subjects should realize the implications of being followed around throughout the day. They must be assured that anything seen or heard will be kept confidential. For recording activities, it is helpful to use a coded notation system that does not involve actual names or details of conversations.

No matter how skillful you are in gaining cooperation, a period of adjustment will be necessary to accustom the person to your presence. Observations may be omitted during this time. Not writing things down during the early sessions will shorten the adjustment period. You might try observing the person in stages—one hour the first day, two hours after that, a morning observation next, and finally an eight-hour session.

Since there are only a few people to be observed, you can expect to be bored much of the time. While you cannot avoid being drawn into conversation occasionally, becoming the person's best friend will detract from the validity of the procedure. Thus, the notation "talking to the observer" should appear infrequently on your scoring sheet.

Person-centered maps are also used in observational studies of children (e.g., in comparing play patterns of children of different ages, of the two sexes, or in different settings). At first, the observer's presence will be noted, but soon the children will habituate and return to their usual patterns of behavior.

Observations can be continuous or periodic. Continuous observations involve following an individual over a period of time (e.g., an 8-hour work shift or an entire school day). Periodic observations involve observing the same individual at intervals throughout the day. This will include a *time sampling procedure* in which the observer prepares a list of specific times when the person's activities will be charted, such as 9:18 A.M., 10:04 A.M., and 2:36 P.M. At the designated time, the observer notes the person's location and activity. Time sampling does not require the observer to watch a single subject all the time. The researcher can schedule other activities, including observational sessions with other subjects, during the intervals.

With people whose schedules and activities are regular and predictable, little is gained by extending the observations indefinitely. At some point, it should be more profitable to move to the next person in your sample. Eventually you may want to return to the first person for a second series of observations, but this is optional. The decision as to how many people to include depends more on economics and interpersonal relations than on theory. How long will subjects permit your observation? How valuable are the additional data? If there is an impressive consistency in people's movements and activities, a small representative sample is probably sufficient.

After you have collected a series of person-centered maps, they can be converted to spatial form. For adults this may be accomplished by using an ordinary city map. The person's travels each day are recorded as single lines, which become thicker with more frequent travel. The maps can also be summarized in tables showing the percentage of time spent in various

BOX 5-1. Behavioral Mapping of Penguins in an Oceanarium

Zoos and animal parks are wonderful places for observing animal behavior, human behavior, and human and animal interactions. Sue Joseph obtained permission from Sea World, a large oceanarium in San Diego, California, to conduct observations in the penguin exhibit. She wanted to learn how use of the various parts of the exhibit changed over the breeding cycle. Her first step was to develop categories of penguin behavior that could be reliably scored by an observer stationed 8 to 10 feet away. She and her assistants used the categories over a 6-month period in observing the penguin exhibit. The categories on the observation sheet (Figure 5-3) were abbreviated and not always meaningful to an outsider. Longer descriptions of each category were given to her assistants during the training sessions in which the reliability of the observers was determined. For example, "ecstatic" refers to a display in which the penguin slowly stretches its head and bill straight upwards while slowly flapping its wings and emitting a staccato vocalization. "Bill-to-axilla" refers to the bird leaning forward at an angle of approximately 45° with slowly flapping wings while rocking its head from side to side with the tip of the bill directed to the base of one wing (after Sladen, 1958). A map of the observation area was drawn and divided into rectangular grids that could be identified through a coordinate system (e.g., Bird 102 was in section B-6 at the time of the observation). Maps of the observation area were placed at the top of the behavioral categories on each score sheet. This score sheet was used for ten 30-second observations of a single penguin throughout a 5-minute period.

locations and activities (e.g., for children on a playground, the amount of time or number of occasions of swing use, sandbox play, climbing, or games).

Safeguarding the privacy of your respondents is exceedingly important. Check your data carefully to ensure that individuals cannot be identified by name. When it is impossible to prevent identification, as in mapping the activities of a lone school nurse, consider omitting detailed information on his or her activities in any published report.

Limitations

Person-centered mapping is both tiring and intrusive. The observer who follows someone around will have difficulty remaining in the background not only for the person observed but for others encountered. Time sampling alleviates some of the tedium but not the intrusiveness of the procedure. Place-centered maps are intrusive in a private location, such as an apartment or personal office; they can work well in public locations. The researcher mapping people's use of a shopping mall may be able to appear as just another customer taking periodic walks through the area.

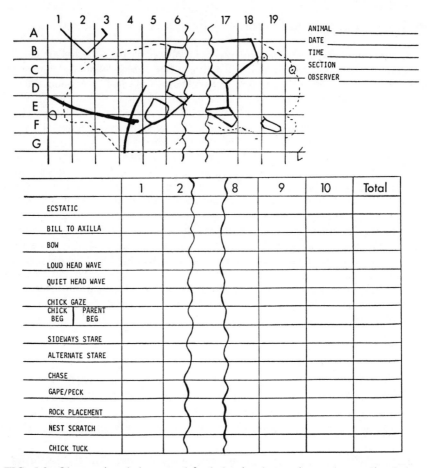

FIG. 5-3. Observational sheet used for behavioral mapping and recording behavior of penguins.

Combining maps from several individuals observed at various times makes interpretation more difficult. A combined behavioral map for 10 observational sessions in a school yard may show 10 dots at a specific location. The reader does not know whether this refers to one child observed at that location for all 10 sessions or 10 children on one occasion. This confusion of within- and between-individual variation makes it difficult to deal with behavioral maps statistically.

Because of the time and effort involved in their construction, person-centered maps tend to involve only a few individuals. This also makes it difficult to test the data statistically.

Finally, person-centered mapping reveals environmental choices with no information as to why these choices are made. For any practical pur-

Behavioral mapping. Several times a day, the location of each penguin in the Sea World Exhibit was indicated by the researcher on prepared maps. (Sea World photo)

Posed picture of behavioral mapping of the penguin exhibit showing the observer with grid diagram on the clipboard and penguins marked with flipper bands. Normally the observations were made from a longer distance away from the birds. (Sea World photo)

pose, the maps must be supplemented with interviews or other data-gathering procedure to find out why certain locations are chosen and others avoided.

Trace Measures

"Moroccans keep out!" North Africa? No. Philadelphia? Yes. And you had better know what it means if you are a local teenager. The message indicates gang activity in the area. This one was a warning to the powerful Moroccan gang to stay out of the territory controlled by its rival. Geographers David Ley and Roman Cybriwsky (1974) analyzed wall writing to chart gang activity in Philadelphia. They found that graffiti are used by teenage gangs to warn outsiders that they are entering someone's turf and must respect local territorial claims.

There are regional and local styles in wall writing. Graffiti in Hispanic neighborhoods in the United States often display a distinctive style of writing (see photograph). Code words are frequently employed, such as *M* for marijuana or *13*, since *M* is the thirteenth letter of the alphabet. *Taboo 12-*

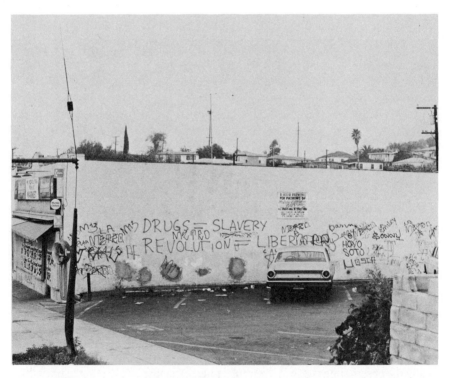

Trace measures: accretion. Graffiti on the side of this East Los Angeles market provides a record of gang activity in the area.

P means that the turf is controlled by Philadelphia's Twelfth and Poplar Street Gang. Street gangs, lacking legitimate ownership of property, take to the walls to assert their claims to turf.

Another type of illegal wall writing is latrinalia, the technical name given to graffiti on public toilet walls. This writing has been studied by anthropologists and others in an effort to learn about cultural values. Latrinalia tend to express attitudes and sentiments that are socially disapproved. Most American toilet walls reveal a preoccupation with sexual experience, excretion, ethnic hostility, and divergent political views. A comparison of latrinalia in Chicago and the Philippines showed far more homosexual writing in Chicago restrooms but about the same amount of heterosexual writing. The American inscriptions were also more likely to be judged humorous, political, and philosophical. The Philippine wall writing had a higher frequency of hostile content and disapproval of sexual ideas (Sechrest & Flores, 1969). The eruption of Mount Vesuvius in 79 A.D. covered the city of Pompeii with a heavy layer of volcanic ash that cooled as it fell to earth. The dense layer of ashes protected the buildings, the walls, and many common household objects for over a thousand years. When the city was excavated, the writing scratched on walls was found to be intact and provided many clues to the day-to-day life of ordinary people.

Trace measures are the physical remains of interaction after the people have departed. Webb, Campbell, Schwartz, Sechrest, and Grove (1981) identify two types of physical traces useful in behavioral research—*accretion* and *erosion*. Accretion refers to the buildup of a residue or product of the interaction—something added to the situation. Erosion refers to deterioration or wear and provides an index of usage patterns. With erosion, something is worn down or removed.

Accretion Measures

Graffiti are a form of accretion; litter is another. While the presence of graffiti has been used to chart gang activity, litter has been employed to study usage patterns in public parks. Garbage, another accretion measure, has been used in the study of human nutrition to determine what and how much people are eating and how much useful food is discarded. Sawyer (1961) made an estimate of people's drinking habits based on the number and kind of liquor bottles found in trash cans.

Erosion Measures

Certain patterns of usage create certain types of erosion or wear. Deterioration of campus lawns and the extent of footprints in the snow reveal informal pathways. Astute university administrators delay installing walk-

Trace measures: erosion. Informal paths shed light on the interaction networks among these apartment dwellers.

ways until after these informal pathways have been located. Such pathways can be used to assess the social relationships between people in different buildings. Footprints do not provide an infallible measure of contact, but this clue may be worth following up if there is a significant number of footprints in the snow going from one dormitory to another and none between that dormitory and another equally close. According to Webb et al. (1981), the floor tiles around the hatching chick exhibit at Chicago's Museum of Science and Industry must be replaced every 6 weeks, while tiles in other parts of the museum last for years. Tile wear, they suggest, is a good index of the relative popularity of exhibits. In the hallways on our campus, the floor tiles with the greatest number of cigarette burns are those directly outside classrooms where students congregate between lectures. Although it is relatively easy to record waiting patterns through systematic observation, cigarette burns increase confidence in the findings.

Limitations

Apart from archeology, trace measures have not found wide acceptance in behavioral research. Most social scientists prefer to study live interaction rather than carpets and lawns. Analyzing garbage and litter can be a dirty business that involves a serious breach of privacy. Park employees in Michigan, for example, objected when they were ordered to dig through garbage barrels as part of a research project on throwaway bottles (Associated Press, 1978).

The information provided by trace measures can be misleading. Deterioration of certain library books, for example, may reflect the activities of a single destructive individual rather than a large general circulation. The absence of graffiti in a restroom may reveal more about the cleaning policies of the janitors than about the social attitudes of the people using the restrooms. The wear on the floor tiles around drinking fountains will be due to a combination of usage and dripping water.

Summary

A behavioral map is a record of people's behavior in space. Behavioral maps can be place-centered or person-centered. A place-centered map shows how people arrange themselves in a particular setting. A person-centered map involves a record of a person's movements and activities over time.

Limitations: Behavioral mapping can be both tiring and intrusive. Further research will be needed to explain the behaviors observed.

Trace measures are the physical remains of interaction after the people have departed. Accretion refers to the buildup of a residue or product of the interaction. It is something added to the situation. Erosion refers to deterioration or wear and provides an index of usage patterns. With erosion, something is worn down or removed.

Limitations: Trace measures are necessarily indirect and may be the result of extraneous factors.

References

Associated Press. (1978, August 31). High priority research stinks, garbage-picking workers say. *Sacramento Bee*, p. B5.

Bechtel, R. (1971). *Arrowhead: Final recommendations*. Kansas City, Mo.: Environmental Research and Development Foundation.

Hester. R. T. (1975). *Neighborhood space*. Stroudsburg, Pa.: Dowden, Hutchinson, & Ross.

Ittelson, W. H., Proshansky, H. M., & Rivlin, L. G. (1970). The environmental psychology of the psychiatric ward. In H. M. Proshansky, W. H. Ittelson, & L. G. Rivlin (Eds.), *Environmental psychology*. New York: Holt, Rinehart and Winston.

Ittelson, W. H., Rivlin, L. G., & Proshansky, H. M. (1976). The use of behavioral maps in environmental psychology. In H. M. Proshansky, W. H. Ittelson, & L. G. Rivlin (Eds.), *Environmental psychology* (2nd ed.). New York: Holt, Rinehart and Winston.

Ley, D., & Cybriwsky, R. (1974). Urban graffiti as territorial markers. *Annals of the Association of American Geographers, 64*, 491–505.

Quan, J. (1978). *Social interaction of Chinese elderly in a skilled nursing home and day health center*. Unpublished manuscript.

Rivlin, L. G., & Rothenberg, M. (1976). The use of space in open classrooms. In H. M. Proshansky, W. H. Ittelson, & L. G. Rivlin (Eds.), *Environmental psychology* (2nd ed.)(pp.
479–489). New York: Holt, Rinehart and Winston.

Sawyer, H. G. (1961). *The meaning of number.* Speech before the American Association of
Advertising Agencies.

Sechrest, L., & Flores, L. (1969). Homosexuality in the Philippines and the United States:
The handwriting on the wall. *Journal of Social Psychology, 79,* 3–12.

Sladen, J. J. L. (1958). The pygoscelid penguins, parts 1 and 2. *Scientific Reports of the Falk-
land Islands Dependency Survey, 17.* London.

Sommer, R., & Ross, H. F. (1958). Social interaction on a geriatrics ward. *International Journal of Social Psychiatry, 4,* 128–133.

Webb, E. J., Campbell, D. T., Schwartz, R. D., Sechrest, L. & Grove, J. B. (1981). *Nonreactive
measures in the social sciences* (2nd ed.). Boston: Houghton Mifflin.

Further Reading

Barker, R. G. (1968). *Ecological psychology.* Stanford: Stanford University Press.

Beckman, L., & Hency, T. (Eds.). (1972). *Beyond the laboratory: Field research in social psychology.* New York: McGraw-Hill.

Holahan, C. J. (1980). Action research in the built environment. In R. H. Price & P. E. Politser
(Eds.), *Evaluation and action in the social environment.* New York: Academic Press.

Webb, E. J., Campbell, D. T., Schwartz, R. D., Sechrest, L. & Grove, J. B. (1981). *Nonreactive
measures in the social sciences* (2nd ed.). Boston: Houghton Mifflin.

Willems, E. P. (1977). Behavioral ecology. In D. Stokols (Ed.), *Perspectives on environment
and behavior.* New York: Plenum Press.

III
Designing Experiments

6 Experimentation

Ratus norvegicus, the white rat so often used in pychological experiments, completed his run along the neck of a T-maze, made a right turn, and gobbled up the rat chow in the goal box (see Figure 6-1.) Why did he turn right? How did he learn to locate the food? Did he know its location in space, or did he simply learn to turn right every time he reached the choice point of the maze? Clark Hull (1943) believed that the rat learned to turn right through practice and reward. Hull developed an influential theory of psychology as to how such responses were acquired. It is called *S-R theory,* or *stimulus-response learning.* Edward Tolman (1932) believed that the rat conceptualized the food's location in space and coined the term *cognitive map.* Tolman's formulations also became an important part of psychological theory. Whether the rat learned only to make a particular response, or instead recognized the location of objects in space, has never been satisfactorily resolved even though experimenters have resorted to clever measures. Some gave the rats wagon rides to the food so that they did not actually run through the maze. Others used elaborate three-dimensional structures with careful laboratory controls for lighting, landmarks, and odor cues.The rats were very good at learning the location of the food.

Linda Acredolo (1978) resurrected the old controversy in her investigations of how infants locate objects and events. She constructed a special room with walls made of curtains. Entry is made through the corner without the necessity of a door. The room has two windows on opposite sides (see Figure 6-2). In the center is a table. At some distance from the center is a chair on rollers that may be moved full circle within the room.

A very young infant is brought into the room by its mother, and both

FIG. 6-1. Rat in a T maze.

mother and baby sit in the chair facing the center table. The windows are to the right and left. A buzzer on the table rings to attract the infant's attention. Then Acredolo looks through the window to the baby's right, smiles and waves, says "Hi, baby," and disappears (see photograph). After a few repetitions, the infant, on hearing the buzzer, looks to the right (Window X) in anticipation of Acredolo's appearance. Now, the question is, has the baby learned the *location* of that event, or has it simply learned to turn its head to the right on hearing the buzzer? It is the old response-versus-place-learning question again. Acredolo's procedure is simply to revolve infant and mother 180° around the table to the opposite end of the room and see where the baby looks when the buzzer rings. If the learning is of response type, the baby will look to its right, to the other window (Window Y), not the one where Dr. Acredolo has been appearing with "Hi, baby." Acredolo

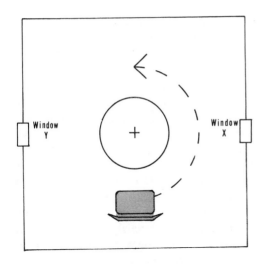

FIG. 6-2. Acredolo's special room.

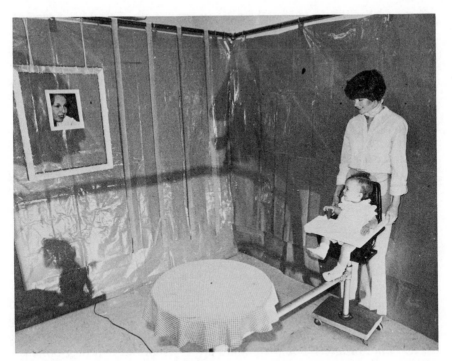

Laboratory experiment. This researcher constructed a special room to study how young children orient themselves in space.

calls the baby's reaction an *egocentric* response, implying that the child has no notion of objective space. If the baby has acquired spatial orientation, place learning should occur and the baby will look toward the initial window (Window X), making a left rather than a right head turn.

This neat experiment is the result of much preliminary work. In order to obtain reliable and valid results, many babies must be tested. Some infants may have a natural response bias to turn right or left. Since rats show turning preferences; the same may be true of babies. Further, infants of differing age and sex must also be tested. Previous experience in the home environment may also influence the outcome. Many other details must be taken into account; thus, experiments are conducted under controlled conditions. Before going on, here are Acredolo's results. The 6-month-old and 11-month old babies showed egocentric (response) learning rather than place learning. They located things primarily with reference to their own bodies. The 16-month-old babies, perhaps as a result of increased individual mobility, tended to be place learners.

The Special Nature of the Experiment

These studies illustrate how the experimental method is used to separate alternative explanations and test them. Among the various research methods, the experiment is particularly suitable for tracing cause-and-effect relationships. Through observation one finds many things that occur together, but observation alone cannot determine whether one thing is the cause of another. All other alternative explanations must be ruled out. A classic example is the relationship between cigarette smoking and lung cancer. Doubts about the contribution of cigarettes to lung cancer were removed when experiments on animals showed that the substances in cigarettes were carcinogenic (cancer causing). Other environmental factors, such as air pollution, may also affect the relationship. The experiment enables each of these factors to be tested in a systematic way. An artificial situation is created in which events that generally go together may be pulled apart.

Variables

A *variable* is any characteristic or quality that differs in degree or kind and can be measured. Examples of variables are height, hair color, sex, running speed, income, IQ, education, social class, and politial party. Variables have *values* or *levels*. Some variables are *continous* in that they possess a sliding scale of value, varying in quantitative fashion. Age is a continuous variable, ranging from zero to over 100 years. A person's age may fall anywhere along that dimension. Other variables are *categorical:* Mutually exclusive categories of value, instead of continuous dimensions, are used. The levels tend to be more qualitative than quantitative. Political party membership is a variable with categorical values, as is sex. A person belongs to one or another party and is usually either male or female. Some variables may be treated as either continuous or categorical. If hair color is measured on a scale of very light to very dark, the variable will have continuous values. On the other hand, if we use mutually exclusive categories of blond, brunette, and redhead, hair color would be considered a categorical variable with three levels.

Independent and Dependent Variables

The variable that is systematically altered by the experimenter is called the *independent variable*. In an experiment, the treatment is the independent variable. The variable that we presume it will affect is called the *dependent variable*.

> Question: Do students do better on an algebra examination when they have studied for a small period of time each day for a week preceding the test (spaced study) or when they cram only on the day before (massed study)?
>
> Experiment: Compare algebra test scores of students preparing with spaced study with those of students using massed study.
>
> Subjects (participants): Algebra students
> Independent variable: Type of preparation
> Two levels (treatment conditions): Spaced study, massed study
> Dependent variable: Score on algebra examination
> Values: Continuous

Experimental Control

The purpose of an experiment is to determine the effect of the independent variable upon the dependent variable. All other influential variables must be either eliminated or their effect controlled in some way to ensure that they are not the cause of a change in the dependent variable. The experimenter should avoid *confounding* or confusing the effect of the independent variable with that of other variables. These other variables to be either eliminated or controlled are termed *extraneous*. They are neither the independent nor the dependent variables of the study. An extraneous variable in one experiment may become an independent or dependent variable in another. Extraneous variables are sources of error, since they mask or cloud the observable effects of the independent variable. For example, in the algebra experiment, if the spaced-study group were more intelligent than the massed-study group, the independent variable would be confounded with the extraneous variable of intelligence. We would not know whether a difference between the groups resulted from the type of preparation or a difference in intelligence. Extraneous variables are associated with the subjects, the experimenter, the setting in which the experiment occurs, and the experimental procedure itself.

Subject Characteristics

The participants in an experiment are called *subjects*. The qualities of the subject are likely to influence the experimental outcome. These include such characteristics as age, education, socioeconomic background, and personality, as well as temporary conditions such as fatigue, nervousness, or preoccupation with other matters. Participants' expectations and beliefs about the experiment may also influence the results.

Solutions:
1. Eliminate or reduce extraneous variables when possible; for example, reduce fatigue by using rested subjects.
2. Make the extraneous variables as similar as possible for all treatment conditions
   a. *Matching groups*—each treatment group shows similar levels of subject characteristics. They are matched by sex, religion, age, socioeconomic background, intelligence, and so on.
   b. *Random assignment*—subjects are randomly assigned to treatment groups. The assumption is that the extraneous variables will be randomly distributed, and thus roughly the same for all treatment groups.

This ensures that extraneous variables will be randomly distributed and roughly the same for all conditions. See Chapter 16 for descriptions of sampling techniques and random selection and assignment procedures.

Experimenter Characteristics

Experimenters, like subjects, possess a variety of characteristics and expectations that might influence the outcome of an experiment. These must be eliminated or kept the same for all subjects.

Solutions:
1. Train experimenters in order to reduce extraneous influences.
2. Use the same experimenter for all subjects.

3. If more than one experimenter is involved, have each run an equal number of subjects in each treatment condition, *or*
4. Randomly assign experimenters to subjects.

The Setting

Qualities of the setting in which the experiment takes place—the functioning of the equipment, time of day, and other situational variables—are also potential sources of error.

   Solutions:
1. Run all subjects about the same time of day.
2. Keep the laboratory conditions (lighting, temperature, noise, etc.) as similar as possible for all subjects (except for the levels of the experimental variable).
3. Check equipment frequently to make sure that it is functioning properly.

The Procedure

The groups treated with or exposed to the different levels of the independent variable are called the *experimental groups*. In addition, many experiments use a *control group*. The control group is deliberately set up to be influenced by all of the variables affecting the experiments groups *except* the independent variable.

   Example:
   A researcher is interested in the effects of a drug on a rat's performance in a maze-running task. Rats are randomly assigned to either the experimental or control conditions.

Subject groups	Treatment condition	Measure
Experimental	Independent variable (drug injection)	Dependent variable (maze-running time)
Control	Same as the experimental group *except* for the independent variable (salt water instead of drug injection)	Dependent variable (maze-running time)

   If changes in the experimental group were due to the experience of being handled or receiving a shot (extraneous variables), the control groups should also show them. The effect of the drug is assessed by looking at the difference between the two groups on the dependent variable (maze-running time). A difference is then attributable to the drug.

Sometimes subject performance is measured before and after treatment; thus, the subjects serve as their own controls. A problem, however, is that change might occur as a result of practice, fatigue, or some other occurrence between trials. Thus, a separate control group is often more appropriate.

Types of Experiments

True Experiments

In a true experiment, three principles must hold: (1) at least two groups or conditions are compared, (2) the researcher has control of or can predict and evaluate the experimental treatment, and (3) subjects are randomly assigned to treatment groups. True experiments may be conducted in the laboratory or in the field—classrooms, homes, public streets, etc. The only difference between laboratory and field experiments is their location.

Laboratory experiments are probably the most common, since they are done in a specially created setting in which the experimenter is able to control a wide variety of extraneous variables. Temperature, lighting, and other aspects of the environment are easily held constant, while distractons such as noise and other activity are eliminated or reduced. In the laboratory, conditions can be created and changed according to schedule and in a manner desired by the researcher. As a convenience to the experimenter, the laboratory is hard to beat. Apparatus is often used in laboratory experiments (see Chapter 14).

Some researchers prefer to do experiments in the outside environment. In a *field experiment* the researcher manipulates the independent variable, but does so in the field (the outside environment) instead of in the laboratory. The design of the field experiment is like that of a laboratory experiment, except for the setting. Field experiments tend to be more difficult to do and interpret than laboratory experiments because there are so many uncontrolled factors that affect behavior: economic conditions, climate, number of people around, and myriad other environmental conditions. Their major advantage is their naturalness compared to the presumed artificiality of the laboratory. Field experiments often possess more external validity than laboratory experiments. That is, the results may be more readily generalized to real-world settings. Experimental psychologists have studied the spatial imagery of taxi drivers (how they learn to find their way around the city), how police are trained to visually process information at the scene of a crime, and the ability of headwaiters to remember customers' names. Henry Bennett (1983), a psychology graduate student, investigated the ability of waiters to remember complicated food and beverage orders. In one study, Bennett and three friends entered a restaurant, sat at a table, and ordered a full-course meal. After the waiter had left the table, the four friends switched places. This was done to see if the waiter associated orders with place or with person. This problem bears some relationship to Acredolo's studies of response versus place learning by infants, described at the beginning of this chapter. Unlike Acredolo's laboratory studies, Bennett's work qualifies as a field experiment. It was done in a natural setting, and the experimenter deliberately changed a single factor (locations at the table) in a systematic way to determine its effect on the waiter's recall. Had the research not been so time consuming and expensive (four full-course meals for each experimental session) Bennett could have expanded the study to compare tables with 4, 6, 8, and 10 customers. He also would have liked to compare customer orders given in a clockwise pattern with those given from random locations at the table.

Actually, Bennett did continue his investigation to include these factors, but instead of doing further field experiments with food orders, he undertook a modified simulation (see Chapter 7). He tape recorded complicated beverage orders from tables containing 7, 11, and 15 individuals and compared the ability of cocktail waitresses and college students to match the orders with table locations. He also interviewed waitresses on the methods of recall they used. This is a good illustration of a multimethod approach to a problem that has traditionally been studied only in the laboratory.

Certain topics are more appropriately studied in the field than in the laboratory. For example, responses to litter and reactions in dentists' waiting rooms are best assessed in the real world. Field studies allow the researcher to go beyond verbal replies to questionnaire or interview items (How often do you litter? Would you pick up an empty beer can lying on the road?), and they avoid the artificiality and distortion of the laboratory. Following the hypothesis that "litter begets litter," it has been found that areas deliberately littered by the experimenter will be more littered by other people than those areas kept neat and clean (Finnie, 1973).

Quasi-experiments

The distinguishing characteristic of a *quasi-experiment*, also known as a *natural experiment*, is that the third condition for a true experiment *(random assignment)* is not met. These are studies of naturally occurring events in which it is impossible to randomly assign subjects to treatment groups or conditions (Campbell & Stanley, *1963*). Examples of quasi-experiments are:

Comparing school achievement in two communities having different student-teacher ratios.

Studying the rate of highways accidents before and after the setting of a national speed limit of 55 miles per hour.

Analyzing residential patterns before and after the compulsory busing of school children

In these instances the researchers do not have direct control over the application of the independent variable, although its effect can be evaluated. These studies gain much in external validity, because they take place in the real world. Unfortunately they lose internal validity. Because subjects are not randomly assigned to conditions, there may have been self-selection or some other form of bias that in turn confounds the results. For example, people living in the town with the lower student-teacher ratio may be wealthier, so that differences in school achievement may in fact be due to home environment rather than to classroom variables.

How to Do an Experiment

Selecting a Topic

Although you may begin with fairly vague ideas, these must be formulated clearly before you design an experiment. Many ideas are suitable for experimentation, but some questions are more important than others. You

Quasi-experiment. To learn how much distance motorists kept between themselves and a bicyclist riding at different speeds, a bicyclist rode on a straight path along a road with separate 25-mile, 35-mile, and 45-mile speed limits. Another researcher photographed the "shy distance" kept by cars in each speed zone.

might ask yourself the grandmother question, "Why is a grown person like yourself concerned with this question?" If you are not sure about your answer, either give the queston more careful thought or change topics. You should be able to explain in clear language what you are doing and why you are doing it.

Developing Hypotheses

The experimental question concerns the relationship between two or more variables. This is generally phrased as a *hypothesis*, a testable proposition.

> *Example*
> Question: Do students in desegregrated classes show a change in IQ scores?
> Hypothesis: Students in desegregated classes will show an increase in IQ scores over time.

This hypothesis is stated positively: there will be a change. It is also possible to rephrase the question as a *null hypothesis*, which predicts that there will be no change.

> *Example*
> Question: Do students in desegregated classes show a change in IQ scores?
> Null hypothesis: Students in desegregated classes will show no change in IQ scores.

After the hypothesis has been formulated, you can consider whether an experiment would be helpful and, if so, what type of experiment—laboratory, field, or natural. At the conclusion of the study, the hypothesis will either be accepted or rejected, depending on the results.

Operational Definitions

The concepts included in the hypothesis must be operationally defined. An *operational definition* involves defining something by the way in which it is measured. Intelligence may be operationally defined as a score on an IQ test. Operational definitions sometimes vary from experiment to experiment. Worker satisfaction may be defined by a number of operations—turnover rate, productivity, expressed satisfaction on a questionnaire, and rate of absenteeism. However, while operational definitions may vary, they are not arbitrary. They must show a logical relationship to the concept under study.

The primary reason for using an operational definition is to specify clearly and precisely what is being measured so that the study may be repeated by someone else using exactly the same procedures and measurements. Using operational definitions reduces the likelihood of misunderstanding.

Designing the Study

The purpose of the experiment is to assess the effects of one or more independent variables on some dependent variable(s). The experimental design must accomplish this and control for the effects of extraneous variables in order to generate conclusive results.

> Problem: Are words that refer directly to sense experience (high-imagery words), such as *sun, brown, loud,* and *sweet,* learned more easily than words which do not refer directly to sense experience (low-imagery words), such as *sent, ask, idea,* and *certain?*
>
> Hypothesis: High-imagery words will be better recalled than low-imagery words.
>
> Operational definition: Ease of learning defined as a number of words recalled correctly.
>
> Independent variable: Degree of imagery
>   Values: High
>   Low
>
> Dependent variable: Number of words of each type recalled after exposure to them.
>   Value: Continuous
>
> Extraneous variables: Familiarity of words, word length, ability of subjects, fatigue, distraction in the setting.

Alternative Research Designs

1. All participants are presented with a mixed list of words.

Subject groups	Treatment condition (Independent variable)	Measure (Dependent variable)
All subjects	Mixed list—high- and low-imagery words	Number of high- and low-imagery words recalled correctly

2. Participants are randomly assigned to group 1 or group 2.

Subject group	Treatment condition (Independent variable)	Measure (Dependent variable)
Group 1	High-imagery word list	Number of high-imagery words recalled correctly
Group 2	Low-imagery word list	Number of low-imagery words recalled correctly

3. *Counterbalanced* design: Both groups receive the same lists of words, but in different order.

Subject group	*Treatment condition (Independent variable)*	*Measure (Dependent variable)*
Group 1	First list—High-imagery words followed by recall	Number of high-imagery words recalled correctly
	Second list—Low-imagery words followed by recall	Number of low-imagery words recalled correctly
Group 2	(reverse of above)	

The purpose of *counterbalancing* is to balance out effects due to order of presentation. Counterbalancing is one way of dealing with possible confounding of variables. If the low-imagery list were presented last to everyone and subjects did more poorly on recall of low-imagery words, it would not be clear whether the results were due to the low imagery or to some other factor, such as fatigue. If they did better, it might be due to practice; hence the need for counterbalancing.

Subject Selection and Assignment to Treatment Conditions

Follow the procedures outlined in Chapter 16 that describes the various techniques for obtaining subject samples. Be sure that the project follows local guidelines for the use of human or animal subjects.

Pilot Testing

Before actually running the experiment, it is essential to run a pilot study in order to be sure that the equipment is working and that directions are easily understood. Pick a small number of persons to use as pilot subjects. Do not use anyone you intend to use in the actual experiment because the pilot test experience might affect their later responses. Think of the pilot study as a last-minute check on the details. Make it as similar to the anticipated experiment as possible. If major problems are encountered, correct them and conduct another pilot test before running the actual experiment. The importance of the pilot test cannot be overemphasized. A preliminary run may save considerable time and effort later.

Running the Experiment

If the pilot test has been successful, the actual experiment should proceed smoothly. Be sure to follow the procedures specified in the design. If you are working with animals, each should be handled in the same manner,

BOX 6-1. Experimentation Checklist

A. Design considerations, preliminary to performing the experiment
   1. Is the rationale of the research question spelled out and are the hypotheses clearly stated?
   2. Are the independent and dependent variables specified and operationally defined in a logically justifiable manner?
   3. Does the research design control for
      a. Subject error?
      b. Experimenter error?
      c. Environmental error, including apparatus, setting, and time of day, and so on?
   4. Is the subject sample representative of the population of concern?
   5. Have you met local requirements concerning the use of human (or animal) subjects?
B. Pilot test (trial experiment)
   1. Are directons clearly understood?
   2. Does the apparatus work correctly?
   3. Is the experimenter performing correctly?
C. Correct any anticipated problems. If they are extensive, do a second pilot test, and upon satisfactory completion proceed with the experiment.
D. On completion, debrief participants and thank them for their cooperation. Answer any questions and explain where and when the results will be available.

except for the specific treatment constituting the independent variable. If you are studying human beings, each person in each group is to be treated in identical fashion—same instructions, same interaction with the experimenter, and so on. All of the considerations mentioned earlier about the control of extraneous variables apply during the experiment.

Be sure to thank participants for their assistance and cooperation. Offer to answer any questions they might have, explain the purpose and uses of the data, and mention when and where the results will be available. See Box 6-1 for a list of steps involved in experimentation.

Limitations

Artificiality is both a major strength and major weakness. Experimental design provides for the separation of variables and enables either control or measurement of extraneous variables. Nature, however, does not operate in accord with this approach. Variables are combined and often interactive. Science is an imposition of a theoretical structure upon the natural world. The structure fits better in some cases than in others. Predictions derived from good experimentation are valid only for settings similar to those in which they were obtained. The more one uses the advantages of the experiment—separating and controlling the effect of variables—the further one moves from the natural world. Subjects in the laboratory may behave differently from people (or animals) outside. Some problems are not suitable for experimentation either for ethical reasons or for cost.

Summary

An experiment involves the creation of an artificial situation in which events that generally go together are pulled apart. The participants in an experiment are called subjects. The elements or factors included in the study are termed variables. Some variables, like age and income, are continuous in that they range along a continuing scale. A variable whose categories are, at least in theory, separate and exclusive, such as membership in a political party or eye color, are termed categorical.

Independent variables are those that are systematically altered by the experimenter. Those items that are affected by the experimental treatment are the dependent variables. Those variables that are not eliminated or controlled are termed extraneous. The most common extraneous variables are those associated with the subjects, the experimenter, the setting, and the experimental procedure.

The experimental groups consists of those subjects exposed to the independent variable. Other subjects not exposed to the independent variable may be included in the study as a control group.

In a *true experiment*, subjects are randomly assigned to treatment conditions. Laboratory experiments permit control of a wide variety of extraneous variables. Experimental control is more difficult in the field. However, field experiments often have more external validity than laboratory ones. In a *quasi-* or *natural experiment*, subjects are not randomly assigned to conditions, but, rather, studied as the conditions naturally occur. Quasi-experiments take advantage of situations that arise as a result of social policy or natural events.

A hypothesis is a testable proposition. The concepts included in the hypothesis must be operationally defined. An operational definition defines something by the way it is measured.

Limitations: While allowing the researcher an impressive amount of control over variables, the experiment in behavioral research is limited chiefly by its artificiality. Conditions in the laboratory may be different from those in the outside world, and people will behave differently. Some behavioral issues are not suitable for experimentations for ethical reasons or cost.

References

Acredolo, L. P. (1978). Development of spatial orientation in infancy. *Developmental Psychology*, 14, 224–234.

Bennett, H. L. (1983). Remembering dring orders: The memory skills of cocktail waitresses. *Human Learning*, 2, 157–169.

Campbell, D., & Stanley, J. (1963). Experimental and quasi-experimental designs for research on teaching. In N. L. Gage (Ed.), *Handbook of research in teaching*. Chicago: Rand McNally.

Finnie, W. C. (1973). Field experiment in litter control. *Environment and Behavior*, 123–144.

Hull, C. L. (1943). *Principles of behavior*. New York.: D. Appleton-Century.

Tolman, E. C. (1932). *Purposive behavior in animals and men*. New York: Century.

Further Reading

Anderson, B. F. (1971). *The psychology experiment* (2nd ed.). Belmont, CA: Brooks/Cole.

Cozby, P. C. (1981). *Methods in behavioral research* (2nd ed.). Palo Alto, CA: Mayfield.

Elmes, D. G., Kantowitz, B. H., & Roediger, H. L. (1985). *Research methods in Psychology* (2nd ed.). St. Paul, MN: West.

Howard, G. S. (1985). *Basic research methods in the social sciences*. Glenview, IL: Scott, Foresman.

Keppel, G., & Saufley, W. H., Jr. (1980). *Introduction to design and analysis: A student's handbook*. San Francisco: W. H. Freeman.

Solso, R. L., & Johnson, H. H. (1984). *An introduciton to experimental design in psychology* (3rd ed.). New York: Harper & Row.

7 Simulation

What is a simulation?
Limitations
Summary

"It's painfully close to the bone," said a dazed role-playing city politician, a man who works on the staff of New York City's Administrator for Environmental Protection. "APEX has all the frustrations of a real city government. You can't get anything done. No one listens to you. You can't get money for programs. And you have to make decisions without nearly enough time or infomation."

"It's uncanny," said a real-life air control officer playing himself. "What you meet here is a bunch of clowns just like the ones we have to deal with almost every day" (Lindsay, 1972). These were some of the responses of people playing the Air Pollution Exercise (APEX), a simulation game intended to teach people about environmental politics.

What Is a Simulation?

Behavioral simulations are imitations of actual situations. They are intended to resemble the true situation in many of its functional characteristics without being mistaken for that situation. An APEX player learns that air pollution control involves more than scientific formulas, cost/benefit ratios, and state and federal laws. There is also a matter of working with local politicians, private developers and industrialists, city and county planners, and air pollution control officers. APEX is one of the many experimental games used in teaching and research.

Situations like air pollution control are difficult to study either in the laboratory or as they occur naturally. The deliberations of business firms or city planning departments are often confidential and occur over a period of years. A simulation involves a complex social situation in which many variables are deliberately mixed together with no effort made to untangle them, as distinct from a laboratory experiment in which variables are introduced systematically so that their specific effects can be measured. Once a simulation has begun, such as when people are asked to imagine that they are participants in a city council meeting on air pollution, it develops its own dynamics and proceeds at its own pace. The researcher lacks the control over the session that would be considered necessary in a laboratory experiment. Simulations have many uses in teaching and clinical practice that will not be covered here. For example, asking people who have been divorced to play a part of a former partner may help them to understand the other person's view of the situation. Readers who are interested in nonresearch applications of simulation will find interesting information in the periodical *Simulation and Games,* published by Sage Publications.

Simulations vary in cost and complexity. They may be as modest as asking students in a class to imagine themselves participants in a UN conference or as complex as constructing a stationary space capsule in the basement of a NASA laboratory. While the mock-up of a space ship and the detailed monitoring of people's responses cost thousands of dollars, an actual flight trial of a space ship would cost tens of millions. Because it depends heavily on the ability of particpants to "fill in" omitted items through imagination, a simulation is less expensive than constructing the actual object.

Simulations also tend to be more economical in terms of time. A graduate student in comparative psychology became interested in improving the information signs at the local zoo. At first, she considered making her own new signs and trying them out on the actual cages. She was interested both in different types of signs and in placing them in different locations outside the cage (e.g., at eye level, at the bottom, at the side). It quickly became apparent that five different signs in five locations would mean 25 experimental conditions. While this would be very awkward and time consuming for a field experiment, it would be a natural problem for a simulation. Once the student created the five different signs, she could photograph these in each of the five locations on the cage. Zoo visitors could then be shown a display of color photographs and asked for their preferences. Testing could be done at a booth in the zoo. Simulation would reduce an otherwise unwieldy field experiment with 25 different conditions to manageable proportions.

Physical handicaps and sensory deficits can also be simulated. This avoids the criticism that the blind or crippled are a select group so well adjusted to their handicaps that they don't recognize how their behavior has changed. However, one would not want to draw conclusions about the world of the blind or the deaf solely on the basis of college students wearing blindfolds and earplugs. It would be necessary to interview blind and deaf people too.

A research team composed of both handicapped and nonhandicapped persons tested the University of California, Santa Cruz, campus for wheelchair access. A fleet of wheelchairs had been provided so that everyone, handicapped and nonhandicapped, could experience some of the problems in getting around. For example, many elevator and emergency alarm but-

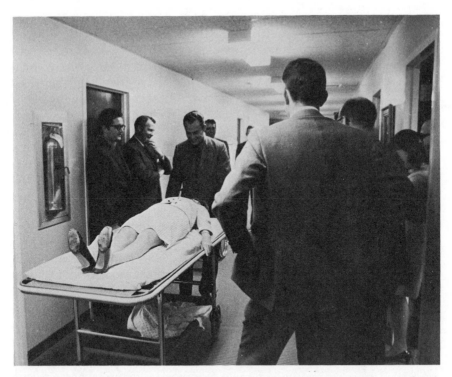

Simulation. To learn some of the problems faced by patients, hospital staff and administrators wheeled each other down the hall on gurneys and tried walking on crutches.

tons were too high to be reached from a wheelchair; so were some copy machine coin slots, many drinking fountains, all upper book shelves, and the top drawers of the library card catalog. Maneuvering through the heavy restroom door in bathroom cubicles, including those designed specifically for wheelchairs, proved very difficult. The team made numerous suggestions for solving the problems they had identified during the exercise (*UCSC Review*, 1978).

Simulation procedures like this can come close to being full-fledged experiments. An experiment involves an artifical situation in which events that generally go together may be separated. A simulation involves an artificial situation, such as a space capsule or wheelchair ride, whose components are left together. To the extent that the researcher attempts to separate items that occur naturally together, the simulation becomes indistinguishable from the experiment. If nonhandicapped students in wheelchairs are asked to perform specific tasks and then timed, the procedure would qualify as an experiment. However, if a person is asked to spend the entire day in a wheelchair and keep notes of everything that occurs, it seems more logical to call this a simulation.

Simulations are most useful in situations where observation and experimentation are not feasible or ethical. For example, a furor was caused when it was found that jury deliberations in Chicago were being taped as part of a research project. Researchers avoid controversy today by using experimental juries composed of paid volunteers. Philip Zimbardo created an artificial jail in the basement of Stanford University's psychology building using paid volunteers as prisoners and guards. The experience had tremendous emotional impact upon the participants. Students playing the guards became cold, aloof, and hostile. Those who became inmates were at first angry and rebellious but in the end became sullen, bitter, and emotionally burned out (Haney, Banks, & Zimbardo, 1973).

Board games such as Monopoly and chess are simulated conflicts. War games were used by the Prussian general staff to train military officers during the nineteenth century, and many other countries have used board games in military schools since then. Training games are also widely used

Simulation. Board games can be used in research on social problems. These people are playing a game designed to teach about social inequality. Some players begin the game with less money and have fewer chances for advancement than others.

in business education. There are probably as many business games as all other simulation procedures combined (Robinson, 1967).

Limitations

Two criticisms of simulations are that they are too realistic in some instances and not realistic enough in others. The imitation jail constructed in the basement of Stanford University's psychology building was extremely stressful for the participants. Even milder forms of roleplaying can be upsetting. People become so identified with their roles that they say and do things they regret later. It is difficult to predict in advance how people will respond in a role-playing exercise and thus protect them from personal revelations or actions that may be harmful to them or upsetting to others. For example, when people take part in role-playing exercises, they reveal themselves in the presence of co-workers, friends, fellow students, supervisors, and others. When the mayor and the county air pollution officer play APEX, each has the opportunity to observe the other's performance, and if the mayor is in charge later on, this may have serious implications for the air pollution officer's job. Ethical problems of simulation exercises outweigh their usefulness as a research tool in many situations. Simulation should be considered primarily when other methods are unavailable or inappropriate.

The second major criticism of simulations is that they are artificial and unrealistic. Playing games is not the same as real life. The actors and the researcher are unrealistic when they try to generalize from imitation to real life. Board games such as chess and Monopoly are less a copy of actual conflict situations than another level of reality (i.e., game playing). The brief duration of play, the fixed rules, and the illusory quality of the rewards and penalties make the situation different from ordinary life.

Summary

Behavioral simulations are intended to resemble actual situations in many of their functional characteristics without being mistaken for them. Simulations include experimental games, role-playing exercises, and large-scale models. Compared to actual situations, simulations are economical in terms of time and money.

Limitations: When a simulation is not sufficiently realistic, it will lack validity; however, if it is too realistic, it can be stressful for the participants. Simulation is used primarily when other methods are unavailable, inappropriate, or too expensive.

References

Haney, C., Banks, C., & Zimbardo, P. (1973). Interpersonal dynamics in a simulated prison. *International Journal of Criminology and Penology, 1,*69–97.

Lindsay, S. (1972, May 13). *Saturday Review,* 55–57.

Robinson, J. A. (1967). Simulation and games. In P. H. Rossi & Bruce J. Biddle (Eds.), *The new media and education.* New York: Anchor Books.

UCSC Review, 1978, *3,* 3.

Further Reading

Cohen, R., McManus, J., Fox, D., & Kastelnik, C. (1973). *Psych city: A simulated community.* New York: Pergamon.

Rapaport, A., & Chammah, A. (1965). *Prisoner's dilemma.* Ann Arbor, Mich.: Univeristy of Michigan Press.

Wrightsman, L. S., O'Connor, J., & Baker, J. N. (Eds.) (1972). *Cooperation and competition: Readings in mixed motive games.* Monterey, CA: Brooks/Cole.

IV
Survey Design

8 Interview

Face-to-face interviews provide an excellent way of exploring complex feelings and attitudes. The following interview was designed to explore the psychological accompaniments of early adolescence and puberty.

Question: Could you characterize your feelings, attitudes, and behavior in general during the period of puberty?

Answer: I was silent and observant, afraid to become involved. Religious origin—the world was the enemy. Very fundamentalist. I was a wayfarer, so the world was my enemy and so were young people outside of church. I had greatly intensified sexual urges. I felt guilty. I was taught, "A man is what he thinks," so thoughts were as bad as action. I continually felt condemned. Earlier there was joke telling among my friends, before puberty. We exploited each other's knowledge.

Q: At what age would you say that you became physically mature— you felt, "This was it!"

A: Intense sexual arousal in the 7th and 8th grade, around age 11 or 12. Couldn't fight it off. Earlier I could forget. Now it was driving and obsessional. (Dreams?) Oh boy, I was very superstitious. Believed in the supernatural. Frightened of the dark. The biggest fear of nightmares. These were the word from the supernatural. Had wet dreams—guilty of committing the act. I was in a real turmoil. I lavished in sensations, but was a very frightened young person.

Q: How would you characterize your feelings at that specific time?

A: I became very emotional, became depressed easily. Had heightened experiences. Fears intensified. I felt more emotional activity.

This was a 27-year-old man's recollections of his adolescence. The interviewer wanted to find out the defining events of puberty, people's responses to the physical changes that were taking place, and their attitudes toward family, friends, and the other sex. The research question was how people *remembered* this period in their lives. This was a combination of what actually happened and how people recalled it later. Had the researcher been solely concerned with the experience of puberty, she would have interviewed boys and girls from ages 11 to 15.

Because memories of early adolescence are often murky and emotionally charged, the interview seemed a more appropriate research tool for this study than the written questionnaire. The interviewer was able to follow up half-answered questions and encourage the respondent to answer more fully. When the session was over, many of the respondents thanked the interviewer for listening to them describe for the first time what puberty had meant to them (Sommer, 1978).

There are times when interviews will produce more accurate information than other types of procedures that seem on the surface to be more rigorous and objective. Researchers found that interviews were more accurate in detecting alcoholism than were laboratory tests. The best of the laboratory tests used in the study detected only a third of those with serious alcohol problems while interview procedures detected 95 percent of excessive drinkers (Bernadt, Mumford, Taylor, Smith, & Murray, 1982).

Interviews constitute a rich and fascinating source of information for research. Their intrinsic interest stems from the personal interaction that is the core of the procedure. Modern technology has led to a broadening of the face-to-face concept to include interviews by telephone, video, and other extended means of communication. However, the key element of the interview is the verbal give-and-take between two persons with the questions and answers providing its form. Another way of describing an interview is that it is a "conversation with a purpose" (Bingham & Moore, 1959).

It is surprising to discover all that people are willing to talk about. With encouragement and the recognition of genuine interest on the part of the interviewer, people will reveal a great deal about themselves and about their beliefs and feelings. In collecting case histories on sexual behavior, Alfred Kinsey and his associates appealed to the willingness of people to contribute information that would be of scientific value and of help to others. The basic pitch was to altruism, but its mode varied for each group interviewed. Professional people responded when they recognized the social significance of the study. Less educated people responded positively when told simply that doctors needed their help in knowing more about these things. The researchers were also quick to show their appreciation and esteem for those who helped. The success of the studies of sexual behavior was due not only to the scholarly competence of the investigators but also to their recognition of the fundamental importance of the human interaction which occurs between the interviewer and the respondent. The Kinsey group respected their interviewers and appointed them trustees of the Institute of Sex Research and members of the policy-making board. Over a period of 22 years, nearly 300 persons were considered as possible interviewers, from whom a total 9 was selected (Pomeroy, 1963). One outcome of this concern for the quality of interviewing is that the Kinsey studies remain an important landmark in the study of human sexual behavior.

Uses and Types of Interviews

The interview is particularly useful for the exploration of topics like puberty and sexual behavior, which are complex and emotionally loaded. Interviews are also useful in areas where opportunities for observation are limited. They can be used to assess beliefs and opinions as well as personality characteristics. A person's answers may reveal both manifest and latent content. *Manifest* content is that which is obvious and conveyed in the spoken information of the interview. It refers to what the person says. *Latent* content is the less obvious or more hidden information conveyed by hesitations and nonverbal responses, such as avoidance of eye contact, nervous gestures, or restlessness. Latent content indicates what the person means. The interviewer pays special attention when the latent content contradicts the manifest content. When interviews are recorded on videotape, the analysis of particular movements, gestures, and facial expressions, as well as changes in voice quality, hesitations ("um . . . you know . . ."), and pauses, provide a wealth of data for assessing the latent aspects of the communication. Such material may then be tabulated in a content analysis (see Chapter 11).

Interviews may focus on personality characteristics rather than on the content. One example is the *psychiatric interview*, an in-depth exploration of personality. These purposes may be combined. Social work interviews often serve the dual function of obtaining necessary factual information as well as gaining insight into a client's personality. Job interviews also combine these goals, where character as well as competence is evaluated. Newspaper and television interviews provide factual information to the viewer but also gives glimpses into the respondent's personality. In watching an interview with Fidel Castro, most of us are as intersted in what he is like as in what he says. Research interviews also provide this dual function. As we explore facts and opinions, we learn about the respondent.

A further advantage of the interview is that people who may be unwilling or unable to write out a long, coherent answer are often willing to say it to an interviewer. Of course this may also become a disadvantage when the interviewer encounters a long-winded respondent who wanders off the subject and won't stop talking. In such cases, the interviewer needs to be firm but polite in guiding the respondent back to the point.

Structured and Unstructured Interviews

Interviews may range form highly structured to unstructured interactions. In a *structured or standardized interview*, the questions are formulated beforehand and asked in a set order and in a specified manner. The structure is provided to obtain consistency from one situation to the next. In survey research where hundreds of people are contacted by several different interviewers, structured formats are essential in getting information which can be combined. The Gallup and Harris polls utilize mostly structured interviews to make their projections of public opinion.

In an *unstructured interview* the main goals are to explore all the alternatives in order to pick up information and define areas of importance that might not have been thought of ahead of time, and to allow the respondent to take the lead to a greater extent. The interviewer has in mind a general topic and may want to ask specific questions. However, there is no predetermined order or specified wording to the questions.

Whether the interview will be structured (standardized) or unstructured will depend on its purpose. If information from a number of respondents is to be combined, as in an attitude survey or opinion poll, then a structured interview is desirable. An unstructured interview is desirable as a preliminary step in developing a structured form for an interview, or a written questionnaire, or may stand as part of a qualitative study.

If data are to be meaningfully combined across respondents, then the questions must be asked in the same way, thus requiring a more structured or standard format. However, some questions still may be left open ended, for example, "What do you think about X?" and "Why do you feel that way?" The important point is that the same questions must be asked in the same manner for all respondents.

Sometimes it is necessary to design a *semi*structured interview where all respondents are asked the same questions, but the order in which they are asked differs from one person to the next. In some cases, even the manner in which they are asked varies, for example, changing the wording or sentence structure to better fit the respondent or the situation. This arrangement may be more suitable for obtaining in-depth information where the interviewer does not want to be restricted by a prescribed question order but would like the advantage of having asked the same questions of all respondents. Interviews with a cross section of the population may require adaptation of wording and sentence structure to better fit the respondent's age or social background.

Using a semistructured interview, one loses the consistency provided by following the same procedure for all respondents. The further one moves from a structured procedure, the greater the likelihood of interviewer bias.

Depth Interviews

The *depth* or *intensive interview* is a special form of unstructured interview. The interviewer follows the respondent's answers with a request for more information at an increasing level of depth. It is this process of using the respondent's answers to delve more deeply into the topic that gives the depth interview its name.

> *Example*
> Does your school operate on a semester or a quarter system?
> How do you feel about that? (rather than "Do you like it") Why?
> Could you be more specific?

As one line of questioning runs out, the direction is shifted.

> Have you ever attended a school with a different calendar system?
> How did that work?

or

> Do you have friends at colleges with the (semester/quarter) system?
> What did they think about it?
> What would you do if the current system at your school were changed?

In pursuing the topic, the tone of the questions remains neutral, giving the respondent as much freedom as possible to express feelings on the topic.

It requires practice and sensitivity to know when to change direction. When a new topic emerges in the discussion, it is difficult to know whether to follow it and risk losing continuity or stay on the major theme and risk the omission of additional information. The decision should rest on your assessment of the respondent and how much shifting of questions can be tolerated. Some people are easily confused and distracted by sudden shifts. Others become bored with a direct and obvious sequence. If the respondent begins answering questions before you ask them, consider picking up the pace and expanding the scope of your interview.

How to Interview

The most effective learning of interview techniques will come from practice combined with feedback. Practice with other people before doing the actual interviews. Such role playing will give you a chance to familiarize yourself with the procedures and provide an opportunity for feedback.

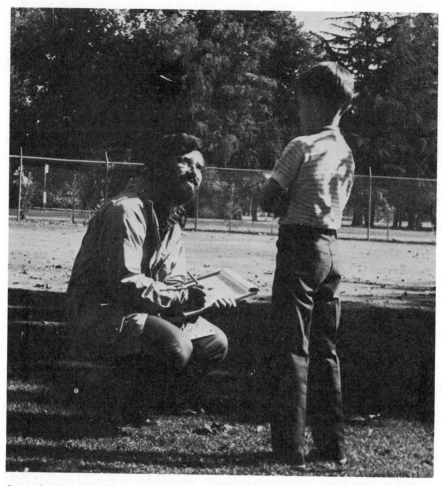

Interviewing children poses special problems. This interviewer felt that getting down to the child's own level increased rapport.

Videotaping and watching a playback of yourself conducting an interview will be helpful in improving your skills. Also, watching skilled interviewers and evaluating their performance provides learning. If a group of you are planning to work on a project, practice on each other and evaluate each other's performance.

Deciding What to Ask

In many cases, the topic will not be a matter of choice but instead is determined by the demands of the situation. The interview process will be con-

siderably simplified if you pick a topic with which most people are familiar. If your questions refer to rare experience or knowledge, you will spend
a lot of time searching for people who know something about the topic.
Another consideration is to select an issue that is nonthreatening. Ethical
considerations require care in interviewing about illegal or taboo subjects.
The respondent should be protected from any possible harmful effects of
the interview, for example, against court subpoena of interview records or
publication of embarrassing information. Sensitive topics must be pursued
sensitively. If they are not, the likelihood of a successful completion of the
interview is markedly reduced.

A final consideration is to pick a topic you find interesting. Your interest
or lack of interest is likely to be conveyed to the respondent. A ho-hum
reaction on the part of an interviewer quickly extinguishes any enthusiasm
a respondent might have about answering the questions.

Begin with the more general and more interesting questions. By starting
in a general manner, you are less likely to inadvertently influence the
answers. A specific question may establish a *set* (a tendency to respond in
a particular way), that then influences subsequent answers. Remember,
respondents tend to make judgments about what a questioner wants to
hear. Starting with more general questions reduces the likelihood of this
happening. The reason for beginning with interesting questions is fairly
obvious—to engage the interest and attention of the respondent. Also,
questions that might be more challenging or complicated are better asked
early. The routine ones that require little thought can be placed at the end
when fatigue is more likely—information covering name, birth date, place
of birth, and so on. This procedure relieves some uncertainty because the
respondent knows exactly what content will be associated with his or her
identification.

Questions should follow one another in a logical order without abrupt
changes in subject. If a change is necessary, a bridge statement from the
interviewer eases the transition.

> *Examples*
> Now, to change the subject, are you in favor or opposed to _____?
> Changing the subject, what do you think about _____?
> The next few questions will deal with _____.

Each subsection of the interview should contain questions which move
from the general to the specific.

The first questions asked should determine whether or not the respondent has knowledge of the topic you wish to cover. *Don't assume anything.*
A graduate student was once interviewing a young man hospitalized for a
suicide attempt. The patient explained that he had quarreled with his lover
and had then become despondent. After having already asked several questions which the respondent had willingly answered, the student asked,
"How long had she been living with you?" The respondent said heatedly,

"It's not a she, my lover is a man." There was an awkward pause as the graduate student readjusted his frame of reference. The interview continued, but there was a loss of rapport between interviewer and respondent.

Obtaining the Interview

Before considering a household survey, you should find out if it is legal. In an effort to regulate the activities of door-to-door salespeople, many communities require a license for any sort of solicitation. Because this was designed for salespeople, it probably won't affect a legitmate research study. However, some unscrupulous salespeople use the "I'm doing a survey" approach to get a foot in the door. This has given survey research a bad name. To be on the safe side, you should check with the local police department before embarking on a community survey. The police like to know what is going on around the precinct in case they receive telephone inquiries. There are certain neighborhoods where researchers may require police protection. Under those circumstances, it would be wise to switch to another data-gathering technique or another neighborhood. Some projects send out interviewers in pairs, one of whom always waits outside while the interview is in progress.

The interviewer's task becomes easier when people expect them or at least know that the survey is being undertaken. Knocking on doors will provoke many refusals from people who are disinterested, suspicious, or afraid of strangers. An advance phone call announcing that the interviewer is coming will be useful. Another helpful device is a leaflet placed in the mailbox or under doors the day before announcing that the survey is being undertaken and explaining its goals. Having the sponsorship of a recognized community agency will make your work easier. Sometimes even government sponsorship may not be sufficient, as in this case of responses of Minnesota farmers toward interviewers from the United States Department of Agriculture:

> The farmer scowls. "I won't give you anything, I'm disgusted." The interviewer walks away empty handed. Later the farmer explains his reaction to a reporter. "When she says 'Department of Agriculture,' I see red."
> The interviewer is accustomed to such treatment, especially nowadays, with agriculture in a near depression and many farmers blaming Washington for much of what is wrong. Although the majority continue to discuss their business and plans with federal pollsters when asked, thousands refused, and not always politely (Birnbaum, 1982).

First impressions are important. Appropriate dress and grooming will reduce reluctance or suspicion. Make a clear and honest introduction, giving your name and institutional affiliation and an explanation of the purpose of the interview. Your manner and voice should be friendly, courteous, and nonthreatening. Overfamiliarity should be avoided. In explaining the purpose of the interview, be sure to give the person time to understand what you are saying. It may be the fortieth time you have rattled it off, but it will be the first time your potential respondent has heard it.

Example
Good afternoon. My name is Robin Jones and I represent the International Research Corporation. We are doing a household survey on transportation needs in the community. May I please ask you a few questions on this topic? The interview should take no more than 15 minutes of your time.

It may be difficult to obtain an unbiased sample in a household survey. Who is at home will vary by time of day. In the afternoon there will be a disproportionate number of homemakers, older people, and children. It is also difficult to interview people in a crowded household. Securing privacy is a problem, and there are the distractions of chores, children, telephones, and television.

Street Corner Interviews

To avoid the problems of a house-to-house survey, some researchers prefer to collect their interviews on street corners, in parks, shopping malls, and other public locations. Again, it is important to gain the permission of the agency or corporation that controls the space. Local police should be consulted about a street corner survey, and the management of a shopping mall regarding a survey conducted on its premises. Most of the time people are willing to oblige a worthwhile and legitimate project. However, some of them may have been burned by individuals or groups promoting political causes, religious concerns, or commerical projects in the guise of doing a survey. Frequently it will be helpful in gaining an interview if you can state factually that the management of the shopping center or the park department has agreed to let you do the survey. Such permission adds legitimacy to your study.

Stopping people walking on the sidewalk may not be as easy as it sounds. Many people are in a hurry and others have developed a tunnel vision for strangers. They simply won't see you as you approach. It is best to dress neatly and carry an obvious clipboard that conveys your purposes at a glance. If you are mistaken for a panhandler, then you are doing something wrong.

Choose a location where people can see you from a distance. That way you won't surprise them with your request. This will enable them to convey through their actions their own curiosity, willingness to help, or clear disinterest. The best sort of location is where people are seated or moving slowly. Interviewing office workers eating lunch in a courtyard outside their building will be easier than stopping them on the street as they leave the building after work. Your success rate will be higher if you pick people who are strolling or window shopping than those who are walking hurriedly toward an obvious destination. Don't try to stop people who are rushing to catch the 5:02 train or trying to get on a bus. If you can get permission from the manager, an airport where people spend hours with nothing to do is a fine place to conduct a survey. Parks, beaches, museums, and shopping areas are also good locations for interviews.

Ingenuity and a knowledge of the characteristics of the population to be studied contribute to the success of an interview. A team of architects and social scientists studying housing preferences in the Navajo nation was having difficulty obtaining information through conventional means. The Navajo had been surveyed so often with so few results that they were uninterested in answering questions. Knowing the Navajo interest in traveling about their territory, the research team gained much of its information from hitchhikers. They picked up and interviewed riders as they drove them to their destinations. Under these circumstances, people were very cooperative (Snyder, Stea, & Sadalla, 1976). Sometimes you have to be creative in approaching the people you want to interview (see Boxes 8-1 and 8-2).

Setting the Stage

A major consideration in putting another person at ease is to be at ease yourself. Role playing and practice interviews will increase your confidence. Respondents generally are more likely to give candid responses

---

BOX 8-1. Creative Technique for Interviewing Bicyclists

The easiest way to find bicyclists, the research team decided, was to seek them out on the streets. A door-to-door survey would be unlikely to turn up more than a handful of dedicated riders. The first problem was to get the cyclists to stop long enough to be interviewed. The research team stationed themselves on a clear stretch of road frequently traveled by bicyclists. They placed a sign 100 feet ahead of them, "Bicycle survey ahead." This aroused the curiosity of most cyclists. The researchers carried obvious clipboards and had big signs across their chests that read "Bicycle survey". Most cyclists, alerted by the earlier notice and spotting the two sign-bedecked interviewers frantically waving their arms, pulled over and answered the questions (Kroll & Sommer, 1976). The novelty of the approach proved successful in that situation. Undoubtedly, if the procedure were repeated many times, the novelty would wear off. How would you go about conducting a survey about the attitudes of motorcyclists? Would you use the same procedure as in the bicycle survey or would you have to do something different?

BOX 8-2. Interviews in a Multimethod Study

Psychologist Donald Norman (1983) combined several research techniques in his studies of people's use of hand calculators. Norman gave people a series of arithmetic problems that were to be solved on a hand calculator. Participants were requested to "think aloud" as they solved the problems while Norman watched and recorded their words and actions. When all the problems were completed, Norman questioned the participants about the methods used and about their understanding of the calculator. Although all the people were reasonably experienced with the machines on which they were tested, they also seemed to have a distrust of the calculator or in their understanding of its operation. As a result, they would take extra steps or decline to take advantage of calculator features that were known to them. Those who had experience with several different calculators often confused features of the different machines. They were unsure which feature applied to which calculator and had various superstitions about the operations of the keyboard. For example, people would hit the CLEAR button several times saying such things as "You never know—sometimes it doesn't register." A similar pattern applied to the use of the ENTER button. People would push it repeatedly, often while commenting that while they knew this to be excessive, "It doesn't hurt to hit it extra" or "I always hit it twice when I have to enter a new phase—it's just a superstition, but it makes me feel more comfortable." The combination of observation and interview used in this procedure was superior to either method used alone.

when they are convinced that their responses will be kept confidential and when they perceive that no moral evaluation of them is being made by the interviewer. This observation was borne out by the researchers in the Kinsey studies of human sexual behavior. Despite the extremely intimate and sensitive nature of their questions, they obtained remarkable cooperation. The need for a nonjudgmental attitude and for assurances of confidentially connot be overemphasized. Human beings are very good at detecting deceit. If the interviewer is making strong moral judgments, it will come across during the interview. Such feelings must be reduced prior to the interview. This may be accomplished by recognizing the legitimacy of other people's views. Another means of reducing the emotional intensity of feelings is through discussion, which may make a topic less sensitive. If your own feelings remain strong, perhaps another person should be found to do the interviews.

Find a place for the interview that is free from distraction and serves to maintain confidentiality. Your respondent is not likely to be candid within earshot of others. Also, telephone calls and other interruptions interfere with the respondent's train of thought. Be sure your own needs for a writing surface and a comfortable location for recording are taken care of before you start. Otherwise, you may have to interrupt the session and you may miss important information.

Nonverbal Aspects

A degree of eye contact is important in establishing rapport between interviewer and respondent. However, don't stare. An unbroken or penetrating gaze will make the respondent uncomfortable. On the other hand, the absence of eye contact makes you appear untrustworthy or uncomfortable. Again, the best preparation for interviews is practice and getting honest feedback from classmates, colleagues, or friends.

The rest of your face, as well as your eyes, communicates your feelings, particularly those of approval and disapproval. Respondents are very likely to pick up even flickers of feeling. Thus, it is very important for an interviewer to show an attentive but nonjudgmental interest. As most of us are not trained actors, we will probably perform best when asking questions that interest us but that do not arouse intense emotions. For emotionally sensitive questions, a considerable amount of practice is essential in desensitizing feelings.

While conducting practice interviews, notice the set of your mouth, your body posture, and your position in relation to the respondent. When do you lean forward? When do you lean back? What might these behaviors communicate? Also, pay attention to your hands. Do you tend to cover your mouth when asking a question? The latent message of that movement is that you don't really want to ask it. Just as videotapes are widely used in training psychotherapists, so are they of value in providing feedback for research interviews. Observe the professional interviewers on television. Notice the effects of their behavior upon the respondents, and vice versa.

The quality of the interview data rests on the interaction between interviewer and respondent. Good questions can be ruined by improper techniques. Poor questions may be salvaged by a good interviewer. Remember, the purpose of an interview is to obtain information about another person's beliefs, opinions, feelings, or attitudes. Responding to the person's answers in a positive way is essential. One need not be vigorous in approval, but rather, through an occasional nod or eye contact, indicate attention and respect for the views expressed.

Interviewing people of different ethnic background, nationality, or social class brings special problems of nonverbal communication. In some cultures, for example, avoidance of eye contact is a sign of respect rather than an indication of untrustworthiness. Physical distance between interviewer and respondent has different meanings for persons of different backgrounds. Northern Europeans and Anglo-Americans often become uncomfortable within the close range quite acceptable for those of Latin background (Hall, 1959). Familiarity with the slang expressions of another social stratum may be necessary. A respondent will soon lose interest if the interviewer can't understand what is being said; for example, probing the drug culture requires knowledge of the various terms used for the drugs and persons associated with them.

Characteristics of race and sex as well as social class can affect the interview. However, the heart of the issue is the degree to which these characteristics will detract from obtaining candid responses. Persons of the same social or ethnic background also introduce a bias of conformity to expected attitudes. The quality of the interview depends more on the interviewer's capacity to convince the respondent of a nonjudgmental attitude and a sincere interest in and respect for the respondent's point of view than upon the specific characteristics of race, sex, or class. However, in some situations, these characteristics may be particularly influential and require a matching or deliberate contrasting of interviewer and respondent characteristics.

Pacing and Timing

A major mistake of beginning interviewers is the failure to allow enough time for the respondent to answer. The interviewer, especially after having formulated the questions, becomes very familiar with the outline and may forget that it is totally new to the respondent. A person needs time to think about each question and to prepare an answer. The interviewer must learn to be comfortable with long silences, yet recognize the point at which the silence is no longer productive and is making the respondent uncomfortable. If an answer is not forthcoming, a reformulation of the question may be appropriate. Sometimes the discomfort caused by silence may be used to the interviewer's advantage. It may lead the respondent to be more self-revealing than he or she originally intended.

To practice how to tolerate delay, look at a watch or clock with a second hand and observe the passage of 30 seconds. As silence, it may seem a conspicuously long period of time. Yet, while attempting to formulate an answer to a complicated or controversial question, 30 seconds is hardly time at all. The main point is for you to become less self-conscious about silence.

The interview should not be allowed to drag. When the respondent has finished answering a question, move on to the next. Otherwise, boredom, irritability at the interviewer's unpreparedness, or rambling into irrelevant comments may ensue. The interview should move at a pace that is rapid enough to retain interest but slow enough to allow adequate coverage of the topic.

Probes

When a respondent gives an unclear or incomplete answer, it is necessary to probe for additional information. A *probe* is a question or comment designed to keep the person talking or to obtain clarification. If the respondent does not seem to understand the question or strays from the topic, it may be sufficient to repeat the question. If that does not work, or if only a partial response is given, other probes are necessary. An expectant pause accompanied by the usual facial expressions of waiting, or repeating the respondent's reply followed by a pause, should draw added comment. Failing that, use neutral questions or comments or simply ask for further clarification.

> *Examples of probes:*
> (Interviewer repeats all or part of question)
> Anything else?
> Could you tell me more of your ideas on that?
> What do you mean?

It is very important that probing questions or comments not bias the response. They should not direct a person to a particular answer.

Recording the Information

The degree to which notes reflect exactly what was said depends on how the interview will be used. When the information is the final source of data, a precise transcript is essential. The most common means of recording is to write down the respondent's replies exactly as spoken. This generally requires a rapid notation system in order to avoid the respondent's losing interest. On the other hand, it is flattering to have someone write down one's statement in detail. Thus, there is a positive aspect even though some delays and interruptions are required.

The type of interview and scoring system will help determine how much the interviewer should record. Slips of the tongue, pauses, and defensive gestures, that would be very important in a clinical interview probably won't be worth recording if the responses are going to be put into categories of agree/disagree or satisfied/dissatisfied. The task of classifying answers into fixed categories is called *coding*. This task becomes more time consuming when the coder must wade through a lot of irrelevant detail. *Verbatim responses* are those written down exactly as spoken and would include ungrammatical statements, requests for more information, and so on. *Paraphrased responses* are the interviewer's impressions of what the respondent meant. Things that are irrelevant, unnecessary, or ungrammatical are omitted.

> *Example*
> Verbatim statement: "I think . . . umm . . . that he is . . . well . . . doing that best he can. They are good . . . they are trying hard. It is not easy to be in the White House for any man."
> Interviewer's paraphase: The President is doing a good job.

Such interpretations by an inexperienced interviewer would be risky. It is probably better for the beginner to write down more, rather than less, detail. What is irrelevant can be ignored at the time of coding. When dealing with groups of people who have a special way of expressing things, such as adolescents or professional engineers, it is important to record statements exactly as they are said. On the street, "bad man" may be a term of respect. Direct quotations can be used to make a report more readable. Instead of talking about the gang members' attitudes towards authorities, the researcher can express their attitudes in the words of the gang members.

Various shorthand techniques, long practiced by stenographers, may be used. Kinsey and his associates developed a very elaborate code system that required 3 months to learn and 6 months to practice with ease. No written words were used, only mathematical signs and numbers. These coded data have never been transcribed into a longhand or typewritten account. The coding during the actual interview served several functions. It enabled the interviewer to record all pertinent data without slowing up the interviewing and risking loss of rapport. It preserved the confidence of the record since the code has never been publicly explained. It facilitated the transfer of the data from the original interview notes to statistical analysis. Had a written record been used, the data would have required coding anyway. Thus an intervening step was omitted by coding the information as it came from the respondent.

Tape recorders provide an advantage of precision and also will record hesitation phenomena, the various "ahems" and "ahs" and "ers" made by the respondent. However, transcription is a long process, taking four or five times the amount of time spent in the interview itself. Many respondents are made uncomfortable by the presence of a tape recorder, and confidentiality may be compromised. Thus, tape recorders are not recommended for most interviews.

Where replies are likely to be lengthy, various shorthand codes may be developed and used. In many interview situations, a self-developed notation is adequate, especially if notes are gone over immediately following the interview, with scribbles and shorthand terms correctly spelled out while the conversation is fresh in mind. A common convention is the use of a hash mark (/) to indicate where a probe has been made.

Example
Question: What do you think about forced retirement at age 65?
Answer: Well, it is probably a good idea in general, but then for some people not so good. / Well because some people are still pretty sharp and have a lot of experience to offer. / Like judges and politicians, things like that.

Other conventional marks may be adopted in an interview project. The University of Michigan Survey Research Center (1976) uses a standardized set of abbreviations for probes (see Table 8-1).

TABLE 8-1. Abbreviations for Probes Used by the University of Michigan
              Survey Research Center

Interview's probe	*Standard abbreviation*
Repeat question	(RQ)
Anything else?	(AE or Else?)
Any other reason?	(AO?)
Any others?	(Other?)
How do you mean?	(How mean?)
Could you tell me more about your thinking on that?	(Tell more)
Would you tell me what you have in mind?	(What in mind?)
What do you mean?	(What mean?)
Why do you feel that way?	(Why?)
Which would be closer to the way you feel?	(Which closer?)

In many instances an exact word-for-word transcription is not necessary, nor is it necessary to code the material for statistical analysis. In conducting in-depth interviews as a preliminary step to questionnaire construction, discovering categories of response is more important than recording every single word or anticipating statistical analysis. Jotting down notes from significant responses will be sufficient.

Tact and Diplomacy

You must learn when to probe and when to end a line of investigation. This is particularly important in the less structured situations. Depending on format or procedural constraints, an interviewer may choose to vary the order or phrasing of the questions, adapting them to the situation and mood of the respondent. Another aspect requiring tact is to recognize when a respondent is being untruthful or wandering off the subject. A direct indication of mistrust on the interviewer's part may terminate the interview. On the other hand, false information is of little value unless its assessment is a purpose of the interview. There are no simple guidelines to deal with these problems. If you are working in an area where misinformation or irrelevancies are likely to crop up, you should plan beforehand how you will deal with them.

If the respondent becomes tense or hostile, it may be desirable to terminate the session, either permanently or until another time. People occasionally take out their resentment about an issue on the interviewer. Because of the number of violent confrontations that occur during questioning, police in several cities have switched to bulletproof clipboards. You will probably not need to consider such extreme measures, but you should be alert to the possibility and, over time, the inevitability of someone becoming upset and angry. Know how to end an interview politely and quickly when this happens.

Ending the Interview

At the outset, tell the respondent how long the interview will last and stick as close to that limit as possible. If it is a paid interview, the means and time of payment should be explained. On completion, express appreciation for the person's time and effort. The respondent should be encouraged to ask any questions about the research, and should be told how the results will be used, and where and when they will be available.

> *Example of a closing sequence of comments:*
> Thank you very much for you time and effort. Is there anything you would like to add to the interview? (pause) The results of our survey will be sent to the State Department of Transportation. You will receive a check for $5.00 in the mail in about 2 weeks. If there is any problem, please telephone. You have my card. Do you have any further questions about the survey? (pause) Thank you again. Goodbye.

The ethics of research require as much feedback as possible to the respondents about the nature, purposes, and intent of the project. Common courtesy requires acknowledgment of the value of a person's time and effort.

Analyzing the Results

Keep your survey data in a safe place. The unspoken fear of researchers is graphically depicted in a newspaper report of an apartment house fire:

> Alan Rosin, who had lived in one of the buildings for 14 years, had just completed a political poll. Now, the damp and partially burned surveys containing 1,352 interviews lay in a mound of debris on the sidewalk. "All the (data) were in my apartment. Now they are all over the street," he lamented. (Lambert, 1984).

When the interview is the primary source of research data, it becomes necessary to devise systematic ways of summarizing information. The first step is generally to provide for transcription and quantification. Transcription refers to putting the responses into clear form for data analysis, such as transcribing answers from a tape recorder to typed copy, or recopying handwritten notes clarifying abbreviated terms. Quantification means presenting the results in numerical form.

Coding

Often responses are coded. This requires establishing categories of response. Coding is the means by which lengthy statements are reduced and sorted into specific response categories. The easiest items to code are sex, age, religion, occupation, and other categorical characteristics. These are categorical in that a person clearly belongs in one or another category (e.g., male, below age 25, and Catholic). Code categories are generally numerical. However, the choice of numbers is arbitrary.

Example
Question: When in your life did you decide upon your present career?
Coding categories:
1 = Childhood (10 yrs. or under)
2 = Adolescence (11 through 17 yrs.)
3 = Young adulthood (18 through 24 yrs.)
4 = Later years (25 yrs. or older)
5 = Still undecided about career

It is very important to keep a record (in duplicate) of the coding numbers used. Your data summary won't make sense if you have 354 cases of code 6 under religion and cannot remember whether these are Catholics or Protestants.

The coding process is more complicated for more complex answers. Box 8-3 illustrates the coding process for an item taken from college students' recollections of their experience of puberty. Another example of coding can be found in Chapter 11 on page 152.

BOX 8-3. Coding Open-ended Responses from Puberty Interviews

A. The first step in analyzing the responses is to read them over and generate a set of categories into which they can be classified. The following categories were constructed from the answers to the question: "What social changes or events did you, at the time, associate with puberty?"

Code #
1. Interest in other sex; social activity with other sex—dances, dating, parties, going steady.
2. Increased independence and/or responsibility.
3. Self-consciousness; attention to appearance.
4. Need for social acceptance, seeking friendship, joining clubs and organizations.
5. Withdrawal from family, problems in communication with family.
6. Increased social sensitivity (i.e., awareness of cliques, feeling social pressure, conformity concerns).

---

7. Other (if too many of the responses fall into this category, it should be made more specific, as those above).
8. No changes, or can't recall.

B. The next step is to check the reliability of those categories. Find a person willing to assist you and provide a description of the coding categories. Independently score a sufficient number of interviews to test the reliability of the scoring system. If the rate of agreement is low, then revise your coding categories and check reliability again.

C. In this example each response is scored using more than one category. For example, the social changes mentioned might have been both interest in the other sex (code 1) and withdrawal from family (code 5). In other cases you may wish to assign responses to one category only. The choice will depend on the nature of the answers, and whether it is feasible to place them in mutually exclusive categories.

Code #	Male respondents
6,4	More aggressive, needed to prove self and to be accepted.
1,5	Increased social activity, less interaction with parents and family.
3,1	Shy, withdrawn. Girl friends—or at least I tried!!!

	Female respondents
1,6	Dances, relationships with guys more than girls, pressure to conform, and I began a relationship with a guy when I was not really ready.
8	Not much.
5,4	Trouble communicating with family, turned more to friends.

D. Following the coding, responses are summarized by category:

Code #	Coding category	Number of females mentioning category (N = 14)*	Number of males mentioning category (N = 14)
1.	Interest in other sex	4	5
4.	Social acceptance	2	3
3.	Self-consciousness	3	1
6.	Social sensitivity	3	1
2.	Independence/responsibility	1	1
5.	Withdrawal from family	1	1
7.	Other	0	1
8.	No changes, can't recall	2	1

*N refers to the number of people in the sample.

Reporting Interview Results

You are not bound to the interview format when presenting the results. It is not necessary to give the answers to question 1 first, then question 2, and so on. Instead, the order should reflect the importance of the findings. The most clear and significant results should be described first. Areas of less agreement and importance come next. Trivial or irrelevant findings need not be mentioned.

Indicate the number of people contacted, the number of refusals, replies that had to be discarded for one reason or another, and the final number of respondents. Discuss the means by which people were contacted, the dates, time of day, and something about the training and background of the interviewers.

Remember to safeguard the identity of your respondents. This can be done through the use of code names rather than real names and the removal of statements that contain identifying information not essential to the reader's understanding of the study.

Limitations

What people say is not always what they do. The information obtained in interviews is limited to the spoken content and to inferences made by the interviewer. The data are highly subject to bias introduced by the human interaction of the interview process. Interviewers may unintentionally encourage or discourage the expression of particular facts and opinions. While no research method is absolutely free of subjectivity, the interview is more open to bias than most other research methods. However, this is not to say that bias is inevitable; rather, to warn that great care in constructing the question format and in training interviewers is essential if valid information is to be gained. The necessary care may be costly. The need for training, coupled with the time-consuming aspects of the interview itself, creates an economic disadvantage. A written questionnaire distributed to a hundred people takes a small fraction of the time required for individual interviews. The coding of the open-ended questions used in interviews is time-consuming and also expensive. Results from more than one interviewer may not be combined unless each has proceeded in the same manner.

Summary

The key element of an interview is the verbal give-and-take between interviewer and respondents. Interviews are particularly useful for exploring complex and emotionally loaded topics. Interviews can be used to explore beliefs, opinions, and personality characteristics. In a structured interview, questions are formulated beforehand and asked in a set order in a specified manner. In an unstructured interview, the interviewer has in mind a general topic, but no set questions or a predetermined order to the questions.

In an in-depth interview, the interviewer follows the respondent's answers with a request for more information at an increasing level of depth. The classification of the respondent's answers into categories is called coding. Interview techniques are learned best through practice combined with feedback.

Limitations: Compared to questionnaires, the interview is time consuming and expensive. The responses are subject to bias introduced by the human interaction during the interview process.

References

Bernadt, M. W., Mumford, J., Taylor, C., Smith, B. & Murray, R. M. (1982, February 6). Comparison of questionnaire and laboratory tests in the detection of excessive drinking and alcoholism. *The Lancet*, 8267, 325–326.

Bingham, W. V. D., & Moore, B. V. (1959). *How to interview* (4th ed.). New York: Harper.

Birnbaum, J. H. (1982, December, 22). Farmers need savvy, as do agents who ask for data. *The Wall Street Journal*, p.1.

Hall, E. T. (1959). *The silent language*, Garden City, N.Y.: Doubleday.

Kroll, B., & Sommer, R. (1976). Bicyclists' response to urban bikeways. *American Institute of Planning Journal*, *42*, 42–51.

Lambert, M. (1984, October, 8). Apartment fire leaves only sorrow. *Sacramento Bee*, p. B1.

Norman, D. A. (1983). Some observations on mental models. In D. Gentner, & A. L. Stevens (Eds.), *Mental models* (pp. 7–14). Hillsdale, NJ: Erlbaum.

Pomeroy, W. B. (1963). Human sexual behavior. In N. L. Farberow (Ed.), *Taboo topics*. New York: Atherton Press.

Snyder, P. Z., Stea, D., & Sadalla, E. K. (1976). Socio-cultural modifications and user needs in Navajo housing. *Journal of Architectural Research*, *5*, 4–9.

Sommer, B. *Puberty and adolescence* (1978). New York: Oxford University Press.

University of Michigan, Survey Research Center (1976). *Interviewer's manual* (rev. ed.). Institute for Social Research, University of Michigan.

Further Reading

Converse, J. M., & Schuman, H. (1974). *Conversations at random: Survey research as interviewers see it*. New York: Wiley.

Gordon, R. L. (1975). *Interviewing: Strategy, techniques, and tactics* (rev. ed.). Homewood, IL: Dorsey Press.

Stano, M. E., & Reinsch, N. L., Jr. (1982). *Communication in interviews*. Englewood Cliffs, NJ: Prentice-Hall.

Weinberg, E. (1971). *Community surveys with local talent*. Chicago: National Opinion Research.

9   The Questionnaire

Sir Francis Galton, a nineteenth-century versatile English genius, was fond of measuring things. He set up a booth at the 1884 International Health Exhibition to measure people's physical responses, including their reaction time, strength of pulling and squeezing, hearing, seeing, and color perception. The testing was later moved to the South Kensington Museum in London. The apparatus stood on a long table at one end of a long, narrow room. After paying a three-penny admission fee (which helped to support the research), each individual performed the various tests while an attendant recorded the responses. The goal was to determine the range of human sensory capabilities. Galton hoped to test the entire population of Great Britain so that the nation would know the exact state of its mental resources. He was never able to fully realize his dream. By the time the program ended, however, he had tested 9337 individuals, quite an achievement for his time.

Galton was also interested in visual imagery—the ability to picture things in one's mind. This was something that could not be observed or tested directly. To assess visual imagery, Galton presented people with a list of written questions about their ability to picture breakfast that morning. Was the image dim or clear? Was it in color or black and white? Were

106

the colors distinct and natural? This was one of the first uses of the questionnaire in psychological research. Respondents were asked to rate the vividness of their images along a scale from 0 (no image at all) to 100 (clear and distinct as the original).

Galton found that artists reported better imagery than scientists. Some scientists, in fact, doubted that imagery existed. They felt that the expression "Seeing in the mind's eye" was only a figure of speech and that the very notion of mental pictures was fanciful. Galton discovered not only important differences in the way people think but also the value of the questionnaire as an instrument for studying behavior that could not be observed or experimented on directly (Galton, 1907).

A *questionnaire* is a series of written questions on a topic about which the respondents' opinions are sought. It is a frequently used tool in *survey research*—the systematic gathering of information about people's beliefs, attitudes, values, and behavior. There are two general types of questionnaires: self-administered, which respondents fill out themselves and interviewer administered, in which the interviewer asks questions and records the responses. The self-administered form is more efficient in time and effort. For example, copies of a questionnaire can be distributed to 100 employees, filled out by them, and collected within an hour's time. Conducting 100 individual interviews would be much more arduous and time consuming. However, a self-administered questionnaire requires clear instructions and a very careful wording of items. The most difficult aspects of a questionnaire are its construction and the interpretation of the results. Distributing and scoring a well-contructed questionnaire are usually easy (although the amount of data to be processed can be extensive). Overall, it is difficult to surpass a questionnaire for economy. That is why it is such a popular and widely used research tool.

Questionnaire Construction

There are two general aspects to every questionnaire: its content and its format. The *content* of a questionnaire refers to the subject matter. The *format* pertains to its structure and appearance—how the items are worded, their appearance on the page, and the form used for answering the questions.

Content

In general, it is best to restrict a questionnaire to a single issue. If you want to find out what college students think about the cafeteria, stay with that topic. Don't ask about teaching methods or the adequacy of the library. If others are interested in these topics, let them do another survey. It will be easy for students sitting in the cafeteria to see the relevance of questions about the food and service.

Is yours the first survey on this issue? Sometimes a beginning researcher is halfway through a survey before discovering that someone else studied the same topic a year earlier. The cafeteria manager or a long-term employee may be a good source of information on this. It is surprising how many surveys are finished, filed, and forgotten. You can save considerable time and effort if the previous survey developed suitable questions. You can always add new questions, but try to include some of the old ones. Wherever possible, retain the same wording. If the previous questionnaire asked whether the employees were "helpful," don't change the word to "courteous" even though you believe this means the same thing. Even a slight change in wording can invalidate the comparison between answers from two surveys.

Assuming you are going to construct your own questionnaire, you will start by using two other methods: casual observation and interview. The purpose of casual observation is to learn the *range of activities* about which questions must be asked. You need to know what goes on in order to ask questions about it. This requires brief inspection rather than systematic observation with detailed categories. Interviews should accompany the observations to learn the range of opinions students hold regarding the food. At this stage, a loose, open-ended interview is preferable. This will avoid suggesting answers to people. Replies will be used primarily to find out which topics should be included in the questionnaire. The following brief list of questions would probably be appropriate for a casual interview on this topic:

> Hello, my name is _____. The Campus Planning Committee is doing a survey of student attitudes about the cafeteria. I would like to ask you a few questions. This will only take a few minutes. Your answers will help us improve food service on campus.
> 1. What do you think of the food here?
> 2. What do you like most about it?
> 3. What do you like least about it?
> 4. What do you think about the service and facilities?
> 5. Is there anything else you would like to say about the food or the service?

These general questions would not be sufficient for a formal interview. However, the purpose is not to use the answers as primary data but only to learn what questions should be asked on the questionnaire.

Format

Open-ended and Closed Questions

There are two major categories of questions: open ended and closed. With *open-ended questions,* the respondents write in their own answers:

Example
What do you like most about this cafeteria?
What do you like least about this cafeteria?

Closed questions, also known as *multiple-choice questions,* ask the respondent to choose among alternatives provided by the researcher.

Example
What do you think of the salads here?
(like) (dislike) (indifferent)
What do you think of the cost of the meals here?
(too expensive) (very reasonable) (about right)

An open-ended format is desirable (1) when the researcher does not know all the possible answers to a question, (2) when the range of possible answers is so large that the question would become unwieldy in multiple-choice format, (3) when the researcher wants to avoid suggesting answers to the respondent, and (4) when the researcher wants answers in the respondent's own words. Multiple-choice (closed) answers are desirable (1) when there is a large number of respondents and questions, (2) when the answers are to be scored by machine, and (3) when responses from several groups of individuals are to be compared.

The beginning researcher often prefers open-ended questions because they allow respondents more freedom to answer as they please. This infatuation with open-ended questions tends to be short lived. Once the researcher attempts to compare one person's answers with another's, and the replies from one group with those from another group, the disadvantages of open-ended questions become quickly apparent. People tend to ramble in their answers to open-ended questions. It is therefore necessary for the researcher to go through lengthy statements in order to pick out the respondent's intent or meaning. Often it shows more respect for people's opinions to let them classify their answers themselves as positive, negative, or neutral than for the researcher to do this for them.

Salience refers to the importance of an issue in people's minds. Open-ended questions are very useful for determining the salience of opinions. It is generally assumed that in answering an open-ended question, those items that stand out in a person's mind will be mentioned first. Another method for determining salience is to ask respondents to *rank* a list of items in terms of importance. This can be done using either an open-ended or a closed format.

Example (open ended):
List those qualifications you would look for in hiring a secretary. Place a 1 next to the most important qualification, a 2 next to the second most important, and so on, until all qualifications on your list are ranked.

Example (closed):
Rank each of the following qualifications in terms of its importance for a secretary in your office (1 = most important).

___ Typing speed
___ Typing accuracy
___ General clerical skills
___ Taking dictation
___ Telephone answering skills
___ Meeting the public
___ Other (please specify)

Ranking versus Rating

Rank-order questions tend to confuse many respondents. They are also more difficult to analyze. Some people will list only their top choices or use check marks instead of numbers. Others interpret the scales in the wrong direction, using 5 for the most important skill and 1 for the least important skill, even though the instructions say the opposite. Other people will list two number 3's and omit number 4 entirely. The larger the number of items to be ranked and the more complicated the format, the more mistakes will be made. With more than 10 items, rating is more efficient than ranking. Sometimes a combination of rating and ranking can be used.

Example
Rate each of the following qualifications in terms of its importance for a secretary in your office. Please use the following scale:

1. Very important
2. Moderately important
3. Slightly important
4. Not at all important

___ typing speed
___ typing accuracy
        etc.
___ meeting the public

Now place a check next to the single most important qualification and two checks next to the second most important qualification.

Matrix Questions

Arranging the items and answers in a matrix is very efficient. By matrix, we mean using answer headings across the top, and listing the items down the side, as illustrated in this example:

For each statement below, please indicate whether you Strongly Agree (SA), Agree (A), are Undecided (U), Disagree (D), or Strongly Disagree (SD).

	SA	A	U	D	SD
The food in the cafeteria is well prepared	( )	( )	( )	( )	( )
Lines are too long	( )	( )	( )	( )	( )
Table arrangements encourage conversation	( )	( )	( )	( )	( )

The degree of detail desired by the researcher determines the number of response categories. If earlier interviews revealed that the students either strongly liked or strongly disliked the cafeteria food, there would not be much point in using 10 categories. Because the students do not expect the cafeteria to be the equal of a fine restaurant, there is little reason to include an "excellent" category. Three terms would probably be sufficient: "good," "ok," and "poor." Those terms will take up little space, will be easily understood by the respondents, and will serve to distinguish between positive, neutral, and negative opinions. In other situations where a finer differentiation of opinion is required, 5 or 7 categories can be used.

Examples
Excellent, good, satisfactory, poor, terrible
Strongly agree, moderately agree, slightly agree, undecided, slightly disagree, moderately disagree, strongly disagree

Measuring the Middle Position

The middle position refers to a neutral or undecided stance. When a respondent checks "undecided," it isn't always clear what this means. Sometimes it means a balance between positive and negative feelings on the issue; other times it means a lack of interest or knowledge on the topic. Some investigators eliminate the middle position creating a forced-choice item where the respondent must agree or disagree, or take some kind of a stand. Other investigators prefer use "don't know" as a middle-ground response. Having a middle category will decrease the number expressing a clear opinion at one end or the other. Not surprisingly, middle category responses occur more often when people don't have strong feelings on the issues (Schuman & Presser, 1981). Although it is possible that people who actually have an opinion might use the middle ground, others may, in fact, feel neutral about an issue. We favor providng the middle alternative in order to avoid forcing a false appearance of opinion one way or the other, and out of respect for the respondent's right to neutral feelings. Several students interviewed in the cafeteria expressed these types of opinions.

The food's okay, I guess.
What do you expect of cafeteria food?
It's better than what you get at Jack-in-the-Box.

A neutral category seems appropriate for vague opinions like these. Some terms useful for the middle category are: "neutral," "undecided," "neither good nor bad," "satisfactory," "OK." Often it is helpful to include the additional response category "not applicable (NA)" for questions that are not relevant. Students who never eat a particular food item may feel more comfortable checking NA than saying that it is neither good nor bad.

Example
What do you think of the desserts served here?

Good   OK   Poor   NA

Combining Question Types

Following the chapter on multimethod approach, it will come as no surprise that the authors recommend a combination of closed and open-ended items, ratings, and ranks, rather then relying on a single type of item. The customary procedure is to use open-ended, general questions at the beginning of a questionnaire, followed by more specific, multiple-choice rated and ranked items. Coupling several types of items provides checks on each. In a survey designed to learn student attitudes toward library reading areas, students were first asked an open-ended question, "What do you like most about the library reading areas?" The most common response was the quiet in the library compared to the student's dormitory room or apartment. Later, students were asked to rate specific aspects of the library environment as "excellent," "satisfactory," or "needs improvement." Surprisingly, the item of library environment that provoked the largest number of complaints was the noise.

This illustrates the value of including both open-ended and closed questions in the same survey. If only the general question about why the student came to the library had been asked, the researchers probably would have concluded (incorrectly) that the noise situation was good. Yet the ratings indicated just the opposite. Students came to the library in search of quiet, but serious noise problems still existed.

Number of Questions

Beginning researchers often include too many items in a questionnaire. In their desire to omit nothing, they forget that the respondents will become fatigued and lose interest as they plod through an unending barrage of questions. For most purposes, the shorter the instrument, the better. Avoid complex formats, such as, "If yes, skip to question 9, part B. If no, answer question 7, part A."

Wording Your Questions

Your questions should be clear and meaningful to the respondents. Terms should not be too difficult. Don't overestimate the vocabulary level of your respondents. Define all difficult or jargon terms. It is helpful to include synonyms. Instead of asking a question about *nuclear power,* you can ask about *nuclear* or *atomic power.* The synonym may reach some people who miss the primary term.

Avoid loaded terms, scare words, and phrases that immediately raise a red flag. Don't ask questions about *dangerous* drugs, *noisy* trucks, or *excess* government spending. Such adjectives produce a reflexlike negative response. If you want to know what people think about cocaine, ask them directly; don't ask about dangerous drugs. *Noise* is a technical term for the unpleasant aspects of sound. Asking employees to evaluate the *sound level* in the office is preferable to asking them about noise, which by definition is unpleasant.

Avoid double-barreled questions. Ask about one thing at a time. Don't ask about the cost *and* efficiency of municipal services. It is preferable to divide this into separate questions, one concerned with efficiency and the other with cost.

Whenever possible, avoid phrasing questions in the negative. It is surprising how often people confuse "do" and "don't," "will" and "won't," "can" and "cannot." If you must use a negative, be sure to underline it or have it printed in italics so that it will not be missed.

Example
Of all the classes that you took in high school, which was the single class that you liked *least?*

A common mistake in writing questions is to use jargon terms. Many employees do not know the meaning of "FICA" or "SSI" even though social security payments are deducted from their paychecks every week. Some words have more than one meaning. When a survey team asked residents of a fundamentalist community about the need for government to regulate profits, they were surprised to find exceptionally strong resistance to the idea. Subsequent interviews disclosed that some people thought the question referred to regulation of prophets!

Balance

Balance refers to the neutrality of questions, or providing sufficient items so that the number leaning toward one view are balanced by an equal number leaning toward the other view. The goal of balance is to counteract implicit influence from the questions themselves. The following shows imbalance in questions about cafeteria food.

Is the meat too salty?
Are the vegetables overcooked?
Is the coffee watery?

This set of questions is unbalanced at two levels. Individually, the items imply a direction to the answer. Balance can be provided by asking "Is the coffee too weak, too strong, or about right?" The second level of bias is that the implied responses for all the items are in the same direction—that the food isn't very good. An alternative to balancing each individual item is to balance them overall. For example, leave the implicit bias in the question "Are the vegetables overcooked?" but balance it with another item of the reverse implied bias, such as "Is the meat properly prepared?" Providing balance not only reduces the effects of a possible response bias, it also makes the survey itself seem more fair, and thus more difficult for partisans of one view or another to ignore or dismiss.

Don't be discouraged if your questionnaire isn't perfect on the first try. It is extraordinarily difficult to anticipate all sources of ambiguity and confusion. Experienced survey researchers always construct a preliminary version, pretest it, and then revise it before distributing the actual survey. The secret of learning to write clear questions is practice, feedback, more practice, more feedback, and still more practice. No one writes a perfect questionnaire the first time.

Checklist for Evaluating Questionnaire Items

1. Is the question necessary? How useful will the answers be?
2. Is the item clear and unambiguous?
3. Will the respondent be competent to answer the question as asked?
4. Will the respondent be willing to answer the question as asked?
5. Have double-barreled questions been eliminated or revised?
6. Is the item as short as possible, while remaining clear and precise?
7. Do the multiple-choice questions provide a comprehensive set of choices? Do they include a "don't know" or "not applicable" category? Is there an "other" category, if appropriate?
8. Is the answer likely to be affected by social desirability (saying the "right thing")? If so, can the question be altered to reduce this bias?
9. Have negatives such as "no" and "not" been eliminated insofar as possible?
10. Are the questions balanced so that the number of favorable items equals the number of unfavorable items?

Layout

A self-administered questionnaire must begin with an introductory statement, present the questions in an easily read and easily answered format, and close with a note of thanks or appreciation. For interviewer-administered questionnaires, instructions at the beginning will help to ensure consistency from one interview to the next.

Introductory Statement

At the top of the questionnaire, briefly describe the purpose, identify the person or group conducting the survey, request assistance, and provide general instructions. For example,

The purpose of this questionnaire is to learn about attitudes toward the cafeteria. The survey is being conducted by Ms. Jones and Mr. Smith, social science students at _____ College. We would very much appreciate your assistance in answering the questions below. Please do not write your name on this form in order that the replies remain anonymous.

Additional instructions might be included. For some rating scales, the respondent is asked not to dwell on the choice, to just check the first response that comes to mind. In other cases a well-considered response is requested.

Question Order

Begin with factual, noncontroversial questions. These help to establish a good relationship that can smooth the way for more difficult or controversial questions later.

General questions on a topic should precede specific questions, as in this example.

1. What do you think of this playground?
2. Is there enough play equipment?
3. Do you feel that any of the play equipment is dangerous?

This sequence avoids suggesting danger to the respondent on the first two questions. If danger is mentioned in the first two answers, it is likely to be a salient issue and influence subsequent answers.

Maintain a logical order understandable to the respondent. Routine items such as age and gender can be included at the end. The questionnaire should *not* begin with overly personal or sensitive questions regarding illicit activities, sex, or controversial religious or political opinions. If such items are to be included, begin with the less controversial ones.

Answer Format

There are various answer formats in which a respondent inserts a checkmark, number, or letter. The response blanks that are placed either to the right or left of the question usually take one of five forms: _____, $\boxed{/}$, ( ), □, or ○.

With regard to neatness and appearance, the □ has been rated best, and the $\boxed{/}$ was the worst, and the left-hand side was best for presenting the response blanks (Major, Jacoby, & Sheluga, 1976). However, for typed questionnaires, the ( ) or _____ are easy and acceptable. Another acceptable practice is to have the respondents circle their choice.

Arrange the response blanks to permit easy tabluation. This is especially important if the answers are to be key punched and analyzed by computer. Put the answers where the operator can find them. Don't scatter them around the page. Insert computer code numbers close to the answers.

Example

What is your class in school?	Fr Soph Jr Sr	
	1 2 3 4	(1)
Are you a full-time or part-time student?	Full-time Part-time	
	1 2	(2)
What is your sex?	Male Female	
	1 2	(3)
What is your age?	___ years	(4–5)

If the questionnaire is precoded for computer scoring, make these codes as inconspicuous as possible and provide an explanation to the respondent, for example, "Please ignore the numbers in parentheses, which are for computer use only."

Closing Statement

At the end of a self-administered questionnaire ask for any other comments or suggestions, and then thank the respondents for their time and effort—a simple THANK YOU VERY MUCH may be sufficient.

Pretesting

The first draft of your questionnaire will need revision. The need for changes should be accepted gracefully. No matter how carefully you phrase the original questions, there will still be some words that are difficult or unclear, some topics left out. The impressive economy of the questionaire is partially offset by the researcher's inability to clarify the meaning of terms. Elaboration is easy in an interview, almost impossible on a questionnaire. Because there may be no person physically present to help explain the meaning of difficult terms or confusing questions, you must anticipate all possible sources of error. An adaptation of Murphy's Law* applies here:—The slightest opportunity for respondents to go wrong means that some of them will.

The best way to reduce ambiguity is to pretest the questions. Try them out on a group of people who are asked the items *and,* in addition, asked to comment on their wording and clarity. The first draft of the cafeteria questionnaire might be given to eight customers and two cafeteria employees. The respondents would be told that this is a trial version of the survey instrument and that we would like their opinions on the food *and* the questions. Pretesting can be done in a short period of time. There is no need for detailed sampling or statistics. A small sample should be sufficient unless serious problems are found, in which case a major revision and fur-

*Murphy's Law: If something can go wrong, it will.

ther pretesting will be necessary. Pretesting can be done orally. Try it out on a few people who will not be in the final sample but are similar to that sample.

A basic rule in questionnaire construction is that the first draft should never be mimeographed or printed. Write it down in longhand or type it, make 10 copies, but no more. Once you have a stack of printed questionnaires in front of you, it is easy to overlook minor errors and inconsistencies and to continue to use the copies because they are available. If you do this, you will regret it afterward. It is easier to change a first draft than to interpret people's answers to ambiguous questions.

Reproducing the Questionnaire

Eye appeal is important. Make sure all questions are legible. Don't squeeze things together. Use a second sheet of paper if necessary for a clear presentation. A nicely designed and printed questionnaire will increase reader interest. With the advent of low-cost photocopies, this is your most likely means of questionnaire reproduction, although mimeograph or ditto, if available, are cheaper. The latter two do not look as professional and a single ditto master is only good for 200 copies at best. Ditto reproduction (the purple one) also fades with time. Before you distribute your questionnaires, go through them to see that pages are in the correct order and there

---

BOX 9-1. Review of Steps in Constructing a Questionnaire

Content

1. Exploratory interviews of an in-depth type and/or casual observation, if appropriate.
2. Decide on aspects of problem to be covered. Be specific.
3. Generate items.

Format

4. Decide item wording, for example, open-ended vs. closed, etc.
5. Reexamine items (see Checklist for Evaluating Questionnaire Items.)
6. Have a knowledgeable colleague or instructor look at the questions.
7. *Pretest*—pilot test the questionnaire *before* putting it into final form.
   a. Check for confusing or ambiguous items.
   b. Estimate the time needed for administration.
8. Revise questionnaire in accord with pilot results. If new items are added, be sure to pretest them.
9. Final editing—include clear instructions to the respondent or the interviewer.

---

are no blank pages. Numbering the pages will make it easier for you (and the respondent) to notice when pages are out of order or one is missing.

The readability of two-sided copies depends on the thickness of the paper, so try it and see whether the print shows through before committing yourself to multiple copies. If you use the back, be sure to write PLEASE COMPLETE THE REVERSE SIDE at the bottom of the first page. Even with that warning, you can assume that in a self-administered questionnaire, some respondents will fail to complete the back page. The same expectation applies to multiple pages. If the questionnaires are being picked up individually, it is wise to make a general scan to see that all pages have been filled out.

In deciding on the number of copies needed, consider your sample size and request additional copies. You will need these not only for follow-up or spoilage, but also for data tabulation, discussion copies, as appendices for reports, samples for other researchers, etc. Later reproduction of a few copies can be expensive and needlessly time consuming.

Distributing the Forms

If the questionnaire is properly constructed and brief, you will be pleasantly surprised how quickly it can be distributed, filled out, and collected. This is the stage at which the economy of this instrument is most evident. It may take more than a month to get permission to conduct a survey among office workers, another few weeks to write and pretest the questions, get them approved by management, and have the forms printed, but only a few hours to distribute them, have them filled out, and collected. Once you have the instrument already available, a second survey can be carried out in a wondrously short time.

Since a questionnaire is to be answered in writing, it is more easily administered to people sitting down than to those standing or on the move. One would probably choose an interview rather than a written questionnaire for customers in a shopping center or teenagers at the Dairy Queen. The questionnaire is ideally suited for office workers, students, library readers, and others who are seated at desks or tables.

There are various methods of distributing questionnaires to potential respondents. Questionnaires can be circulated at a group meeting, handed to people individually, or mailed. Each approach is likely to work better in some situations than in others.

Group Meetings

When an organization, club, or class meets regularly, you have a good opportunity to distribute a questionnaire. If the survey is brief and relevant to the group's purpose, it may be possible to have the questionnaires filled out during the meeting and returned directly to you. There is likely to be a problem of a biased sample if only a small number of members attend because they may not be typical of the total membership.

Individual Distribution

Questionnaires can be handed to people as they enter or leave a setting with the request that the questionnaire be filled out and either placed in a designated collection box or returned through the mail in an attached postage-paid return envelope. We do not recommend handing a survey to people walking by and asking them to fill it out and return it by mail. Most of your questionnaires are likely to end up on the sidewalk or in a trash can. For maximum returns, the questionnaire should be given out and collected in person. Confidentiality can be assured by not requiring names and enclosing the questionnaire in an envelope.

Mail Surveys

A mail survey is efficient for covering a large geographic area quickly. It is expensive to send researchers to all parts of a city or state to conduct surveys. The advantages of a mail survey are its low labor and travel costs and complete standardization. There is no need to train interviewers, and all respondents receive the same questions posed in the same manner. A mail survey also provides more anonymity to the respondents than is possible in a personal interview. A follow-up study of former employees may secure more valid information when conducted by mail without requiring names to be associated with the responses. If contacted directly, individuals might fear that their opinions would be used against them. However, there will be many other situations where controversial opinions can be explored more fully through a personal interview than in a mailed questionnaire.

Disadvantages of a mail survey are its impersonality, low return rate, slowness, and financial cost. Many commercial firms and political organizations send out fake surveys as promotional tools. Respondents are asked to answer questions deliberately intended to create favorable attitudes toward a product or organization. This misuse of survey methodology has led many householders to classify all mail surveys as junk mail.

A mail survey of households randomly selected from a city telephone directory will probably result in a 10 to 33 percent return rate, thus requiring the researcher to send out from three to five times as many questionnaires as are needed for the final sample. There is also a problem of potential response bias when only a small percentage of questionnaires is returned. The return rate is likely to be much higher if the recipients have a prior interest in the topic of the survey. For example, a mail survey of former high school alumni accompanied by a cover letter from the school principal is likely to yield a return rate in excess of 60 percent of delivered questionnaires.

A mail survey is slower than a telephone survey, which can be done in a few days. Questionnaires take several days to be delivered by mail and weeks before the bulk of replies return. A mail survey is not appropriate when timely information is needed. The costs of printing, mailing, and return postage may seriously deplete the budget of a small organization or agency.

BOX 9-2. Recycling Survey (Johnson, 1984)

A questionnaire was mailed to a sample of 350 households randomly selected from a city phone directory along with a stamped return envelope and a cover letter from the sponsor of the project. Of the 350 sent, 20 were returned by the post office as undeliverable and 140 were returned completed, yielding a return rate of 42 percent on delivered questionnaires. Here are some of the items.

Recycling Survey

To be filled out by the person most likely to make recycling decisions on behalf of the household. Please check the appropriate box or fill in the blank.

Section I. This section asks questions about your current recycling activity.

1. How often does your household currently recycle the following items?

	Do not recycle	Weekly	Every two weeks	Monthly	Other (specify):
Newsprint	☐	☐	☐	☐	☐ _____
Aluminum	☐	☐	☐	☐	☐ _____
Glass	☐	☐	☐	☐	☐ _____
Tin	☐	☐	☐	☐	☐ _____
Other _____	☐	☐	☐	☐	☐ _____

2. For those materials you currently recycle, approximately what percentage of the total amounts used in your home are recycled?

	Do not recycle	1–20%	21–40%	41–60%	61–80%	81–100%
Newsprint	☐	☐	☐	☐	☐	☐
Aluminum	☐	☐	☐	☐	☐	☐
Glass	☐	☐	☐	☐	☐	☐
Tin	☐	☐	☐	☐	☐	☐
Other _____	☐	☐	☐	☐	☐	☐

5. If the weekly curbside program required you to sort glass by color (clear, green, and brown) instead of mixing the colors, what is the likelihood of your recycling glass?

Definitely would *not* participate	Probably would *not* participate	Undecided	Probably would participate	Definitely would participate
☐	☐	☐	☐	☐

Only apartment dwellers answer question #8

8. If containers for recyclables were placed near the refuse containers in your complex, what would the likelihood be of your recycling the following materials?

	Definitely would *not* participate	Probably would *not* participate	Undecided	Probably would participate	Definitely would participate
Newsprint	☐	☐	☐	☐	☐
Aluminum	☐	☐	☐	☐	☐
Glass	☐	☐	☐	☐	☐
Tin	☐	☐	☐	☐	☐

Section III. This section asks background questions that will help us in interpreting this survey. Your honesty is greatly appreciated and all answers are confidential. [Demographic questions follow on original questionnaire.]

Increasing Response Rates

Notifying people about the survey beforehand will increase cooperation. Placing a sign in the library, for example, telling people that a survey is being undertaken and explaining its purposes will arouse interest and encourage cooperation. Office workers could be sent a note describing the goals of the survey and why it is important for them to participate. No matter how fine your motives, people are doing you a favor when they invest time and effort answering your questions. Therefore, try to convince them of the usefulness of their answers. This can be done *both* in the advance letter and in the introductory paragraph of the questionnaire.

Helpful Hints for a Mail Survey

Obtain current addresses. Use the most recent version of the telephone directory or other information source.

Send questionnaires first-class mail so that the post office will return the undelivered questionnaires. First-class letters are more likely to be noticed than bulk mail.

Undeliverable surveys will be returned if mailed first class. Note the use of attractive stamps to increase respondent interest.

Hand address the letters and use attractive stamps. Some market researchers believe that a stamp placed at a slight angle on the envelope increases the return rate.

Arrange for a newspaper article describing the survey to appear shortly before the questionnaires are sent out. The article can describe the nature of the survey sponsorship, what information is being collected, how it will be used, and sample selection (see Box 9-3).

Postcards can be sent before and after mailing to increase return rate. Several days beforehand, you can send a postcard describing the purposes of the survey. A week after sending the questionnaire, a follow-up reminder can be mailed asking people to please return the surveys, and providing an address to which people can write if they mislaid the original survey and would like another copy.

Example
Dear Resident,
About a week ago you were sent a questionnaire about your attitude towards various types of recycling programs. If you have not yet sent in your questionnaire, please do so as soon as you can so that our data will be truly representative

Addressing envelopes by hand increases the likelihood of a response in mail surveys.

BOX 9-3. Newspaper Announcement of a Survey (Birnbaum, 1982)

Major Farm Survey Launched

The U.S. Department of Agriculture is launching a major survey this month on farm production expenses, debts and assets, crop and livestock sales and costs of production.

Letters are gong out to about 24,000 farmers representing a broad cross-section of American agriculture. Interviewers will then visit the farms between January 21st and March 8th to conduct the farm costs and returns survey.

Survey results will be used to determine the economic well-being of farmers.

"This is one of the best ways for farmers to get out their story," said economist Jim Johnson of USDA's Economic Research Service.

Responses to each survey are confidential.

The results will be reported to Congress, farmers, and the public.

[Similar information can be provided to radio and TV stations prior to the start of the survey. Advance publicity should increase interest and levels of cooperation.]

---

of your area. If you have already mailed in your questionnaire, please accept this as a thank you for your cooperation.

Sincerely,

(signature)
(title and affiliation or sponsor)

Scoring

Scoring a properly constructed questionnaire is quite simple. If the instrument is brief and there are fewer than 100 respondents, it may be easier to score by hand than by computer. Any open-ended questions must be coded by hand. See Chapter 8 for a detailed account of coding. An additional

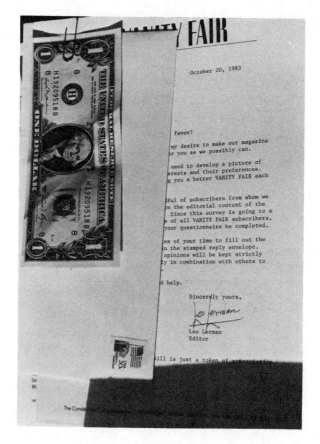

This survey from a national magazine was accompanied by a crisp new one-dollar bill as an inducement, along with a stamped return envelope.

benefit of hand scoring is that you stay closer to the data and get a better sense of the responses to the questions. However, if the number of items and respondents is large, or if you wish to make many comparisons among the questions, the computer may be desirable. Nothing surpasses a computer for speed and accuracy in finding out how the opinions of clerical employees who have been employed for 10 years and who live between 5 and 10 miles from the office compare with those of clerical employees who have been employed less than 5 years and live 10 to 20 miles from the office. If you expect to use a computer in analyzing your results, these comparisons should be planned from the start and the questionnaire designed for computer analysis.

Interpretation

Up to now, everything has gone well. You've written your questionnaire, pretested it, revised it, distributed and collected the final version. You are now the proud owner of 96 completed questionnaires. Two people didn't finish the questionnaire and another didn't follow the instructions. One person didn't take the questions seriously and wrote funny answers. This last is the moron factor, and the response should be disregarded. As long as it is not done to bias the results, it makes sense to discard bizarre answers. A person who puts an exclamation point after "sex" or writes "I am for it" is probably kidding. If some of the person's other replies look humorous, it is probably best to discard the entire questionnaire. On the other hand, someone putting a question mark after "age" may be shy about revealing how old he or she is. Some of your respondents will *always* omit one or two items. Either the question is not clear or the item was missed in going through the questionnaire. Don't be concerned if you don't have replies to all the questions. When you convert to percentages, there will be no problem.

When you deal with people who are rushed or busy, you can expect that some of them won't finish the questionnaire. Generally the replies from the completed portions can be added to the total sample without significant bias. This is not true of people who object to your questions. Even a mild question can upset some people. For example, an employee may use the questionnaire to vent hostility toward an employer. Before discarding these replies, it is best to check with a colleague or co-worker to see that you are not biasing your results. Occasionally an apparently humorous response is meaningful and a refusal is appropriate. Even though you have promised your respondents anonymity, some of them won't believe you. This is not totally unrealistic if they don't know you. Abnormal conditions can provoke abnormal responses. Do not expect to get honest answers from people who believe that the survey results will be used against them.

Removing the two incomplete questionnaires, the person who didn't follow the instructions, and the joker, our sample in the cafeteria survey now consists of 96 respondents—a fairly good ratio. If we had wanted to finish with a perfect 100, we could have aimed for 115 completed questionnaires and put 15 aside as replacements for any rejections. For our purposes, however, there is no significant difference between 96 and 100 completed replies. Assuming we have hand scored the questionnaires—the quickest and easiest approach—we will probably be presenting our results in overall percentages, as in Table 9-1.

This is a straightforward presentation of the data. For many purposes, it is all that is needed. However, if you want to know how the attitudes of male freshmen living off campus compare with female freshmen living on campus, it may be awkward to sort the questionnaires for each analysis. The computer is a very efficient way of making these detailed comparisons, but unless you are careful, the computer can overload you with data. It will cost only a few extra pennies to ask the computer how the replies of 17-year-old Protestant men compare with those of 19-year-old Catholic women. We advise against asking trivial questions. The computer does not indicate which results are important and which are trivial.

Describing Survey Results

People's likes can be as significant as their dislikes. The point of a survey is not to reveal only failure and frustration. Success and satisfaction should also be identified. A beginning researcher often identifies important results with surprises. Can a survey be worth anything if the results are not shocking? The answer is clearly yes. A survey that finds there is no problem may be just as important as one that identifies a source of tension. If your survey tells you, for example, that students are satisfied with the cafeteria food, this is a perfectly valid and useful finding. You have found that your

TABLE 9-1. Student Ratings of the Cafeteria

	Percentage rating		
Aspect of the Cafeteria	*Good*	*OK*	*Poor*
Meats	10	55	35
Vegetables	7	44	49
Salads	53	38	8
Desserts	43	35	22
.			
.			
.			
Seating arrangement	22	62	17
Sound level	0	32	68

cafeteria is better than most. There still may be some room for improvement in other areas, such as noise and crowding.

There is nothing more frustrating to the reader of a report than to have every percentage described. You need not go through all the questionnaire items, one by one. Don't bury your reader under a mountain of statistics. Instead, select the most important results and present them first. Some findings may be unimportant or too ambiguous to have meaning. Don't exaggerate the importance of small differences. Often the similarities among various percentages are more impressive than small differences. The body of the report should be devoted to the major findings. It is realistic to assume that most readers will look only at the summary. It is still necessary to make the actual data available for those readers who want them. The best place to include detailed percentages is in the appendix, where they will not interrupt the flow of the report. Here is the summary from our cafeteria survey:

Report on Students' Attitudes Toward the Cafeteria: Summary

To learn students' attitudes to the food and service, a 25-item questionnaire was constructed, pretested, revised, and distributed to 100 students in the cafeteria during lunch on Thursday and Friday, June 9–10, 1978. Three-quarters of the respondents had purchased cafeteria food and one-quarter brought their meals with them. The main reason students brown-bagged their lunches was the cost of the food. Areas of most satisfaction with the cafeteria were size of portions (very ample), the green salads (tasty and nutritious), cleanliness, fast service, and the possibility of going back into the line for seconds. The problems indicated by at least one-third of the sample included quality of the meats (poor), tastiness of the vegetables (overcooked), noise in the table area, and the drab decor of the cafeteria. On most of the other items, people were satisfied but not particularly enthusiastic.

This summary presents the highlights of the report. It includes what people liked as well as what they disliked. Specific complaints are placed in the context of the overall general level of satisfaction. This is accurate as well as diplomatic. It would have been biased and shortsighted to list only the complaints and omit the compliments. A good summary, like a good report, describes the full range of attitudes, including weak and noncommittal responses. The summary should be brief and to the point. The discussion comes in the body of the report, and the detailed percentage totals appear in the appendix. The raw data, the 100 questionnaires, remain in your files until you run out of room.

Comparison of Interviews and Self-administered Questionnaires

In deciding whether to do interviewing or to distribute self-administered questionnaires, carefully consider your project needs and resources in time and money. Self-administered questionnaires are generally more economical in that they require less time and assistance in scoring, provided that they have been designed with a closed-ended response format. Administration is much quicker. They also have the advantage of offering anonymity, so they may be more desirable for investigating sensitive attitudes or behaviors.

Interviews have the advantage of allowing for observation in addition to answers to questions. Interviewers can assess nonverbal behaviors as well as elements of the setting. Even telephone interviews allow for recording intonation and comments. The interview is less likely to be incomplete and yields a higher return rate. It is better for dealing with complicated issues.

Limitations

A questionnaire is of little use with respondents who are very young, very old, infirm, or uninterested in the topic. As a written document, it is not appropriate for people on the move or who are busy with other activities. The typical questionnaire with multiple-choice answers evokes "bare bones" responses. You can learn the general structure of the situation but not the details. Follow-up interviews will help to make sense out of the trends.

A poorly worded question can create the appearance of attitudes where none exist. People may believe they are helping the researcher by providing answers that he or she wants to hear. Questionnaire replies are more useful for identifying attitudes than for predicting behavior. Do not confuse people's opinions as expressed on a questionnaire with their behavior.

Questionnaires strike many respondents as impersonal, mechanical, and demeaning and the response categories as limited, artificial, and constraining. Unless the researcher asks precisely the right questions, the information will not be very useful. Although this chapter has emphasized the economy of the questionnaire, the work involved in writing questions, pretesting the instrument, and tabulating the responses should not be underestimated. If opinions from only a small number of respondents are needed, the open-ended interview, in which a few general questions are followed by specific questions tailored to the respondents' replies, will be more economical.

Summary

A questionnaire is a series of written questions on a topic about which the respondents' written opinions are sought. Because it is so economical to administer and score, the questionnaire is widely used in behavioral research.

Open-ended questions provide space for the respondents to write in their own answers. With closed or multiple-choice questions, respondents choose among alternatives provided by the researcher. Open-ended questions are desirable when the researcher does not know all the possible answers to a question, when the range of possible answers is so large that the question would become unwieldy in a multiple-choice format, when the researcher wants to avoid suggesting answers to the respondent, and when the researcher wants answers in the respondent's own words. Multiple-choice answers are desirable when there is a large number of respondents and questions, when answers are to be scored by computer, and when answers from different groups of individuals are to be compared.

Salience refers to the importance of an issue in people's minds. Open-ended questions are well suited to determining the salience of an issue. In a multiple-choice format, salience can be determined by asking the respondent to rank or rate a list of answers in terms of importance.

In many cases you will need a middle-response category such as "neutral" or "undecided," and need to include a "nonapplicable" or "don't know" response.

Check all items for clarity. Avoid double-barreled and negative questions. Provide balance. Always pretest the questionnaire before putting it into final form.

The questionnaire is of little use with respondents who are very young, very old, infirm, or uninterested in the topic. The typical questionnaire with multiple-choice answers evokes "bare bones" responses. Questionnaires are more successful in identifying attitudes than in predicting behavior.

References

Birnbaum, J. H. (1982, December 22). Farmers need savvy, as do agents who ask them for data. *The Wall Street Journal*, p. 1.

Galton, F. (1907). *Inquiries into human faculty and its development*. London: Dent.

Johnson, S. L. (1984). *Source separation recycling programs*. Unpublished master's thesis, University of California, Davis, CA.

Major, B. N., Jacoby, J., & Sheluga, D. A. (1976). Questionnaire research on questionnaire construction. *Purdue Papers in Consumer Psychology*, No. 166.

Schuman, H., & Presser, S. (1981). *Questions and answers in attitude surveys: Experiments on question form, wording, and context*. New York: Academic Press.

Further Reading

Backstrom, C., & Hursh-Cesar, G. (1981). *Survey research* (2nd ed.). New York: Wiley.

Groves, R. M., & Kahn, R. L. (1979). *Surveys by telephone*. New York: Academic Press.

Miller, D. C. (1983). *Handbook of research design and social measurement* (4th ed.). New York: Longman.

Rossi, P. H., Wright, J. D., & Anderson, A. B. (1983). *Handbook of survey research*. New York: Academic Press.

Selltiz, C., Wrightsman, L. S., & Cook, S. W. (Eds.) (1976). *Research methods in social relations* (3rd ed.). New York: Holt, Rinehart and Winston.

10 Attitude and Rating Scales

What Is a Scale?

Originally from the Latin word *scala,* meaning a ladder or flight of steps, a scale represents a series of ordered steps at fixed intervals used as a standard of measurement. Rating scales are used to rank people's judgments of objects, events, or other people from low to high or from poor to good. Commonly used scales in behavioral research include attitude scales designed to measure people's opinions on social issues, employee rating scales to measure job-related performance, scales for determining socio-economic status used in sociological research, product rating scales used in consumer research, and sensory evaluation scales to judge the quality of food, air, and other phenomena. These scales provide numerical scores which can be used to compare individuals and groups.

There are various methods for making ratings. With *graphic rating scales,* the respondent places a mark along a continuous line. The ends and perhaps the midpoint of the line are named, but not the intervening points. The person can make a mark at any point along the line. The score is computed by measuring the distance of the check mark from the left end of the scale.

Example
Place a check mark somewhere along the scale to indicate the quality of this loudspeaker system.

130

$$\checkmark$$
_____

Excellent

                                                                          Terrible

(score 7·5 cm)

A *step scale* requires the rater to select one of a graded series of intervals. Intermediate points cannot be used. The intervals can be letters, numbers, or adjectives. For scoring purposes, these may be numbered from 1 to 5.

Example
How would you rate the quality of this loudspeaker system? (circle one)
excellent   very good   good   poor   terrible

Comparative rating scales are commonly used on recommendation forms. The person is asked to compare the applicant with others in the same category.

Example
Compared to other students in the class, how does this student rate in terms of motivation for graduate work?
Top 1%___ Top 5%___ Top 10%___ Top 25%___ Top 50%___ Bottom 50%___

Attitude Scales

An attitude scale is a special type of questionnaire designed to produce scores indicating the overall degree of favorability of a person's attitude on a topic. It is constructed so that all its questions concern a single issue. Attitude scales are used most often in attitude change experiments. One group of people is asked to fill out the scale twice, once before some event, such as seeing a propaganda film, and again afterward. A control group fills out the scale twice without seeing the film. The control group is used to measure practice effects. The change in the scores of the experimental group relative to the control group, whether their attitudes have become more or less favorable, indicates the effects of the film.

Thurstone-type Scale

In 1928 L. L. Thurstone published the article "Attitudes Can Be Measured." The title was radical because many psychologists of his day doubted that something as subjective and vague as an attitude could be measured. Thurstone maintained that people's attitudes on a topic represented the sum total of their beliefs, feelings, knowledge, and opinions about it. He developed an elaborate procedure for measuring attitudes.

Constructing a Thurstone-type Scale

The first step in constructing a Thurstone-type scale is to collect statements on the topic from people holding a wide range of attitudes, from extremely favorable to extremely unfavorable.

Examples of attitudes toward the use of marijuana:

It has its place.
Its use by an individual could be the beginning of a sad situation.
It is perfectly healthy; it should be legalized.

Duplications and irrelevant statements are omitted. The rest are typed on 3 × 5 cards and given to a group of people who serve as judges. The judges need not have any special qualifications other than to be representative of the population whose attitudes you wish to measure. They are asked to sort the statements into eleven piles representing the entire range of attitudes from extremely unfavorable (1) to extremely favorable (11). Pile 6 is for statements that are neither favorable nor unfavorable. The location of the pile in the series indicates the judges' ratings of the item (pile 8 indicates a rating of 8). Thus each statement will receive a rating from 1 to 11 from each judge. The ratings from each statement are averaged, and that average indicates how favorable the statement is on the topic.

Example

	Average rating from 20 judges (11 = extremely favorable)
If marijuana is taken safely, its effects can be quite enjoyable.	8.9
I think it is horrible and corrupting.	1.6
It is usually the drug people start on before addiction.	4.9

Note that the judges do not indicate their personal opinion on the issue; they simply decide how favorable or unfavorable each statement is. Statements about which the judges are unable to agree are not used in the final scale. The statement "Marijuana use should be taxed heavily" was rejected because it was ambiguous. Some judges thought it was pro-marijuana because it implied legalization, while others felt it was anti-marijuana because it advocated a heavy tax.

Administration and Scoring

After the statements have received their average ratings from the judges, they are arranged in random order on a questionnaire. Table 10-1 illustrates a Thurstone-type scale for measuring attitudes toward marijuana use. The average ratings made by the judges are shown in parentheses. These should not actually be reproduced on the final questionnaire.

People filling out a Thurstone-type scale are asked to check only those

TABLE 10-1. Thurstone-type Scale for Measuring Attitudes toward Marijuana

This is a scale to measure your attitude toward marijuana. It does *not* deal with any other drug, so please consider that the items pertain to marijuana exclusively.

We want to know how students feel about this topic. In order to get honest answers, the questionnaires are to be filled out anonymously. Do *not* sign your name.

Please check all those statements with which you agree.

___ 1. I don't approve of something that puts you out of normal state of mind. (3.0)*
___ 2. It has its place. (2.2)
___ 3. It corrupts the individual. (2.2)
___ 4. Marijuana does some people a lot of good. (7.9)
___ 5. Having never tried marijuana, I can't say what effects it would have. (6.0)
___ 6. If marijuana is taken safely, its effects can be quite enjoyable. (8.9)
___ 7. I think it is horrible and corrupting. (1.6)
___ 8. It is usually the drug people start on before addiction. (4.9)
___ 9. It is perfectly healthy and should be legalized. (10.0)
___10. Its use by an individual could be the beginning of a sad situation. (4.1).

*Average ratings from statements sorted into 11 piles, from very unfavorable (1) to very favorable (11). These numbers were *not* included in the actual scale to be filled out by respondents.

statements with which they agree. No indication of the strength of agreement is given. The respondent's score is computed by adding up the average ratings of all the statements checked and dividing by the number of statements checked.

Example: Scoring a Thurstone-type scale
Favorability rating (number in parentheses) of each statement checked.
2.2
1.6
4.9
Total: 8.7 ÷ 3 (number of statements checked) = 2.9 (score)

Likert Scale

The Thurstone procedure for constructing an attitude scale was later simplified by Likert (1932).

Constructing a Likert-type Scale

A Likert-type scale includes only statements that are clearly favorable or clearly unfavorable. Statements that are neutral or borderline are eliminated. Judges are used in making this decision. They rate each statement as to whether it is favorable or unfavorable on the topic. Where there is little agreement or difficulty in deciding whether the item is favorable or unfavorable, the statement is eliminated. Rather than using precise mathematical averages for each degree of favorability, Likert recommended that all items be given the same mathematical weight.

The Likert procedure eliminates the need for establishing precise favorability weights (scores) for each statement. It also simplifies the scoring procedure by using whole numbers (e.g., 1 to 5) for each item rather than numerical averages (e.g., 2.8 or 3.6). A Likert-type scale presents a list of statements on an issue to which the respondent indicates degree of agreement using categories such as Strongly Agree, Agree, Undecided, Disagree, and Strongly Disagree.

Administration and Scoring

The statements are arranged in random order on a questionnaire with a choice of degrees of agreement. Each favorable statement would be followed by five degrees of agreement (strongly agree, agree slightly, undecided, disagree slightly, strongly disagree), which would be scored 5, 4, 3, 2, and 1, respectively. The same procedure would be done with unfavorable statements except that these would be scored in the reverse direction (1, 2, 3, 4, and 5, respectively). Respondents are asked to check their degree of agreement or disagreement with all statements on the list.

Example
Indicate your degree of agreement or disagreement with each of the following statements about marijuana by circling one of the following letters

    SA = Strongly Agree
    A = Agree
    U = Undecided
    D = Disagree
    SD = Strongly Disagree

SA A U D SD 1. Marijuana use corrupts the individual.
SA A U D SD 2. Its use by the individual could be the beginning of a sad situation.
SA A U D SD 3. Marijuana does some people a lot of good.

People with very favorable attitudes would be expected to strongly agree with the favorable statements and strongly disagree with the unfavorable statements. They would earn a high score on the score when the item scores are added together. Conversely, people with very unfavorable attitudes would be expected to strongly disagree with the favorable statements and strongly agree with the unfavorable statements, and would score low on the scale. The Likert and Thurstone procedures for constructing attitude scales are compared in Table 10-2. The simplicity of the Likert scor-

TABLE 10-2. Comparison of the Thurstone and Likert Procedures for
Constructing Attitude Scales

Thurstone procedure	Likert procedure
Statements collected from a wide range of individuals	Same
Statements sorted by judges into piles representing 11 degrees of favorability on the topic	Statements rated by judges as favorable, unfavorable, or neutral on a topic
Statement on which judges disagree as to favorability discarded	Same
Items selected to represent the full range of opinion, from very favorable to very unfavorable, including neutral statements	Neutral statement discarded, leaving only statements clearly pro or con
	Each statement followed by the terms "strongly agree," "agree," "undecided," "disagree," "strongly disagree"
Respondents asked to check only those statements with which they agree	Respondents asked to indicate their degree of agreement or disagreement with all statements
Each statement scored according to average degree of favorability (e.g., 2.1, 4.6)	Favorable statements scored from 5 to 1; unfavorable statements scored from 1 to 5
Mathematical average of all statements checked is computed	Scores for all items are summed

ing system makes this procedure attractive to researchers. Most attitude scales used today are of the Likert type.

Reliability

An attitude scale should yield consistent results. Consistency in measurement is known as *reliability*. There are three common methods for testing the reliability of an attitude scale: test-retest, split-half, and equivalent forms. With the *test-retest* method, the scale is given to the same person on two occasions and the results are compared. Unless something significant happened during the interval, the two scores should be similar. The *split-half* method involves splitting an attitude scale into two halves, which are then compared. This is generally done by combining all the even-numbered items into one scale and all the odd-numbered items into another. The scores on the two halves are compared and should be similar if the scale is reliable. The third method of measuring reliability involves the use of *equivalent forms*. Two different scales on the topic are constructed, Form A and Form B. If the scale is reliable, the scores on the two forms should be similar.

These three methods for determining reliability rest on a comparison between two sets of scores. This comparison is made through a statistical test known as the correlation coefficient, described in Chapter 18.

For readers who do not want to construct their own attitude scales, a good selection of scales whose reliability has already been established is available in Robinson and Shaver, *Measures of Social Psychological Attitudes* (1973). Journal articles on the topic of interest will also provide references to scales currently in use.

Limitations

There are serious questions about the validity of attitude scales. Often they predict behavior poorly or not at all. The words on the printed page bear little resemblance to the actual situation. Another problem with attitude scales is the assumption that attitudes lie along a single dimension of favorability. People's opinions on a topic like marijuana are complex and multidimensional. A person may be in favor of reducing the penalties on marijuana posession but not on cultivation or sale, and may want strict penalties for anyone driving under the drug's influence. A single favorability score cannot reflect the specificity of these concerns. A questionnaire, which treats each item separately, is more widely used than the attitude scale for this reason.

Semantic Differential

The semantic differential is a procedure developed by psychologist Charles Osgood and his associates to measure the meaning of concepts (Osgood, Suci, & Tannenbaum, 1957). The respondent is asked to rate an object or a concept along a series of scales with opposed adjectives at either end.

Example
Rate the park nearest your residence along each of the following scales.

```
    Quiet ___:___:___:___:___:___ Noisy
Dangerous ___:___:___:___:___:___ Safe
      Sad ___:___:___:___:___:___ Happy
```

The semantic differential is a good instrument for exploring the *connotative meaning* of things. Connotation refers to the personal meaning of something, as distinct from its physical characteristics. For example, a panther, in addition to being a large cat, connotes stealth and power. Crepes suzette suggest elegance and expensive dining.

Selection of Terms

In the research that developed the semantic differential, three major categories of connotative meaning were found: value (e.g., good-bad, ugly-beautiful), activity (e.g., fast-slow, active-passive), and strength (e.g., weak-strong, large-small). Table 10-3 presents four adjective pairs high in value, activity, or strength. Not surprisingly, the value dimension (good-bad, valuable-worthless) is of greatest importance in evaluative research. When you want to know whether or not people like something, you will probably want to include good-bad, ugly-beautiful, and friendly-unfriendly. Activity and strength are important dimensions in certain circumstances. A comparison of people's images of cities and small towns found major differences on the activity and strength dimensions. Cities were full of bustle, hurry, and activity, while in small towns the pace was more slow, relaxed, and leisurely. Cities were also rated as larger, stronger, and more powerful than small towns (Sommer, 1965). Other adjectives may be more relevant to a particular topic. An investigation of religious concepts used adjectives closely related to religious belief, such as sacred-profane, mysterious-obvious, and public-private (Heeren, 1963). The nature of the project will determine the adjectives to be used.

Pretesting the adjective pairs is essential for eliminating difficult or ambiguous terms. Even if adjectives have been used by other researchers, it will still be necessary to test them on your particular respondents. Adjectives that have one meaning for one group of people may mean something else to another group.

Length and Layout

Don't burden your respondents with too many scales. After a while, the lines become a blur. We do not recommend using more than 20 adjective pairs to measure a concept; 10 to 12 adjective pairs seem preferable.

TABLE 10-3. Polar Adjective Pair*

High on value dimension	High on activity dimension	High on strength dimension
Good-bad	Active-passive	Strong-weak
Beautiful-ugly	Energetic-inert	Large-small
Friendly-unfriendly	Fast-slow	Hard-soft
Wise-foolish	Excitable-calm	Heavy-light

* Adapted from Osgood, Suci, & Tannenbaum, 1957.

Remember that the value of your results depends on the voluntary cooperation of your respondents.

Counterbalance the order of positive and negative adjectives. Begin some scales with the positive term (happy-sad) and others with the negative term (noisy-quiet). This will prevent the respondent from falling into a fixed pattern of always checking to the right or left.

Make sure that people put their marks in the right place. Most researchers use solid lines for the responses and colons as spacers.

Example:

Light ____:____:____:____:____:____:____ Dark

It is important that answers be marked on the lines and *not* on the dots. Tabulating the responses becomes very complicated when people have checked on the dots. When this occurs, many researchers assign the mark to the right or left line in random order. That is, if a person has checked midway between the second and third line, the response will be scored as a 2 the first time and a 3 the next time this occurs. So long as this is done randomly, the results should not be biased.

Most researchers follow Osgood in using seven-point scales. This includes a midpoint, which is useful when the item is neither happy nor sad or neither light nor dark, but somewhere in the middle. However, if machine scoring limited to a five-point scale can be done cheaply and quickly, this option should be seriously considered. Five-point scales are more easily tabulated by hand, too. Many researchers find that differences among the three scale points to the right or left of the midpoint have little meaning. The direction of response (e.g., whether the cafeteria is seen as a happy place) is more important than whether it is seen as extremely happy, moderately happy, or somewhat happy. If you plan to combine all three categories to the right of the neutral point later, you might as well begin with a smaller number of scale points—five or even three.

Example
Rate this room along each of the following scales:

friendly ____:____:____ unfriendly
   light ____:____:____ dark
  quiet ____:____:____ noisy
  dirty ____:____:____ clean

Scoring

The scale points are given numerical values from 0 to 6 or 1 to 7 on a seven-point scale, going from left to right. The average is computed separately for each pair. Thus, 3 is the midpoint value of the happy-sad scale,

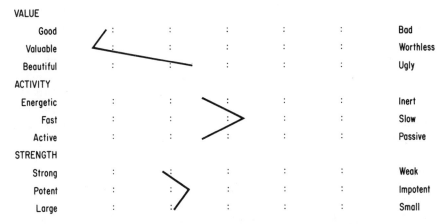

FIG. 10-1. Library reference room, ratings from the semantic differential.

whose end points are 0 and 6. Anything below 3 means that the item is generally happy, and anything above 4 means that the item is generally sad. In presenting the results, it is helpful to the reader to reorganize all the scales so that the favorable end is on the left and the unfavorable end on the right. Note that this differs from the order of the scales given to the respondents. Placing all the favorable adjectives on the left enables the reader to see at a glance how the ratings came out.

The results can be presented graphically as well as in averages. Figure 10-1 shows student ratings of a reading room in a university library. The room is highly valued and strong but relatively low in activity.

Limitations

The semantic differential is usable only with intelligent and cooperative adults. People with little education often focus on the ends of the scale and do not use the middle points. We would not recommend using the semantic differential with children, with people whose command of the language is limited, with older people who would have difficulty seeing the various scale points, or with any group of respondents who are not accustomed to making fine distinctions in their assessments of persons, objects, and events.

Performance Rating Scales

Many companies require the work of all employees to be formally rated periodically. This is intended to ensure some level of competence among workers. It also requires a supervisor to have firsthand contact with the employee's work. Performance scales contain a built-in evaluative component. Behavior is rated along dimensions such as skilled-unskilled, organized-disorganized, competent-incompetent. It is desirable to make the behaviors assessed very specific; instead of asking a general question about work habits, the rater is asked about the employee's response to supervision, ability to work under pressure, relationships with fellow employees, and so on. These items can be collected by asking workers and supervisors about what qualities are important on the job and from previous research on worker productivity. It is important to pretest both the job-related characteristics and the rating scales to eliminate ambiguous or unclear terms.

Experience with performance ratings in industry, the civil service, and the armed forces has been disappointing. These ratings are still used in many settings primarily because no better measures are available. *Halo effects* refer to the tendency to make ratings of specific abilities on the basis of an overall impression. If you like someone, it is easy to see everything he does as good. If you don't like him, it is easy to give poor marks to all his work. Another problem is that raters are not willing to make honest judgments. There are severe pressures against saying unkind things about another person. If a supervisor wants to be known as a "good guy," all employees routinely get good evaluations. Also, low ratings for employees reflect badly on the supervisor.

Because raters know that extremely positive statements are the rule, anything less than the top score is seen as likely to jeopardize the person's career. With a shrug of the shoulders because "everybody does it," the rater routinely checks "outstanding" for all categories. This happened in the U.S. Army Officer Efficiency Ratings. In this scale, "Excellent" was a typical score and "Very Good" became a mark of disapproval (Thorndike, 1962). This tendency to inflate a person's abilities is readily apparent on recommendation forms that use performance scales. A high proportion of recommendation letters describe the applicant as being in the top 5 or 1 percent.

One method used to minimize the tendency to give top ratings to everyone is to make the questions specific and personal. Instead of asking whether an employee is a good worker, supervisors are asked how likely they would be to recommend the employee for advancement in their department. A professor writing a letter of recommendation would be asked not only whether the applicant was a good student but whether the professor would admit the student to his or her own graduate program. Personalizing the questions helps reduce the ho-hum attitude on the part of the rater. The generosity factor may be less apparent in anonymous ratings. While anonymity for raters is impractical in considering applicants for admission or promotion, it is quite feasible in research.

BOX 10-1. Air Force Ends Quota on Top Ratings

As of October, 1978, the Air Force will no longer impose a quota on the number of officers who can receive the highest efficiency ratings. The quota had been imposed in 1975 when it was found that 95% of officers were receiving "ones" which was the highest possible performance rating. Air Force officials decreed that only 22% of the officers within a command could receive ratings of "1" and only 28% could receive the lesser rating of "2". The remainder would have to receive lower ratings from 3 to 6.

Outraged responses from those doing the rating and those being rated forced the Air Force to withdraw the quotas. Critics charged that the quota system did not take into account the quality of officers on a base. In a mediocre command, even average performance could rate a "1" but an outstanding performance on a top notch base might not even rate a "2." The Air Force bowed to the criticism and returned to the older system of permitting an unlimited number of top scores. (Bell, 1978)

Limitations

Performance rating scales have not been very useful in research because of the reluctance of raters to say unkind things about people, halo effects, and a lack of standards for judging employee effectiveness. If other criteria of effectiveness are available, such as production records or customer ratings, the supervisor's ratings may provide useful supplementary information.

Consumer Rating Scales

When checking into a motel room, it is common to find a short questionnaire on the dresser asking for an evaluation of the service, facilities, and food. The purchaser of a new car is likely to receive a questionnaire in the mail from the national distributor asking about the quality of dealer service and maintenance. Consumer organizations collect evaluations of products from members and volunteers. Such ratings of actual products and services are different from market surveys to establish levels of demand. Rating is most appropriate for items with which the person is directly familiar. Surveys of needs and wants are better handled through interviews.

Product rating scales are useful for comparing responses from large groups. It would be awkward and time consuming to compare interviews collected from 50 owners of car A and car B. Comparison would be easier if all persons had rated their cars along the same set of scales. Instead of using a random or representative sample of the community, it is common to use only those who have had direct experience with the product or service. Thus, ratings of an airline would be obtained from passengers during a flight. A questionnaire regarding customer satisfaction with a camera might be attached to the warranty card. Commercial firms employ methods that vary in complexity and sophistication to obtain customer feedback. Some cast their nets widely in the hope of finding something useful; others prefer more detailed surveys with a much smaller, carefully selected sample. Often the latter surveys are undertaken by a national marketing firm.

The first step in product rating is to identify those characteristics that are important and relevant. This is done by examining ratings of similar products and by consulting with suppliers and customers.

The next step is to establish scale points. For a brief questionnaire that accompanies the product or is filled out by customers, a three-point scale is probably sufficient.

Example
Please tell us how you felt about your stay in this hotel.

desk clerk	above average	average	below average
elevator	above average	average	below average
cleanliness of room	above average	average	below average
coffee shop service	above average	average	below average

For children and others not accustomed to making verbal ratings, a series of facial expressions can be used to indicate liking.

Example
Which face shows the way you feel about this product?

Limitations

Ratings through questionnaires attached to the product or left on hotel dressers are subject to response bias. Persons most likely to fill out and send in questionnaires will be those with strong opinions pro and con—and generally the latter. Response rates will vary with the consumers' interest in helping the manufacturer or service agent.

Sensory Evaluation

Sensory evaluation began in the laboratories of early experimental psychologists, who were interested in the basic properties of odors, tastes, sounds and other sensations. The connection between the physical qualities of objects and their sensory attributes is called *psychophysics*. A key assumption in psychophysics is that people can make meaningful ratings of the degree of their sensory experiences (e.g., rating items as more or less bright, loud, sweet, and so on).

The food and beverage industries rely heavily on sensory evaluation. Before a new product is marketed, its consumer acceptance will be tested. Products are often first tested by expert judges who have exceptionally well-developed palates, noses, or visual sensitivity before being tried out on a panel of nonexperts.

The qualities to be rated depend as much on the interests of the investigator as on the objective characteristic of the item. A firm might be interested in the visual appearance of a bar of soap, the texture of canned fruit, or the sound level of fluorescent lights. Deciding what characteristics are relevant should be done in consultation with the client or consumer organization, or it can be based on previous research.

Various methods have been used to present material to the judges. One

Sensory evaluation. The student was asked to rate the flavor and appearance of tomatoes.

approach is to present the judges, at the beginning of the session, with *standards.* For an investigation of taste qualities, the judge will first taste four different compounds, one very sweet, one very sour, one very salty, and another very bitter to use as standards in making subsequent judgments.

Example
Rate the item you have tasted along each of the following scales. Place a check anywhere along the line.

very sweet	not sweet

very sour	not sour

very salty	not salty

very bitter	not bitter

Note that the four taste qualities are rated separately. Sweet is not considered the opposite of sour. Grapefruit and pineapple can be both sweet and sour.

In the method of *paired comparisons,* items are presented two at a time and the person is asked to compare them. This method is useful in deciding whether a change represents an improvement over a standard model.

Example
Compared to B (the standard), item A is:

spicier	less spicy	equal
sweeter	less sweet	equal
more dense	less dense	equal
more fragrant	less fragrant	equal

Since the subject compares only two items at a time, each comparison can be done quickly and easily. There is very little dependence on memory. Comparison procedures are useful with inexperienced judges, who can express a preference for one item over another without being specific as to their reasons.

Example
Which of these two wines is sweeter, A or B?
Which of these two wines would you choose to accompany a steak dinner, A or B?

Such sessions are conducted as *blind taste trials*. The term *blind* indicates that the subject is not aware of the origin or identity of the item being rated. The subject is told its general category (wine) but not the specific variety, cost, or place of origin. Blind tasting minimizes the effects of labels and stereotypes. Subjects may be more likely to give high ratings to wines with expensive labels or fancy names. A further refinement of this procedure requires two experimenters, one who replaces all identifying information with code numbers before the sessions. The second experimenter, who has no information on the coding system, conducts the actual taste trials. This is called a *double blind procedure*, since both the subject and experimenter conducting the tests are in the dark about what is being tasted.

Limitations

Like performance rating, sensory evaluation is subject to a halo effect. When people like a product, they tend to see most things about it as good; if they dislike it, they see everything about it as bad. Without careful explanation, the terms used in sensory evaluation may not be clear to those doing the rating; for example, people may have difficulty distinguishing among fragrant, fruity, and spicy. Expert judges, such as food critics and wine tasters, use different criteria than those used by ordinary consumers. Sensory evaluation requires people to make artificial distinctions. When they taste ketchup on a hot dog, most people do not divide the taste into separate degrees of sweetness, sourness, and saltiness.

Summary

Rating scales are used to rank people's judgments of objects, events, or other people from low to high or from good to poor. They provide numerical scores which can be used to compare individuals and groups.

On a graphic rating scale, the respondent places a mark along a continuous line. On an interval scale, the rater checks one of a graded series of steps without intermediate points. On a comparative rating scale, the person is asked to compare the object or person with others in the same category.

An attitude scale is a special type of questionnaire designed to produce scores indicating the overall degree of favorability of a person's attitudes on a topic. A Thurstone-type scale contains statements expressing a full range of opinions on a topic. Respondents check all those statements with which they agree. A Likert-type scale contains only statements that are clearly favorable or clearly unfavorable. No neutral or borderline statements are included. The respondents rate each statement along a five-point scale of agreement, from strongly agree to strongly disagree. Most attitude scales used today are of the Likert type.

Reliability refers to consistency of measurement. There are three common methods for estimating the reliability of an attitude scale. In the test-retest method, the scale is given to the person on two occasions and the results are compared. The split-half method involves splitting an attitude scale into two halves which are then compared. The third method of measuring reliability involves constructing two equivalent forms of the scale. If the scale is reliable, the person's score on the two forms should be similar. The chief limitation of attitude scales is that they predict behavior poorly or not at all.

The semantic differential is a procedure developed to measure the connotative meaning of concepts. Connotation refers to the personal meaning of something as distinct from its physical characteristics. Three major categories of connotative meaning are value, strength, and activity.

Performance rating scales are used to judge the competence or work output of employees. Experience with their use in most settings has been disappointing. Many supervisors are not willing to make honest judgments. The halo effect refers to the tendency to rate specific abilities on the basis of an overall impression.

Consumer ratings are used to find out people's opinions about products and services with which they are familiar.

Sensory evaluation is used to test the psychophysical properties of products, particularly food and beverages. Sensory evaluation can involve expert judges or average persons. Sometimes judges are asked to rate items along graphic rating scales (e.g., sweet-not sweet, salty-not salty). In the method of paired comparisons, items are presented two at a time and the person is asked to compare them. In a blind taste trial, the respondent does not know the origin or specific identity of the item being rated. In a double-blind procedure, neither the subject nor the experimenter knows the origin or specific identity of the item being rated.

Without careful explanation, the terms used in sensory evaluation may not be clear to those doing the rating. Expert judges such as food critics use different criteria than those used by ordinary consumers.

References

Bell, T. (1978, October 17). Air force ends quota on ratings. *Sacramento Bee*, p. B3.
Heeren, S. D. (1963). *A study of religious concepts.* Unpublished masters thesis, University of Alberta.
Likert, R. (1932). A technique for the measurement of attitudes. *Archives of Psychology, 140,* 1–55.
Osgood, C. E., Suci, G. J., & Tannenbaum, P. (1957). *The measurement of meaning.* Urbana: University of Illinois Press.

Robinson, J. P., & Shaver, P. R. (1973). *Measures of social psychological attitudes* (rev. ed.). Ann Arbor, MI: Survey Research Center, Institute for Social Research, University of Michigan.

Sommer, R. (1965). The significance of space. *A.I.A. Journal 43,* 63–65.

Thorndike, R. L., (1962). *Personnel selection.* New York: Wiley.

Thurstone, L. L. (1928). Attitudes can be measured. *American Journal of Sociology, 33,* 529–554.

Further Reading

Anderson, A. B., Basilevsky, A., & Hum, D. P. J. (1983). Measurement: Theory and techniques. In P. H. Rossi, J. D. Wright, & A. B. Anderson (Eds.), *Handbook of survey research* (pp. 231–287). New York: Academic Press.

Dunn-Rankin, P. (1983). *Scaling methods.* Hillsdale, NJ: Erlbaum.

Maranell, G. M. (Ed.). (1974). *Scaling: A sourcebook for behavioral scientists.* Chicago: Aldine.

Oskamp, S. (1977). *Attitudes and opinions.* Englewood Cliffs, NJ: Prentice-Hall.

Robinson, J. P., & Shaver, P. R. (1973). *Measures of social psychological attitudes* (rev. ed.). Ann Arbor, MI: Survey Research Center, Institute for Social Research, University of Michigan.

Shaw, M. E., & Wright, J. M. (1967). *Scales for the measurement of attitudes.* New York: McGraw-Hill.

V
Other Useful Research Procedures and Materials

11 Content Analysis

Medical Advertisements

Drug advertising is controversial in terms of both the large dollar volume and its contents. Estimates of the amount spent by pharmaceutical firms on promotion and advertising range from $400 million to over $1 billion annually. This amount represents from 12 to 20 percent of the total expenditures by the drug industry depending on the country and method of calculation used. The large number of new drugs on the market each year makes it difficult for physicians to keep abreast of them. The most heavily used sources of information for physicians have been found to be journal articles and conversations with colleagues, followed by promotional literature and visits from manufacturers' representatives (Hess, 1974). One study found that 73 percent of physicians surveyed rated advertisements in medical journals as somewhat important or very important to them as sources of information about drugs (Linn & Davis, 1972).

Social scientists have been concerned that advertising might encourage the use of drugs when other treatments are more appropriate. Two researchers examined advertisements in *The American Journal of Medicine, Journal of the American Medical Association, Medical Aspects of Human Sexuality,* and *Psychiatric News.* Advertisements occupied from 35 to 75 percent of total page space. The dominant advertisers were pharmaceutical firms who had purchased from 56 to 87 percent of the ads and contributed from 64 to 96 percent of advertising revenues. Drug ads tended to be longer, make use of more illustrations, and feature more color than other ads. There was a stereotyped use of male and female models in portraying health professions, with female nurses and male physicians (Sommer & Sommer, 1978).

The first decisions for the researchers who undertook this study

151

involved the selection of journals to be studied (there were many medical journals available) and the particular issues (month and year). The next step was to develop a classification scheme (see Box 11-1). Then the length of each ad was tabulated, as was the use of illustrations, color, models, and so on. The information was coded by hand and analyzed by computer. Advertising rates were obtained from the publishers, and the dollar volume of all advertising was computed.

Quantification in Content Analysis

Content analysis is a technique for systematically describing the form and content of written or spoken material. It has been used most often in the study of mass media. However, the technique is suitable for any kind of written or spoken material, including interview records, letters, songs, cartoons, advertising circulars, and so on. The basis of a content analysis is *quantification* (i.e., expressing data in numbers). Instead of impressions about trends and biases, the investigator comes up with precise figures. In the study of medical advertising mentioned earlier, 96 percent of the models used for physicians were male, while 90 percent of the nurses or lab technicians were female. These figures strengthen the case for a stereotyped role portrayal and allow comparison with other media.

The analysis can emphasize the content of the material or its structure or both. *Content* refers to the specific topics or themes. *Structure* includes location on the page, format, use of illustrations, and so on. How much attention does a president's speech devote to the Soviet Union compared

---

BOX 11-1. Coding System for Medical Advertisements
Ad sheet (Fill out one for each advertisement)

Column	*Variable code*
1	Journal (circle one)
	1. *American Journal of Medicine*
	2. *JAMA*
	3. *Medical Aspects of Human Sexuality*
	4. *Psychiatric News*
2	Issue number (put your issues in chronological order and number them from 1 to 4, giving data below. This will be the same for all ads from a particular magazine. (circle one) 1 2 3 4
3–6	Ad number. Be sure to right align (number your ads chronologically, giving *each* ad a different number. Do *not* renumber when starting a second magazine or issue, but rather, continue on.)

3	4	5	6

7   Ad color (circle appropriate number)
            1. color—any color other than black, white, or gray
            2. black/white/gray

8   Ad format (circle appropriate number)
            1. Illustration—any picture, drawing, or sketch.
               Does *not* include medical symbols or chemical
               symbols.
            2. No illustration

9–12   Size of ad; measure in square centimeters. (If
            classified, measure entire section.)

9	10	11	12

13–14   Content (circle only one)
            1. Prescription—internal medicine: Look for
               warnings of side effects, prescribing
               information, etc.
            2. Nonprescription—internal medicine (e.g.,
               aspirin, NoDoz)
            3. External medications—salves, ointments, jellies
            4. Treatment apparatus—IUD, hypodermic
               needles, enema, etc.
            5. Dietary—cranberry juice, etc.
            6. Lab equipment, hospital equipment, furniture,
               wheelchair, etc.
            7. Clothing
            8. Seminars, workshops, training/education
            9. Books, periodicals, films
            10. Job recruiting, vacancy, availability
            11. Classified section (entire section)
            Unable to determine (please describe)_____

15   Physician (circle one)
            0. no
            1. male
            2. female
            3. both
            4. indeterminate sex

16   Nurse/lab technician (circle one)
            0. no
            1. male
            2. female
            3. both
            4. indeterminate sex

17   Patient (circle one)
            0. no
            1. male
            2. female
            3. both
            4. indeterminate sex

to China? This is basically a structural question. Whether it is anti-Soviet or pro-Soviet, anti-Chinese or pro-Chinese is a content question.

Content analysis allows a person to do social research without coming into contact with people. There is no need to check with a human subjects committee. No laboratory equipment or expensive facilities are required. The materials for a content analysis are probably available in a library or newspaper file. In some cases, it will be necessary to dig for scarce materials in back issues of a periodical that is difficult to locate. A reference librarian can be extraordinarily helpful in finding materials.

Content analysis has additional advantages compared with other techniques. The investigator uses material that is already available. This eliminates the possible bias that occurs when the researcher generates the data in an interview or observational study. Content analysis is unobtrusive. The observer has no effect upon the material analyzed. The material is the same after the study as before. This is not true in an experimental or interview study. Content analysis permits comparison of trends over time. It is easy for one person to repeat another's study since the materials are readily available and unchanged by the previous study. Of all the methods discussed in this book, content analysis scores the highest marks in terms of ease of replication. The technique is well suited to comparisons among different nations.

On the debit side, content analysis can be a tedious and exacting activity. Imagine sitting at a library table with 10 years of magazines stacked in front of you. Each article must be classified along several dimensions. The first few issues are interesting. By the time the twelfth issue is done, it is easy to wonder why you embarked on the study. Content analysis requires patience and attention to detail. It is not a technique for someone who wants to determine the main trends and run. It requires long hours at a library or study table counting, measuring, and classifying. Yet there is an excitement that comes from seeing trends emerge from a mass of printed material. The researchers who undertook the study of medical advertising had predicted that there would be sex stereotyping of the patients. They imagined that most of the patients would be women. Their supposition proved incorrect. The models used to depict patients showed equal representation of men and women. Other researchers studying medical journals also confirmed this. However, a finer-grained analysis by another research team that examined the type of drug did show sex stereotyping. When the ailment was psychological (anxiety, depression, or insomnia), the model tended to be female. When the condition was a physical illness or a work related disability, the model tended to be male (Prather & Fidell, 1975).

Finding Categories

The best way to select categories for classification is first to skim over the materials to identify the major themes. These can be listed as they are found. When the categories begin to repeat themselves (i.e., the material all seems to be covered by the previous categories), you can stop for the moment. Categories that overlap or duplicate one another can be combined. The resulting categories can then be tried on new materials to see how well they fit.

The list of categories must be comprehensive, covering all the items to be analyzed. However, it is legitimate to use an "other" heading for unusual items that belong nowhere else and aren't sufficiently numerous to warrant a separate heading.

Example
Content analysis of responses to open-ended interview question: "What is the single most important reason why you shop in this store?"

Reason	Classification
"Prices are low"	Prices
"Near my home"	Location
"Friendly service"	Employees
"Prices cheap"	Prices
"Convenient"	Location
"Good value"	Prices
"Accompanied friend"	Other
"Store on my way to work"	Location

Establishing categories is not always easy. Cartoons may be difficult to classify with respect to type of humor. Some cartoons may show a combination of categories (e.g., both aggressive and sexual or absurd and sick). Classifying emotional themes in television serials will have a subjective component. In general, structural items such as amount of space, time, and location tend to be more reliable than content themes, which are more subjective.

Sampling

Finding one biased textbook does not necessarily indicate a serious problem with school books in the community; nor is an analysis of one speech sufficient to confirm a political trend. A larger number of school textbooks or speeches must be analyzed. A single edition may be affected by extraneous factors, such as the time of year or some unusual event that may temporarily obscure long-standing policies. The larger the amount of material analyzed, the more valid the conclusions will be. While the more-is-better rule applies in general, at some point the cost of increasing the amount of material will outweigh the benefits. If a monthly periodical is being examined over a 10-year period, there will be 120 issues available for study. For reasons of economy, the researcher may decide to reduce this number through sampling rather than use all of them. Probably a sample of 6 issues per year would be sufficient. However, the sample must be representative. The investigator cannot simply use those articles or speeches that support his or her beliefs.

There are several different ways to obtain a representative sample of material. The researcher may decide to use every third issue of a magazine or every fifth article over a 2-year period. The important consideration is that the choice of material be representative rather than under the arbitrary control of the researcher.

Decisions must also be made about the unit of analysis. One can analyze sentences, paragraphs, pages, or entire articles. In the drug advertising study, some ads ran more than four pages. In counting the amount of drug advertising, should one four-page ad be scored the same as four one-page ads? Is a large editorial cartoon on a topic equivalent to a small one? One approach is to score each item in two ways. First, count each article, advertisement, or cartoon as a separate unit regardless of size (e.g., the number of antipolitician cartoons on the editorial page regardless of their size). Second, tabulate them by the amount of space (column inches) they occupy.

Reliability

Scoring categories must be reliable. Two people doing a content analysis of the same article using a single list of categories should come up with similar results. Reliability is greatest when the scoring categories are clearly stated and do not overlap. Reliability cannot be assumed. Even something presumably as obvious as the sex of advertisement models can be ambiguous. Several of the medical ads showed models who were so blurred and indistinct that their gender was indeterminate. There were even questions about whether some ads were in color or black and white. Sepia tone ads were difficult to classify as to color.

The first step in checking reliability is to train two or more judges in the use of the scoring system. It is important that the training be leisurely and relaxed. The judges must be free to ask questions and express their doubts when they are uncertain. Even a good scoring system may seem unreliable if the judges are not properly trained. Training begins with a detailed explanation of the scoring system and then practice in scoring material under the watchful eyes of the investigator. The material used should be similar to that in the actual research project. When the judge has a problem, this can be discussed with the investigator. It may be that the categories are ambiguous and should be changed. At other times, the problem will be the judge's inexperience in using the system. If the judges still have problems after a few practice trials, then the classification system should probably be revised. It is wasteful to begin a lengthy content analysis if the categories are not reliable.

Limitations

The results of a content analysis are purely descriptive. They reveal *what* the content and structure of communications are but not *why* they are that way; nor does the analysis reveal the impact of a communication upon the audience. This requires further investigation through observation, interviews, or experiments.

The researcher using content analysis is restricted to the materials available. Some topics are more likely than others to be covered in the media. Someone who is interested in media stereotypes of accountants or steamfitters, for example, would have to search a long time and would probably find little that was applicable.

Content analysis deals with communication materials, not necessarily with outside reality. An increase in media coverage of robberies and burglaries may reflect less of an actual crime wave than an editorial decision to highlight crime during a particular month. The investigator must be careful not to assume that trends in written or audiovisual materials automatically reflect changes in the topic being covered.

Summary

Content analysis is a technique for systematically describing written, spoken, or visual communication. The analysis can emphasize either the content of the material or its structure. The basis of content analysis is quantification.

The researcher uses material that is already available; there is no need for interaction with an actual subject. The method is well suited for cross-national comparisons and for examing trends over time. The material chosen for analysis must be selected in an unbiased way, and reliable categories must be used in the scoring.

Limitations: The results of a content analysis are descriptive rather than explanatory. Analysis is limited to available recorded materials and is subject to any biases in these materials.

References

Hess, S. W. (1974). Communicating with physicians. *Journal of Advertising Research, 14,* 13–18.

Linn, L. S., & Davis, M. S. (1972). Physician orientation toward the legitimacy of drug use and their preferred source of new drug information. *Social Science and Medicine, 6,* 199–210.

Prather, J., & Fidell, L. S. (1975). Sex differences in the content and style of medical advertisements. *Social Science and Medicine, 9,* 23–26.
Sommer, R., & Sommer, B. (1978). Advertising in health journals. *Journal of Orthomolecular Psychiatry, 7,* 275–281.

Further Reading

Holsti, O. (1969). *Content analysis for the social sciences and humanities.* Reading, MA.: Addison-Wesley.
Krippendorf, K. (1980). *Content analysis: An introduction to its methodology.* Beverly Hills, CA: Sage.
Stewart, J. S. (1964). Content and readership of teen magazines. *Journalism Quarterly, 41,* 580–583.

12 Personal Documents and Archival Measures

Personal Documents

With all the new household appliances presently available, one would suppose that American women would spend far less time in housework than did their mothers and grandmothers in the 1920s. Not so, concluded researcher Joann Vanek (1974), who examined diaries kept by women as part of a research study sponsored by the U.S. Bureau of Home Economics. Participants in the study had been asked to keep records of their daily activities. It was found that women not holding jobs outside the home spent as much time doing housework as did women in the 1920s. Diaries did show changes in the nature of housework. Time spent in shopping and administering the home had increased. Less time was spent in preparing food and cleaning up after meals. Washing machines, dryers, and abundant hot water made laundry activities much easier. Nonetheless, the amount of time women spent doing laundry has actually increased over the past half century. Also, more time is now spent in travel to food and shopping stores—approximately one full working day per week on the road and in stores, compared to less than 2 hours per week in the 1920s.

These conclusions could not have come from the laboratory, but rather from the study of people in their homes. Up to this point, the major procedure recommended for studying natural behavior has been observation. Another possibility is to ask people to keep journals of their activities or

159

to use diaries that people keep on their own. This method is advantageous when the behavior is private and difficult to observe without being intrusive.

Study Diaries

Diaries have been used by research teams interested in knowing how much time undergraduates spent studying. This answer, too, could not come out of the laboratory. To find out how long students actually study, one must enter the world of dormitories, libraries, and cafeterias. Researchers considered a number of other techniques before deciding on journals kept by individual students. The lack of any specific location for reading discouraged the use of observation. Reviewing notes was found to occur at odd hours—in between cups of coffee in the cafeteria, lying on one's bed listening to the stereo, at the laundromat, and occasionally in the bathroom. There was no single place from which an observer could keep track of all the reading that was done. Interviews about the amount of study during the past week were also unsuccessful. Because of the varied nature of study

Personal documents. Because studying so often took place at odd hours in odd locations, researchers asked students to keep diaries showing how much and where they studied.

and the fact that it was frequently combined with other activities, students were vague and hesitant in their answers. The interviewer received replies like, "Two or three hours, I guess." or "Maybe five hours, I don't know." Another approach considered but then discarded was to track students throughout the day to observe their study habits directly (i.e., behavioral mapping). This would have been extremely intrusive and time consuming. The presence of an observer in a small dormitory room would have been intolerable to many occupants; nor would many students care for an observer accompanying them on a study date. The diary was considered a good compromise between accuracy and nonintrusiveness, especially since the diaries could be supplemented by observations in the library and interviews with students about their study habits (Sommer, 1968).

Most research diaries are limited to specific activities. Few researchers ask people to keep open-ended journals describing everything that has happened. Such accounts would be extraordinarily tedious for both the diarist and the researcher. Most research diaries have time periods indicated directly on the record sheet. The investigation of housework used 5- and 15-minute intervals, and the research on study habits used hourly intervals (see Box 12-1). Finding appropriate time units is very important. Information will be lost if the intervals are too long, but if the intervals are too short, the amount of paperwork increases and cooperation is likely to suffer. When the activity has a clearly defined beginning and end, logs can be kept in minutes (e.g., telephone calls took place between 9:18 and 9:21, 9:36 and 9:45) and so on. With activities that are loosely defined and sub-

---

BOX 12-1. Record Form for Study Sessions

Day_____ Date_____ Initials or Code Number_____

Amount of time (in minutes) spent in:

Time	Reviewing notes	Reading text	Reading other materials	Preparing term report, project, etc.	Other (describe)	Length of study periods	Place where study occurred
8–9 A.M.							
9–10 A.M.							
. . .							
11–12 P.M.							
12–4 A.M.							
4–8 A.M.							
Comments:							

ject to intrusion, records can specify the primary activity that occurred during the period.

Life Histories

The diaries mentioned thus far in this chapter were prepared at the researcher's request. Other sources of information on a topic are published diaries, journals, letters, and autobiographies. In some cases, people have published their own journals, but in other cases it is someone else—perhaps a relative, friend, or historian—who locates an interesting diary and obtains permission to get it published. A researcher, studying grief and bereavement, analyzed diaries of 56 people who experienced the loss of someone close to them. Quantitative and qualitative analyses were used to compare grief responses in the nineteenth century with those of the twentieth century (Rosenblatt, 1983).

Letters written by famous individuals have also found their way into print—for example, Freud's letters to Wilhelm Fliess (Freud, 1957) and Van Gogh's letters to his brother Theo (Van Gogh, 1953). Originally written as private correspondence, they have become public documents available for journalistic, historical, and psychological studies. There are published autobiographies relevant to almost any conceivable topic. Occasionally a sufficient number of autobiographies is available to permit systematic analysis. Numerous scientists and inventors have written accounts of how they made their discoveries. Politicians frequently write autobiographies, as do film stars, singers, musicians, and artists. Over a hundred published autobiographies of prison inmates are available. These accounts cover all time periods and many nations, permitting comparison of prisons across centuries and national boundaries.

Relevant personal narratives are often found in unusual places. For example, interesting material on medical practice can be found in the autobiographical poems of poet/physicians. A good account of blindness is Eleanor Clark's *Eyes, etc.* (1977). Reading first-person narratives is easy and enjoyable. Most can be finished in a single evening.

A reference librarian can be extraordinarily helpful in locating pertinent autobiographies. It is surprising how many bibliographies (lists of books on a topic) and books about books are published each year. Someone has undoubtedly written a master's thesis on the literature of the steel mills of the nineteenth century or the building of the transcontinental railroad. We cannot emphasize too strongly how helpful a librarian can be. An entire profession exists whose avowed goal is to help you gain access to books. Do not hesitate to consult the owner of a used-book store, who is likely to be a book lover. Book dealers can initiate searches through trade newsletters. Purchasing secondhand books is not necessarily expensive as long as you avoid rare editions. For instance, two researchers collected autobiographies of former mental patients using the newsletters of book dealers at an average cost of $5 per volume. The key rule in locating published autobiographies is to use the services of available book people such as librarians, book dealers, archivists, and historical society members. When they do not know where materials can be found, they will often be able to supply the name of someone else to ask for advice.

The most common use of autobiographies in behavioral research is to illustrate findings that have been established through other methods. One social psychologist interested in sensory deprivation quoted the experiences of early Arctic explorers. Researchers who study creativity will include statements by famous inventors. Reports on crime are likely to quote from the diaries of famous swindlers, burglars, and pickpockets. Care must be taken to ensure that the statements are not taken out of context or selected in such a way as to ignore contrary information. The researcher who quotes a prison inmate's description of food as "slop" should be prepared to document this description in other prison writing. This particular description holds up, since virtually every account of prison life describes the food as overcooked, tasteless, and nonnutritious. The most usable quotations have both internal and external validity; that is, similar statements occur elsewhere in the same diary and in other people's journals.

Fact or Fiction?

The line between autobiography and fiction is often blurred. Ken Kesey's novel *One Flew Over the Cuckoo's Nest* (1962) was based on his experiences as an attendant in a mental hospital. Joseph Wambaugh's *The New Centurions* (1970) was based in part on his work in the Los Angeles Police Department. Are such books fact or fiction? A little of both, probably. It is more hazardous to rely on fictionalized accounts than on autobiographies. A novelist is freed from the constraints placed on a person who claims to tell a truthful tale.

A biography is one person's life as seen by another person. Its value as a research document depends on the skill, diligence, and accuracy of the writer. Subjects of biography tend to be even less representative of people in general than are subjects of autobiographies. Few biographers will spend time on an ordinary lawyer or politician. In seeking examples, ideas, or personal narratives for a research paper, our preference is for autobiographies over biographies and for avowedly factual to fictionalized accounts.

Another type of biographical study is the sociological life history obtained through intensive interviews. These personal narratives can add fascinating dimensions to behavioral research, and they provide balance to the biographical studies of more famous or powerful people. Oscar Lewis' accounts of family life and social relationships in Mexico are as compelling as a well-written novel. *The Children of Sanchez* vividly portrays through the words of the respondents, the lives, hopes, despairs, and dreams of the poor (Lewis, 1961). The richness of the accounts reflects a careful distillation of hundreds of hours of interview notes and tape recordings. Lillian Rubin (1976) explored life in working-class families in the San Francisco Bay Area. Robert Coles (1977) illuminated our understanding of minority children in his sociological life histories of *Eskimos, Chicanos, and Indians.* These accounts of personal history are subjective. Although they can be quantified by means of a content analysis, much is lost in the process. Retaining them in narrative form provides *qualitative* data—information not reducible to quantity or amount. It is often difficult to demonstrate the reliability and generalizability of such accounts. Despite this drawback, qualitative information complements quantitative data in increasing our understanding of behavior and social process.

Private Documents

Occasionally a researcher gains access to letters or documents not intended to be made public. Letters of resignation and written complaints fall into this category. The manager of a restaurant is likely to maintain a file of complaints. The personnel director of a restaurant may have exit interviews with departing employees. Such records may be valuable sources of information about personnel procedures or health and safety practices. Their use in social research was pioneered by W. I. Thomas, a Chicago sociologist, who believed that such materials revealed people's views of themselves and of the world (Thomas & Znaniecki, 1958). For his comparison of rich and poor people in Chicago, Harvey Zorbaugh (1929) used as sources letters, personal diaries, and suicide notes. A more systematic study of suicide notes was made by Shneidman and Farberow (1957), who used them to understand the thought processes of people attempting to kill themselves.

Limitations

Published autobiographies are frequently biased. The authors' intentions in writing were to place themselves in a good light or to support some cause. Such people are generally atypical. They are more articulate and intelligent than others who have undergone the same experiences but have not written about them. Police officers who have written about police work are not typical officers. The same is true of the airline stewardess who wrote *Coffee, Tea, or Me* and the school teacher who wrote *Up the Down Staircase.*

Although personal documents can be analyzed in the same way as other written materials using content analysis as described in the preceding chapter, this should be done only with extreme caution. What does it mean that 18 out of 20 letters received by the City Parks Department are complaints? Statistical analysis of such letters is a poor guide to public attitudes. Bias can be assumed even when most of the letters and documents are favorable. Most of the people who write spontaneously on a topic will feel strongly pro or con. Personal documents not intended for publication should be tabulated and analyzed only with extreme caution and with respect for the privacy of the people involved.

Archival Measures

Archives are public records and documents. They contain a wealth of information for the researcher. Over a century ago, the French sociologist Emile Durkheim (1951) examined records of suicides from all parts of Europe where such records were available. He found that suicide rates differed greatly among nations. Those nations that had the highest rates during one time period also tended to have the highest rates at other times. Durkheim's statistics were used to test various hypotheses. A common belief was that suicide increased with the temperature. Durkheim's data did not support this hypothesis; there was no straightforward relationship between temperature and suicide rate. What seemed most important was the cohesiveness of the society. When family ties, social relationship, and politicial ties were strong, the suicide rate was low. When the social fabric began to come apart, the rate rose.

Many statistics are readily available in government reports; other information requires a diligent search through newspaper files, crime statistics, biographical directories, and census records. Most of the other techniques discussed in this book require the researcher to go out and collect original data. For the archival researcher, the data are already available in almost limitless quantity. This creates a high risk of having more information than can be sorted into meaningful categories. The researcher is faced with the task of choosing from among statistics from different regions and time periods.

Public records can be used as a check against interview and case study material. Anthropologists Sylvia Forman and Richard Mazess (1978) matched baptismal records with the stated ages of residents of Vilcabamba, Ecuador, where many residents claimed to live more than a century. Earlier reports stated that residents lived to age 130 and that a large proportion was over 65. However, Forman and Mazess found no one older than 96 and an expected proportion of senior citizens. "It's clear that a few individuals were specifically lying about their age, but most of them believed what they were saying," the researchers reported. "There is apparently a natural inclination of the elderly in Vilcabamba to exaggerate their ages for reasons of status or celebrity . . . and they have been getting encouragement from both tourists and the scientific community to do that." Available records provided a check on the residents' self-reports.

Underreporting and Bias

Today many researchers are skeptical about the value of published statistics on suicide. Many families will conceal a self-inflicted death regardless of the method used by the victim. Some automobile accidents, particularly those involving a single automobile, are believed to be suicide attempts, although they are rarely classified as such. Whether or not death from drug overdose is classified as suicide is often a matter of chance. When there is underreporting of some condition, official estimates of its occurrence will be too low.

Researchers have dealt with underreporting in various ways. One method is to try to estimate the extent of error and correct for it statistically. Like suicide, incidents of robbery are also significantly underreported. The *victim survey* has been used to correct robbery statistics. Instead of relying only on police records, researchers ask a representative sample of people in a district whether or not they have been robbed during the past year. If 15 out of 100 residents report a robbery while police statistics show a rate of only 5 per 100, there is an assumed underreporting factor of 66 percent. If this error rate is found in other victim surveys, the police crime statistics in similar districts can be corrected by 66 percent to yield a more accurate picture of the number of robberies.

Another approach is to seek out those cities and agencies with the most detailed and accurate social statistics. For example, public health researchers in the United States have often been frustrated in keeping track of schizophrenics. When these people move, all contact with public agencies in the first city is lost. To get around this problem, researchers on schizophrenia make use of records in Denmark and Switzerland, where social statistics are more accurate and comprehensive than those in the United States. Records of birth, death, family relationships, and hospital admissions going back hundreds of years can be found in district offices. While information obtained in Denmark can be generalized only with caution to the situation of schizophrenics in the United States, it can contribute to a multimethod research strategy. The Denmark data have different limitations than studies of mental patients in the United States, which tend to cover a large geographic area over a short time period.

Another way of correcting for bias is to supplement social statistics on large populations with detailed case studies and interviews with smaller samples. Public records are invaluable in a multimethod approach. What they lack in depth can be compensated for by their greater comprehensiveness and coverage over time. Unlike data collected for a research study, which tends to be a one-time activity, government records are collected repeatedly. Once an agency begins publishing statistics on some topic, it seems difficult for them to stop. This is advantageous to the researcher who wants to compare trends over time. However, the researcher must check to see that the methods of data collection have not changed. For example, annual listings of major crimes provided by the Federal Bureau of Investigation have undergone several significant revisions, making it difficult to directly compare crime figures from two time periods. Further analysis is necessary to correct for bias resulting from changes in the method of data collection.

Because public records come in so many forms, no attempt will be made to discuss methods of analysis. Using census data or other social statistics to study characteristics of groups is termed *aggregate data analysis*. Specific references for handling these data are listed at the end of the chapter. In general, aggregate data are more useful for making predictions about groups than about individuals. Some distortion and error may be assumed in all statistics, no matter how carefully they have been collected and assembled. The important question is whether the errors rule out the use of the records in a particular study. Some statistics, such as those for victimless crimes, have been proved so erroneous that they are virtually useless. Records for robbery and rape are clearly underestimated, but this bias can be corrected to some degree. Some records are useful for certain groups in society but not for others. Census figures are generally considered more accurate for the white middle-class sections of the community than for racial and ethnic minorities and the poor. Census figures reveal very little about illegal aliens, who are heavily concentrated in specific areas of the country. Many older people sink into poverty and disappear from public records.

Finding Unusual Sources

In seeking information, the researcher is not limited to the most obvious reports, such as crime statistics, voter registration lists, and census reports. Numerous private firms keep detailed records of their activities. In studying the community response to a crime wave, it would be interesting to examine the sales of deadbolt locks and burglar alarms. Since no central records for this exist, it would be the researcher's task to visit locksmiths in the community and compare sales for the same month over several years.

The number of telephone calls between two cities provides an index of social contact. Most long-distance calls from Montreal go to other French-speaking cities in Quebec, the heart of French Canada. Matching for size and distance and adjusting for cost, a call from Quebec is five times more likely to be destined for another Quebec city than for a city in the adjacent largely English-speaking province of Ontario (Mackay, 1958). Mail and visiting records were used to study the desocializing effects of a long stay in a mental hospital. A newly admitted patient was 45 times as likely to receive a letter and 20 times as likely to have a visitor during a given week than was the patient who had been in the hospital several years (Sommer, 1958). Letters and visits indicate family interest, which is considered a valuable asset to the patient's recovery.

Limitations

The quality of record keeping varies significantly from one agency or city to the next. The classification system used in different jurisdictions may not suit the researcher's purposes. A felony in one state may be a misdemeanor in another. Methods used in gathering and classifying information are likely to have changed over time. Many statistics, such as crime and illness rates, tend to be underreported. Other figures, such as unemployment and cost-of-living statistics, are occasionally manipulated for political purposes. Researchers tend to be justifiably suspicious of statistics compiled by individuals and agencies with little interest or stake in accurate records.

Summary

Personal documents provide a subjective view of events. They are especially useful for understanding private behavior. The most common use of autobiographies in behavioral research is to illustrate findings that have been established through other methods. The line between biography and fiction is often blurred. Some books are a combination of both.

Limitations: Autobiographies are frequently biased accounts by unusual individuals. Letters received by public agencies also have limited generality because they may not reflect the views of the larger population.

Archives include public records, documents, and statistical reports. Public records are often useful as a check against interview and case study material.

References

Clark, E. (1977). *Eyes, etc.: A memoir.* New York: Pantheon.
Coles, R. (1977). *Eskimos, Chicanos, and Indians: Children of crisis* (vol 4). Boston: Little, Brown.

Durkheim, E. (1951). *Suicide*. Glencoe, IL: Free Press.

Forman, S., & Mazess, R. B. (1978, March 10). They either lie or forget. *Daily Democrat* (Davis, CA), p. A2.

Freud, S. (1957). *The origins of psychoanalysis. Letters, drafts, and notes to Wilhelm Fliess, 1887–1902*. (M. Bonaparte, A. Freud, & E. Kris, Eds.) Garden City, NY: Doubleday.

Kesey, K. (1962). *One flew over the cuckoo's nest*. New York: Viking.

Lewis, O. (1961). *Children of Sanchez: Autobiography of a Mexican family*. New York: Random House.

Mackay, J. R. (1958). The interactance hypothesis and boundaries in Canada. *The Canadian Geographer, 3*, 1–8.

Rosenblatt, P. D. (1983). *Bitter, bitter tears: 19th-century diarists and 20th-century grief theories*. Minneapolis: University of Minnesota Press.

Rubin, L. B. (1976). *Worlds of pain: Life in a working class family*. New York: Basic Books.

Shneidman, E. S., & Farberow, N. L. (Eds.) (1957). *Clues to suicide*. New York: McGraw-Hill.

Sommer, R. (1958). Letter writing in a mental hospital. *American Journal of Psychiatry, 115*, 514–517.

Sommer, R. (1968). The social psychology of cramming. *Personnel and Guidance Journal, 9*, 104–109.

Thomas, W. I., & Znaniecki, F. (1958). *The Polish peasant in Europe and America*. New York: Dover.

Vanek, J. (1974). Time spent in housework. *Scientific American, 231*, 116–120.

Van Gogh, V. (1953). *Verzamelde Brieven*. Amsterdam: Wereldbibliotheek.

Wambaugh, J. (1970). *The new centurions*. Boston: Little, Brown.

Zorbaugh, H. (1929). *The gold coast and the slum*. Chicago: University of Chicago Press.

Further Reading

Allport, G. W. (1942) *The use of personal documents in psychological science*. New York: Social Science Research Council.

Borgata, E. F., & Jackson, D. J. (1979). Aggregate data analysis: An overview. *Sociological Methods and Research, 7*, 4.

Gottschalk, L., Kluckhohn, C., & Angell, R. C. (1945). *The use of personal documents in history, anthropology, and sociology*. New York: Social Science Research Council.

Landis, C. (1964). *Varieties of psychopathological experience*. New York: Holt, Rinehart and Winston.

Selltiz, C., Wrightsman, L. S., & Cook, S. W. (Eds.). (1976). *Research methods in social relations* (3rd ed.). New York: Holt, Rinehart and Winston, Ch. 11.

Wasserman, P., & Paskar, J. (Eds.). (1977). *Statistics sources* (3rd ed.). Detroit: Gale Research.

Webb, E. J., Campbell, D. T., Schwartz, R. D., Sechrest, L., & Grove, J. B. (1981). *Nonreactive measures in the social sciences* (2nd ed.). Boston: Houghton Mifflin.

13   Case Study

The tornado that struck Xenia, Ohio, in 1974 killed 33 persons and injured 1200 others. Four hours after the tornado hit, a research team from the Disaster Research Center of Ohio State University arrived to conduct an 18-month study of the tornado's effect on the psychological health of the community. Contrary to what many people had expected, there was an extremely low rate of severe mental illness as a result of the disaster. A large percentage of the townspeople felt stronger and healthier for the experience. For example, 84 percent learned that they could surmount crises better than they had expected. Social relationships within the town seemed improved. Morale was high, and people put aside their own problems to help others. Everything was not rosy, however. Sales of tranquilizing drugs such as Librium and Valium increased 50 percent; the use of sleeping pills rose; 20 percent of the houses were destroyed and another 25 percent were damaged. More than half of the jobs in town were at least temporarily interrupted as factories and stores were forced to shut down. Eighteen months later, about two out of five persons reported an overall increase in problems in everyday living (Taylor, 1977).

Advantages of a Case Study

Unusual events like this call for innovative techniques. When there is no opportunity for a controlled experiment or before-and-after observations, the researcher may still want to undertake a careful investigation after the fact. Basically a case study is an in-depth investigation of a single instance. It can involve a unit as small as an individual or as large as an entire community. It provides the opportunity to apply a multimethod approach to a unique event.

The case study has a long and honorable history in clinical medicine.

170

What is lacking in breadth and generalizability may be compensated for by greater depth. When a physician comes across unusual symptoms, it is important to examine the patient's background and experiences in great detail. Has any member of the patient's family shown anything like this? Has the patient been exposed to toxic substances? Any recent foreign travel? If there appears to be a connection between the symptoms and some specific factor, a report may be published in a medical journal even though it is based on a single set of observations. The author hopes that others have come across patients with similar symptoms and can supply confirming or negative instances. When several case reports link the symptoms to a specific cause, then it is time to undertake a survey or experimental study. The first case report can begin a chain of events that produces an important discovery.

The case study approach emphasizes the individuality and uniqueness of the participants and the setting. One is not merely talking about disaster victims in the abstract, but about Henry Smith clearing away the debris and rebuilding his house, and his concerns about the possible relocation of the factory where he has worked for the past 20 years. The reader can visualize Henry Smith as a homeowner, father of two children, volunteer firefighter, assistant foreman in a factory, and most of all, a human being struggling to make the best of a bad situation.

Choosing a Topic

There are no rules for selecting a topic worthy of detailed investigation. Most researchers choose things that are unusual and newsworthy, such as natural disasters, serious illness, riots, fads, and fashions. This has created the false impression that a case study can be used only with unusual events. There is no theoretical reason why the method cannot be applied to ordinary people doing ordinary things. The practical objection, of course, is that it is likely to make dull reading and no one will publish it.

Consider the possibility of a comparative case study of two communities rather than one. A nearby city of the same size and population characteristics that did not experience a tornado might have made a good comparison for Xenia. You might also be able to find comparison groups within the research setting, such as families who lost their homes and those who didn't. The use of comparison groups can convert a case study into a quasi-experiment or experiment-in-nature.

In most case studies, the researcher begins after the fact. It would have been desirable to possess detailed information on Xenia before the study, but it may not be available. Many important records were destroyed or damaged in the disaster. Usually the researcher will have to *reconstruct* the prior situation after the fact. This limitation exists in most types of historical research.

Obtaining Cooperation

The researcher's first task in a case study is to obtain the cooperation of the people involved. This is not as easy as it sounds. People who have lost their homes or livelihoods are struggling to survive. A recent tragedy may be so intense that they do not want to talk about it. The researcher will not be able to offer people fame, fortune, or anything tangible. Probably the investigator will offer the very opposite—a firm guarantee of anonymity. The researcher promises to conceal the respondent's identity. The opportunity to help science may induce some people to cooperate even without tangible remuneration. However, the deciding factor is usually not financial gain or an abstract goal but a personal relationship with the researcher.

You will gain or lose people's cooperation by your manner of approach and interview style. An anthropologist interviewing natives in the Canadian Arctic had a difficult time explaining his purposes. The natives could not comprehend why he wanted to know the intimate details of their lives. He wasn't getting any cooperation until he admitted that his employer told him to get this information. *That* they could understand. Compliance with the boss's orders required no further explanation. The anthropologist was perceived as another person doing his job. In your own case study, you will find that people open up because they like you, trust you, and want to help you. This is particularly true if the study continues over a long period and involves personal revelations. Of all the research methods discussed so far, the case study places the most emphasis upon the researcher's style, approach, and personality.

With poor or needy individuals, money is helpful in obtaining cooperation. It conveys the researcher's seriousness of intent and the value placed on the information. Even with an affluent respondent, a token payment can be helpful. There is widespread belief in this society that something obtained for nothing is not appreciated. However, there are situations in which money cannot be used. One could not, for example, offer $100 to the mayor or city planner to discuss zoning policies. Offering payment would be insulting, unethical, and perhaps illegal.

Avoid overselling your project in order to gain people's cooperation. Listen to their objections to your study before you begin. Encourage them to express any doubts they might have, such as fears for their privacy, the possibility of bad publicity for the community, and so on. It may be easier to work out ways to deal with these objections at the outset than in the midst of gathering data.

Make sure that you touch bases with the key individuals involved with the issue you are studying. At the close of an interview, ask people specifically for the names of others who should be contacted. There is nothing more embarrassing after you have finished your study and left the area to find out that you neglected to interview important sources.

Cross Verification

A statement about the tornado made by a single observer should be regarded as tentative. When three or four people independently provide similar accounts, it seems more substantial. Cross checking the accounts of independent observers is one means of assessing validity in a case study. If a tornado victim tells the researchers how he tried to help other people after the twister struck, the researchers would write this down. Later on, other people may indicate that the first individual was dazed and groggy and had to be led to safety. Do not conclude that the first respondent is an unreliable liar. Distortion becomes a topic of investigation. How consistent are people's accounts of their own actions during and after a calamity? We are led directly to a study of how people put unwelcome thoughts out of their minds.

A researcher should not challenge the respondent even when an account seems biased or incorrect. You are not the district attorney conducting a cross examination. The goal is to obtain the respondent's point of view. Verification comes afterward. You must convey the impression of being a good listener. The respondents' knowledge that you have access to neighbors, newspaper reports, and public records will keep them from straying too far from the truth. Deliberate collusion among townspeople in concocting a false story is a possibility, but it does not occur often.

Differences between two accounts may reflect the way each person saw the situation. The person who spent several days in an evacuation camp after the tornado may have a different view of events than the person who stayed in town removing debris. Each of the views is accurate but based on a limited range of experience. Inconsistencies in people's narratives can provide valuable leads. The researcher is a bit like the psychoanalyst who pays special attention to distortions and omissions. Asking for further elaboration is a better way of internally checking a story than challenging people as to their truthfulness or objectivity.

Public and Private Records

Because a case report is likely to involve a newsworthy event, public records are valuable sources of information. If you are lucky, you may gain access to private records, such as letters written by people after the tornado or diary entries (see Chapter 12 on the use of personal documents). Studies of pharmacy records following the Xenia tornado showed an increase in prescriptions for tranquilizers. The records of individual physicians were also of interest to the researchers, but they had to deal first with the ethical problems connected with medical records. Unlike reporters who might enter a community in lightning fashion to conduct interviews and depart the next day, the case study team will spend weeks or months becoming familiar with the community and its people. This will inevitably turn up information that would be missed in a quick survey. The researcher may find it profitable to invest several weeks in getting to know the town before beginning to question people. It is this intensive familiarity over time with the respondents and the locality that distinguishes the case study from other techniques that cover the same topic but in less depth.

Limitations

Generalization from a case study is necessarily limited. No matter how many people were interviewed in Xenia, and no matter how much time was spent in the town by the research team, this is only a single instance of a natural disaster. It is appropriate to draw conclusions from the data (e.g., sleep disturbance was common weeks afterwards), but these cannot be generalized to other communities without further study.

Often an event is selected for a case study because it is atypical. This increases the problems of generalizing to more typical occurrences. Because so much depends upon the observer's personality and approach, a case study is difficult to repeat. The situation of two researchers conducting *independent* case studies of the same event virtually never occurs.

Because a case study usually takes place after the fact, the researcher must depend upon the people's recollections of events. Such memories, particularly after a crisis, are likely to be selective and distorted. It is difficult for a researcher to set time limits on a case study. Effects continue on up to the present. Some consequences of the Xenia tornado are probably just now becoming evident. There are not clear rules about when a case study is concluded.

Summary

A case study is an in-depth investigation of a single instance. This method emphasizes the individuality and uniqueness of the participants and the setting. Validity is obtained through cross verification of people's accounts. Public and private records are useful in a case study.

Limitations: Generalization from a case study is necessarily limited. The event studied is likely to be atypical. People's recollections of past events are likely to be selective and distorted.

Reference

Taylor, V. (1977, October). Good news about disaster. *Psychology Today,* pp. 93–94.

Further Reading

Caudill, W. (1958). *A psychiatric hospital as a small society.* Cambridge, MA.: Harvard University Press.

Erickson, K. T. (1976). *Everything in its path: Destruction of community in the Buffalo Creek Flood.* New York: Simon & Schuster.

Riley, M. W. (1963). *Sociological research: A case approach.* New York: Harcourt, Brace, & World.

Withers, C. (James West, pseud.) (1945). *Plainville, U.S.A.* New York: Columbia University Press.

14 Apparatus

Instructions to Subjects in a Perception Experiment

I am going to show you some figures in the viewer. They will be the same figures that you saw in the first part of the experiment, either the whole figures or parts of them. Exposure times will be very brief, so be alert. I will give you notice every time that a figure is going to be shown. Please write down the name of the figure on the score sheet in front of you. Feel free to guess if you aren't sure which figure it is. If you don't recognize it at all, please describe in your own words what you saw in the viewer. Are there any questions? Then, we'll begin the series.

These were the instructions read to participants in a perception experiment. The subjects were secretarial students in a business school who were paid small fees for their participation. From the subjects' standpoint, the room would probably be described something like this: "Small, dimly lit, rather empty except for a table, two chairs, and a big wooden box that looks as if you are supposed to look into it. A few gadgets on the floor, but I can't make out what they are." The big wooden box was a tachistoscope, an apparatus for presenting visual material in very brief exposures. The viewer portion stood on the left side of the table; the timing mechanism and exposure switch were housed in a metal cabinet on the floor out of the subject's view. The viewer portion had an opening, with a forehead rest, into which the subject looked. There were two visual fields that could be presented to the subject. One was a square field of bright white light. When the experimenter pressed a lever on the electronic timer, a picture would appear in the viewer for 200 milliseconds. The picture was seen at the same distance and intensity as the previous white light. Several features of this tachistoscope made it useful for the particular study:

1. The bright white field served two purposes. It provided orientation for the location at which the picture appeared, and it prevented afterimages following exposure of the picture.
2. The use of "neon daylight" tubes presented the colors of the pictures accurately and without distortion.
3. The electronic timing circuit used no relays and therefore was silent in operation.
4. Electronic timing is highly reliable (± 1 millisecond) if it is checked periodically.

Note to the reader: You need not be concerned about the technical aspects of the tachistoscope or the particular experiment. This example was used to show some of the considerations involved in selecting the right piece of apparatus for an experiment.

Borrow or Build Your Own

It may not be necessary for you to buy your own apparatus, particularly if you are on a limited budget. It is surprising how much good apparatus exists unused in the storerooms of research and teaching institutions. A piece of expensive equipment bought for a single experiment will gather dust afterward. It may also be possible to use someone else's apparatus on a timesharing basis. Plates for measuring color blindness cost as much as $50, but they are widely available in the offices of optometrists and ophthalmologists and in personnel departments in industry. Searching for apparatus is good training for a researcher. If you decide to continue in behavioral research as a career, you are likely to be searching for apparatus, supplies, and funds throughout your professional life.

Your needs may be so specific that nothing suitable is available on the commercial market. Then you will have to build your own equipment. The tachistoscope described earlier was built by a research assistant in a psychology department workshop. Linda Acredolo, whose work was described in Chapter 6, constructed a special room for testing how children learn spatial concepts. Access to a good workshop is necessary if you plan to construct your own equipment. Most research institutions and psychology departments have a workshop supervised by a knowledgeable technician. With permission, you may be able to construct your apparatus in the workshop, or at least obtain technical advice. A shop technician is also a good source of information on what equipment is available and on its condition.

Apparatus Supply Firms

Most of the research described in this book requires no more equipment than a typewriter, a mimeograph machine with an endless supply of paper, and access to a calculator or computer. Occasionally, further materials will be necessary. Laboratory research almost always involves special equipment. This may either be built by the experimenter for one-time use or it may be a standard machine that is available from a commercial supplier. Physiological research may use brain wave recordings from an EEG machine. Studies of group activities may use recorders or special-purpose machines for recording interactions. Often the simplest hardware is the best, but there are times when a more complex machine can yield results otherwise unavailable.

Many different kinds of apparatus for behavioral research are available commercially. Manufacturers of behavioral equipment publish catalogs listing items in stock or that can be custom made. The catalog of one major apparatus supplier includes such varied items as hand steadiness tests, plates for assessing color blindness, optical illusions, eye movement recorders ($4000 and up!) and biofeedback apparatus.

There are both major and minor suppliers of apparatus for behavioral research. Two of the larger suppliers that will send catalogs free upon request are the Stoelting Company (1350 South Costner Avenue, Chicago, Illinois 60623) and the Lafayette Instrument Company (P.O. Box 5729, Sagamore Parkway North, Lafayette, Indiana 47902). Many smaller firms specialize in custom-ordered apparatus and will quote prices on request. To locate an apparatus supply firm nearby, check with people doing behavioral research in your locality. These can include psychologists working for industry or at a university. If the opportunity arises, you can also visit the equipment display booths at the annual conventions of your regional psychological association. Equipment suppliers demonstrate their newest apparatus and have their current price lists available at these conventions.

Mechanical Failure

Any machine will eventually break down or wear out. Over a period of time, mechanical malfunction is the rule, not the exception. Jam-proof slide trays will jam, automatic cameras will give the wrong light readings, and computers will reject perfectly punched cards. This does not mean that human beings are more accurate than machines. No machine has been known to deliberately deceive its owner. Rather, it means that the possibility of mechanical error must be considered at every stage of the research, from presenting materials to subjects in the laboratory to computer analysis of the data. A book could be written about all the things that can go wrong with a slide projector. It is wise to carry spare parts, such as an extension cord and an adapter to convert three-pronged to two-pronged electrical plugs. Have a screw driver or, even better, a Swiss Army knife for making repairs on the spot. It is not an evil spirit that breaks machines at the worst possible moment—for example, in the middle of a crucial meeting or during an experiment—but rather the pressures on the researcher, which cause minor but significant technical operations to be omitted, such as pressing the record button or loading the camera with film. Most researchers have come to realize that dependence on hardware can be a mixed blessing.

The Camera and the Recorder

There are three major uses for cameras and recorders in behavioral research:

1. *To present materials to respondents.* There may be some value in putting audio instructions on tape so that all the participants will hear the identical words. The same is true of visual stimuli projected from slides or shown on videotape. The use of cassette recorders and slide projectors allows the researcher to standardize the method of delivery and presentation to a degree impossible any other way. Even when an interviewer deliberately tries to approach each respondent in the same manner, there are likely to be subtle differences from one time to the next depending on the interviewer's mood, the location, or even the time of day. Putting the introduction on tape or slides minimizes these sources of error.

2. *To obtain data.* When researchers use cameras and recorders to obtain data, they can expect to spend a great deal of time typing transcripts of taped sessions and analyzing records of interaction, body posture, and so on. For this reason, obtaining data is *not* the most common use of cameras and recorders in behavioral research. The most common uses, in fact, are presenting materials to the respondent and illustrating the results obtained through other research methods. Only a small percentage of behavioral studies uses photographs and recordings as primary data because of the cost and effort involved in transcribing materials. While it is relatively easy to record a group conversation, obtaining a typed transcript is difficult and time consuming even under the best of circumstances. Unless you have a special audio tape recorder with a foot-reverse pedal (and very few tape recorders have this), the typist will have to reverse the tape by hand whenever a word or phrase is unclear. Since most conversations are full of half-spoken and half-heard phrases, transcribing an audiotape accurately will involve as many as eight hours per one-hour tape, with many words or phrases omitted entirely or incorrectly transcribed. Unless there was an observer with the tape machine keeping written notes of who was speaking, the typist will have difficulty identifying people's voices, particularly when only brief statements or interjections are

made. This problem is reduced in the case of videotape, but the process of transcription is equally cumbersome. The presence of a recorder may inhibit some participants and induce them to avoid sensitive topics. The machine will run out of tape, the cassette will have to be changed or turned over, and this will disrupt the event. However, the most serious disadvantages of audio and video recording are the time and expense of transcription. Until you yourself have tried to do this, you can't realize how boring, time-consuming, and frustrating transcription is.

Few behavioral researchers have used still or movie cameras as primary data sources. Transcription problems are not as severe as with tape recordings, since photographs can be developed and printed commercially. Large prints, which may be necessary for analyzing interaction, will run up the costs. Another problem with the still or movie camera is that, like the recorder, it is very intrusive. Many people do not want to be photographed. Zoom and telephoto lenses make the researcher's life easier. Movie cameras and videotape capture ongoing actions, but the scoring problems that arise during transcription are equal to or greater than those involved in analyzing audio tapes.

3. *As illustrations.* The camera is invaluable for illustrating results. When you are trying to describe what a town looked like after the tornado hit or the lack of privacy in dormitory rooms, slides and photographs will be helpful. Audio recordings are far less useful. Unless an audio recording is professionally made and edited, there are likely to be fuzzy and unintelligible spots that are confusing and frustrating to the audience. Editing requires expensive equipment, trained personnel, and much time and effort. Some audiences become restless and bored hearing an audiotape without seeing anything on the screen. Audiotapes are not as useful as slides for presenting the results of behavioral studies.

When using a camera in field work, you must plan for adverse conditions. Picture taking is generally forbidden in bars, gambling establishments, prisons, and hospitals. Adverse environmental conditions can include rain, power failure, and illumination too dim for most natural light photography. There are three solutions to the low-light problem. The first is the use of an inexpensive strobe attachment, whose chief disadvantages are distortions in color and light reflection as well as intrusiveness. It is difficult to remain in the background when you are using a strobe. Another possibility is to use high speed films and "push processing." The speed of the film is written as the ASA number on the side of the film. The higher the number, the more useful the film will be under low light conditions. If necessary the film speed can be "pushed" even higher through special processing. You should discuss this with a camera store owner before you take the pictures to learn the maximum "pushing" that can be handled locally. The third method for handling weak illumination is to use time exposures. This requires a tripod along with a shutter release. Good pictures are possible in a dimly lit area if exposure time is sufficiently long. The chief disadvantage is that any movement will blur a portion of the picture.

Wind, rain, and snow create problems for a field photographer but they are all solvable with the right equipment and advice. Cameras made for underwater photography can be used in the rain. Cheap protection can be obtained by wrapping the camera in a transparent plastic bag. This will produce some distortion, perhaps not unpleasant from an aesthetic visual standpoint. There are also methods for making sound recordings under adverse weather conditions. Advice can be obtained from local radio personnel or audio-visual specialists.

Helpful Hints in Using a Still Camera in Behavioral Research

A supersophisticated and expensive camera is unnecessary, but on the other hand, an Instamatic is unsuitable. You'll probably need a single lens reflex camera that will cost about $200 for the basic camera and lens.

Inexpensive lenses are adequate for most behavioral studies. The need is for functional pictures rather than works of art. Besides the standard 50mm lens that comes with the camera, you will probably want a wide-angle and a telephoto lens. The wide-angle lens will be invaluable indoors, the telephoto lens outside. For telephoto pictures we recommend an inexpensive 135mm automatic lens. Incidentally, the cost of the same lens varies greatly from one camera outlet to another. So, be sure to shop around before you buy and check the prices listed by advertisers in reputable photography magazines. *Consumer Reports,* which is available in most libraries, provides detailed evaluations of photographic equipment. For a wide-angle lens, a 35mm or 28mm automatic lens is recommended.

Instead of considering a long expensive lens, such as a 300mm or 400mm, you can achieve practically the same results for less money with your 135mm lens and an inexpensive 2X teleconverter. These are available in any good photo supply store and list between $20 and $35 depending on lens quality.

There are ethical and legal considerations in photographing people as part of a research study. Since laws vary from place to place, it is worthwhile to check with a local photographer before undertaking a research study involving camera work. A professional photographer can also supply valuable assistance in dealing with unusual lighting or haze conditions.

While tiny cameras hidden in matchboxes are important in spy movies, you probably won't need them in your study. Researchers who use a camera professionally tend to rely on telephoto lenses operated at a distance rather than spy cameras up close.

Helpful Hints in Using a Recorder in Behavioral Research

Audio Recorder

An inexpensive tape recorder can do most of the things an expensive one can do. You don't need tremendous fidelity for most purposes. The omni-directional (all-directional) microphone that comes with most tape recorders is satisfactory for recording the normal range of voice frequencies. You will probably want to obtain an inexpensive stand to avoid holding or laying the microphone on a table where it will be frequently jarred. *Consumer Reports* is also a good source of information about audio equipment.

Try to obtain a recorder that can be battery-operated as well as plugged into an outlet. This will allow greater flexibility in your operations. Be sure to carry an extra pack of batteries and extra cassettes.

If you are going to have the tape transcribed, check on the availability of a machine that has a *foot reverse* pedal. This is an expensive built-in feature which most tape recorders lack. Note that we are talking about a foot *reverse* pedal and not simply a foot pedal.

If you want to play tapes to an audience, you will probably need a good player with at least two speakers. The separate speakers will enable you to aim the sound to different parts of the room. A good amplification system makes the difference between a clear presentation and a confused, bored, and irritated audience.

As with spy cameras, there are very few situations in which we would recommend the use of hidden microphones. There are serious ethical problems in using them.

An audio specialist can help you select the right equipment for a special recording situation. Some microphones, for example, completely block out background noises; others record background and foreground equally. Know what is available and choose accordingly.

Videocamera

Videocameras are becoming increasingly common in research laboratories, especially when there is field work (outside study) to be done. Also, facilities for showing videotapes are becoming commonplace in classrooms and conference centers. When used to gather data, a videocamera is particularly useful for recording complex interactions that are difficult to observe and analyze at the time they occur. Behavior can be recorded at one time and analyzed later when observers are available. Material can be played many times so that fine detail and complex interactions can be accurately noted. Early models were large, heavy, and bulky, and primarily useful for studio recording. Newer models are lighter, more portable, and more flexible for research use. If the camera is to be carried into the field, check out the weight with the battery pack. See that it comes with a shoulder strap or harness to aid in carrying it.

The technical aspects of videotape recording have also improved. Now this is a very convenient method for collecting information. The researcher zips in a cassette and the machine takes over. Cameras may also be wall mounted or used with tripods for stationary recording. Videocameras differ in special features and some are much easier to use in the field than others. Special lenses are available for the cameras, including wide-angle lenses useful for indoor recording, telephoto lenses for long-distance pictures, and macro lenses for close-up work. Some machines have built-in microphones and head sets for continuously monitoring audio quality. Other models allow for remote operation both in recording and playback. Some cameras allow for the insertion of titles, date, and elapsed time, and combine both recording and playback systems.

It is more common in behavioral research to code videotape data (as in a content analysis) than to transcribe it literally, which would be very arduous and time consuming (i.e., describing every word and movement). See Chapters 8 and 11 for a discussion of coding procedures. Coding videotapes is more complicated than dealing with most other types of material because they include both verbal and visual material. One potential disadvantage of videotape recording is the tremendous amount of information collected. This can encourage the researcher to postpone dealing with the tapes. The result will be a huge library of uncoded and unanalyzed videotapes.

Taking pictures of everything going on can be very wasteful and time consuming for data analysis. A better approach is to have some idea in advance of what you want to record. Viewing angle is very important, especially if there is to be a systematic analysis of the data that requires consistency in what is being recorded from one time to the next.

Videotaped interviews require planning and a warm-up period. Don't go into a setting cold and expect to interview people there. Check out the location in advance, particularly the lighting and sound environments. Is there too much background noise from a ventilating system or street traffic? Such considerations should be checked out prior to the formal taping session. No matter how well you know the person and the place, the presence of a camera can change the quality of interaction and a warm-up period will probably be needed. Arrange beforehand to have some friendly and interesting questions or comments to offer before the filming, or in the early stages. The important thing is to get the respondent's attention off the camera and on to the interaction with you. A shoulder- or hand-held camera is both awkward and intimidating during an interview. It is preferable to keep the camera off to the side while talking to another person.

Videocassette Recorder (VCR)

A VCR can be used to record programs made earlier or for presenting videotape selections to an audience. These capabilities have a number of applications in behavioral research. Programs recorded on network television can be subjected to a content analysis (e.g., the length and type of commercials, violence on prime-time shows, etc.). A VCR is also used for playing back tapes made with a videocamera. The various types of VCR machines are not necessarily compatible with one another or with home television sets. Professional models cost more than consumer models and produce a higher quality picture. Tapes for professional models are usually more expensive than those for consumer models. The choice of machine for research depends on the needed quality level and compatibility between recorder and playback machine. A videotape made on a Beta-type machine must be shown on a Beta-type VCR.

Some machines allow the possibility of playing tapes in slow motion. This may be a useful feature in interaction analysis. A "search mode" enables the researcher to locate needed items on a tape visually. For any type of content analysis, a PAUSE or FREEZE FRAME control will allow for the extended analysis of single frames. In some machines the frozen frame may be too fuzzy or unstable for serious analysis. For on-air recording, a counter will be helpful for making notes of significant features for later analysis. Video printers are available for making hard copy from video images. Slides and movie films can be transferred to videotape for presenting research results to an audience.

Summary

Apparatus supply firms manufacture equipment for behavior research. Sometimes researchers must build their own equipment.

Still cameras, audio recorders, videocameras, and videotape cassettes are often useful in behavioral research. The camera and audiotape are used more often for presenting material to respondents and for illustrating talks presented to audiences than for obtaining primary data. Videocameras and videotape cassettes are often used in field study for recording complex interactions for content analysis and other purposes. Limitations: The cost of transcribing audiotapes and videotapes makes these methods cumbersome and time consuming for data collection and analysis.

15 Standardized Tests and Inventories

Not surprisingly, many students are anxious before taking exams. To investigate this phenomenon, a researcher administered a standardized test for state anxiety (which is connected with a mood or situation) to a research methods class early in the semester. The inventory used, the State-Trait Anxiety Inventory, consisted of 20 statements, such as "I feel calm" or "I feel upset" to be rated by the student in terms of how well the term applied: not at all, somewhat, moderately so, and very much so (Spielberger, Gorsuch, & Lushene, 1970). This inventory yields an overall state (situational) anxiety score.

A few weeks later, on the day of the first exam, the inventory was given again. A comparison score from the two administrations showed a significant increase in state anxiety on the day of the exam. However, there was no relationship between the amount a student's anxiety had increased and his or her actual exam performance. That is, students whose anxiety levels soared did neither better nor worse on the average than students whose anxiety levels changed very little. Also, there was no relationship between anxiety on the day of the exam and how well the student performed on the exam.

What Is a Test?

A test in the behavioral sciences is a systematic procedure for comparing people's performance, feelings, attitudes, or values. The tests most useful

185

in behavioral research are those that have been standardized. This means that the test has been published and is widely available, and that its questions and methods of administration are so fixed that the scores of people tested at different times and places can be compared. A standardized test usually has norms, or standards of normal performance, which can be used in interpreting results (Cronbach, 1984). A test is *valid* to the extent that we know what it measures or predicts. *Reliability* refers to the stability of measurement over time. If we measure a person's typing skills on two occasions, the scores should be similar unless something significant has happened in the interval between tests.

When tests or inventories have been given to many people and the results have been compared to those of other measures, estimates of reliability and validity can be made. A standardized test will have a manual that provides instructions for administration, normative data (results from specific samples against which individual and group scores can be compared), and reliability and validity information.

Some tests are designed for group administration, while others are constructed for individual administration. Most group-administered tests can be administered by a relatively untrained person and many can be scored by computer. However, the interpretation of the results (what the scores on the various parts of the test mean) must still be done by a test specialist. Most individually administered tests are specifically designed to be scored and interpreted by a trained examiner.

Technically speaking, standardized tests are less a method of research than tools, like apparatus. Such tests are used most frequently in research in education and psychology, less often in anthropology, sociology, and geography. Some of the most commonly used standardized tests are IQ tests, personality tests, occupational inventories, and school achievement tests (Box 15-1). There are also specialized instruments for assessing hospital adjustment, work environment, study habits, and preference for leisure activities. Most can be given to groups of people and scored by machine or with a set of templates that accompanies the scoring manual. These tests are better suited for determining differences between groups than for individual prediction. The research use of tests is therefore somewhat different from their use in personnel selection or career planning. Other tests are designed to be individually administered, scored, and interpreted by a trained examiner. Standardized tests can be contrasted to improvised personal instruments, such as a questionnaire used for a single project or an examination given by a college teacher. With sufficient development, revision, distribution, and the compilation of norms, these instruments could become standardized tests.

The advantage of standardized tests is that someone else has done the work. You need not develop your own measure of employee morale or hypnotizability; there are tests that do this for you. Booklets and answer sheets are already printed and standardized norms are available. Norms will disclose how a person's score compares with those of others taking the

BOX 15-1. Common Types of Standardized Tests in Educational and Psychological Research

Test type	Purpose	Examples*
School achievement	To determine a person's academic level	Metropolitan Achievement Test, Stanford Achievement Test
Intelligence (group administration)	To measure how a person's intelligence compares with that of others in the same age group	Differential Aptitude Tests, SRA Primary Mental Abilities
Intelligence (individual administration)	To obtain a detailed picture of an individual's intellectual abilities, primarily for clinical use	Wechsler Adult Intelligence Scale, Stanford-Binet Intelligence Scale
Personality	To measure various dimensions of normal personality, such as introversion, independence, practicality, etc.	California Psychological Inventory, Bernreuter Personality Inventory
Mood	To assess emotional state	POMS (Profile of Mood States), the Adjective Check List (Gough), STAI (State-Trait Anxiety Inventory
Clinical	To identify patterns of behavioral dysfunction	MMPI, IPAT Depression Scale
Occupational interests	To determine interest in specific vocations as well as general occupational categories	Strong-Campbell Interest Inventory (SVIB-SCII), Ohio Vocational Interest Survey
Specialized abilities	To measure abilities in such areas as music, art, languages, etc.	Seashore Measures of Musical Talents, Modern Language Aptitude Test, General Clerical Test

*Only a few tests in each category are listed here. Many others can be found in the catalogs of test distributors.

test. Some tests are accompanied by scoring sheets or keys that allow you to score the answers yourself; others must be mailed to a testing service, where they are scored and analyzed for a fee.

Unfortunately, standardized tests are often unsuitable for your specific needs. Very few of the research problems discussed in previous chapters are suitable for standardized testing. No commercial questionnaire will tell you what college students think about the cafeteria food; the same is true of student attitudes toward peer counseling, financial aid, or alcohol use. Few standardized instruments with appropriate norms are available for attitude measurements. Even those standardized tests on which the most work has been done, such as measures of intelligence and school achievement, have many limitations and may not be usable for the particular groups you want to test. However, if you decide that the standardized instrument comes close to your needs, do not tinker with it. If you change the procedure or reword the items, you will lose the advantage of having the normative data (usually presented in the test manual) with which to compare your findings. Also, your results will have more meaning if they can be compared with the findings of other researchers using the same instrument in the same manner.

Locating Suitable Tests

Your first task is to find out whether appropriate tests are already available. This can be done in several ways. First, you can look at previous research on the topic. Have studies similar to yours employed standardized tests? If not, the answer may be that none is available. You can ask people knowledgeable in the field whether they know of any appropriate measuring devices. You can consult the catalogs of test suppliers who distribute tests to professionals. A partial list of suppliers is provided at the end of the chapter. Names and addresses of other firms that distribute standardized tests can be obtained from faculty in departments of education and psychology, personnel managers, school guidance counselors, and others who use standardized tests in their work. It will not be easy for a beginner to sort through numerous catalogs and find the right test. Discussing your needs with a qualified test specialist is helpful. The Educational Testing Service (20 Nassau Street, Princeton, New Jersey), which provides for the testing of millions of students in the United States and 50 other countries, distributes several free pamphlets, including *ETS Builds a Test,* which describes how a test is constructed, and *Selecting an Achievement Test,* which provides guidelines for interpreting and using test results. Other sources of information on available tests are the *Mental Measurements Yearbook* and *Tests in Print,* both edited by Oscar Buros, which list more than a thousand tests, along with data on their use and validity, critical reviews by tests experts, and a directory of test publishers. These two books are available in most reference libraries.

Obtaining the Tests

Some tests are available only to members of professional societies, such as the American Psychological Association. Access to these tests is restricted to prevent their unauthorized use. Information on availability is contained in most test catalogs. If the test you are considering has restricted distribution, you must either be personally qualified or involve someone who is. The personnel department of your company or the counseling bureau of your school probably has a qualified test professional. This person may have a copy of the test on file or can obtain a sample copy for you to examine. Most test suppliers distribute (for a small charge) sample kits containing a single copy of the test booklet, a test manual containing norms, and scoring sheets. The sample kit should be closely scrutinized before any decision is made about ordering mutliple copies. You may find that the questions on the test are too easy, too difficult, or inappropriate for the sample in your study.

Constructing a Test

If you cannot locate the test you need in catalogs from test suppliers or published work on the topic, a remaining option is to develop a test of your own. This will be a time-consuming procedure so the decision should not be made lightly. Making up a standardized test, with score sheet, norms, etc. requires far more time and effort than composing a questionnaire or list of interview questions.

The sequence of steps involved in compiling a standardized test is shown in Box 15-2. The first task is to define the performance or behavior to be measured. This is a more difficult task than it may sound, because it involves important policy decisions. Let us use bicycle riding as an example of a common ability for which few or no standardized tests are available. If you wanted to compare the bicycle riding skills of individuals or groups, you would probably have to make up your own test. Defining the skill will raise some important questions. Should the ability to operate motorized bicycles be included or should the test be restricted to pedal-powered vehicles? Shall we include the skills required for long-distance touring or racing? These are certainly "skills," but they may not be particularly relevant if our concern is with safety in local bicycling. One approach to defining the topics to be included in a test is to consult previous research. What aspects of performance have been deemed important or relevant by other investigators? Another possibility is to consult with recognized authorities. What sorts of skills do leaders of cycling clubs and safety officials feel are important for bicyclists? General statements must be made specific and defined in terms of observable operations.

The behavioral items collected from all sources must be examined to remove obvious duplications and inconsistencies. See that important issues are covered and that the instrument is not too long. The revised list of items can be tried out on an exploratory basis with a small number of respondents. The goal at this point is to get the bugs out of the procedure. This will require several successive revisions of the preliminary version of

BOX 15-2. Steps in Constructing a Standardized Test

1. Define the performance to be measured
   Check previous research
   Include your own experience
   Consult with recognized authorities
   Translate statements into behavioral measures
2. Compile potentially useful items
   Eliminate duplications and inconsistencies
   Decide on length and format
3. Pilot test
   Revisions (several)
4. Compose final version
   Item analysis
5. Check reliability
   Administer test to same individuals on two occasions
6. Check validity
   Compare scores with known abilities or performance
7. Compile norms
   Administer test to different groups
   Compile scores according to relevant categories (e.g., age, education, experience, etc.)
8. Publish or disseminate test

the test. This will produce an almost-final version of the test to be further refined through an *item analysis*. Detailed methods for undertaking an item analysis, can be found in Anastasi (1976). An item analysis shows the degree to which the various items "hang together." Items that produce responses unrelated to those of the other questions are probably measuring a different type of ability and can be removed from the instrument.

Establishing the reliability of the revised instrument is done by administering the test to the same individuals on two separate occasions. If the test is reliable, those individuals who score high on the test the first time should also score high on the second administration. Many standardized tests will also have alternate versions. Constructing alternate versions requires additional effort but it will increase the practical and research usefulness of the instrument.

The *validity* of the test is the degree to which it actually measures bicycling ability. One approach to validity is to administer the test to people known to be high or low in the skill being measured. Presumably a group of experienced cyclists should perform better on a test of bicycle skills than a group of inexperienced cyclists. Another approach to validation could test individuals who have been involved in bicycle accidents. We could predict that when matched for age, cycling experience, amount of riding per week, and other relevant background factors, individuals who have been involved in a bicycle accident should perform worse on a test of bicycle skills than individuals who have not been involved in an accident. These are only a few of the ways in which a standardized test can be validated.

The next step is to compile norms from various groups. A test of bicycle skills should probably include norms for different age groups. The norms would be compiled by administering the test to samples of respondents at different age levels and tabulating the results. This will allow scores of people to be compared with those of their own age groups.

If all of the above steps have been done, and the test appears promising in predicting bicycle skills, the next step will be to publish the results and make them available to researchers and cycling organizations. Encouraging researchers to try out the test will assist in developing norms for other geographic areas and types of samples.

Projective Tests

Tests that have not been standardized are sometimes useful in research. The absence of norms or score sheets may mean that the test is new and the investigator wants to try it out. Some instruments, which rely on subjective interpretation by a trained examiner, do not lend themselves to standardization. There is a class of research techniques in clinical psychology called *projective tests* that lacks usable norms. They are called "projective" because the questions or stimuli are deliberately vague or incomplete. It is assumed that the respondents fill in the blanks by *projecting* their personal concerns and experiences. Often the style of responding (e.g., hesitation or embarrassment) is more important than the content of the response. The two most widely used projective tests are the Rorschach and the TAT (Thematic Apperception Test). The Rorschach consists of ten inkblots developed by the Swiss psychiatrist Herman Rorschach. This was the successor to the Stern Cloud Pictures Test, in which the respondent was shown pictures of clouds and asked what they looked like. Multiple-choice versions of the inkblot test suitable for group administration are also available. The TAT consists of a set of blurred pictures of people in various situations. It was developed at the Harvard Psychological Clinic by Christina Morgan and Henry A. Murray.

Limitations

Standardized tests are not available for many topics that an investigator wants to study. When tests are available, the norms may not be appropriate for groups other than those on which the test was standardized. Many standardized tests have been criticized as being culturally biased. Their norms are likely to be inappropriate for people who speak another language, have been out of school a long time, or who are institutionalized. Standardized tests are primarily useful for people similar to those on whom the norms were standardized. The apparent precision of test scores is often misleading. The important issue is how well the test measures what it is supposed to measure.

Personality tests tend to stigmatize people who diverge from conventional social norms. Some of the questions on personality tests are intrusive. You must be sensitive to the way the question appears to respondents and outside agencies. It is difficult to defend some of the questions about personal habits and sexual preferences included on major personality tests.

The research value of all projective tests is limited by their low reliability. Two psychologists examining the same record are likely to develop different interpretations.

Summary

Standardized tests, which are available from test supply firms, have norms that can be used in interpreting results. Validity refers to whether a test measures what it is supposed to measure; reliability refers to the stability of measurements over time. Nonstandardized tests may be so new that norms have not been developed. Or they may be deliberately vague, as with the projective tests used in clinical psychology, so the subject can give an individual interpretation to the questions.

Constructing a new standardized test is a difficult and time-consuming task because of the need to establish reliability and validity, and to collect norms from different segments of the population.

The most common types of standardized tests measure school achievement, intelligence, personality, clinical symptoms, occupational interests and skills, and specialized abilities in areas such as music, art, and languages.

Limitations: Many standardized tests are not appropriate for groups other than those on whom the norms were established.

Publishers of Tests and Inventories

Consulting Psychologists Press
577 College Ave.
Palo Alto, CA 94306

EDITS/Educational and Industrial
  Testing Service
P.O. Box 7234
San Diego, CA 92107

Institute for Personality & Ability
  Testing
1602 Coronado Dr.
Champaign, IL 61820

Psychological Test Specialists
Box 9229
Missoula, MT 59807

The Psychological Corporation
757 Third Ave.
New York, NY 10017

Western Psychological Services
4311 Wilshire Blvd.
Los Angeles, CA 90025

Test Corporation of America
330 W. 47th St., Suite 205
Kansas City, MO 64112

References

Anastasi, A. (1976). *Psychological testing* (4th ed.). New York: Macmillan.
Cronbach, L. J. (1984). *Essentials of psychological testing* (4th ed). New York: Harper & Row.
Spielberger, C. D., Gorsuch, R. L., & Lushene, R. E. (1970). *Manual for the State-Trait Anxiety Inventory*. Palo Alto, CA: Consulting Psychologists Press.

Further Reading

Anastasi, A. (1976). *Psychological testing* (4th ed.). New York: Macmillan.
Buros, O. K. (Ed.) (1974). *Tests in print II*. Edison, NJ: Gryphon Press.
Buros, O. K. (Ed.) (1978). *The eighth mental measurements yearbook*. Edison, NJ: Gryphon Press.
Cronbach, L. J. (1984) *Essentials of psychological testing* (4th ed.). New York: Harper & Row.
Eliot, J., & Smith, I. M. (1983). *An international directory of spatial tests*. Atlantic Highlands, NJ: Humanities Press.
Gough, H. (1976). Personality and personality assessment. In M. D. Dunnette (Ed.): *Handbook of industrial and organizational psychology* (pp. 571–607). Chicago: Rand McNally.

VI
Sampling, Statistics, and Reports

16 Sampling

A physical education teacher wants to study the possibility of sex differences in running speed among elementary school children. This will involve a comparison of the running time of boys and girls in different age categories. For practical reasons, the teacher is unable to test all the children in the school. This is a common situation in behavioral research. Rarely can an investigator test all the people in a given category. Some selection of subjects is necessary, but this must be done in an unbiased way. The entire group of people in a category is called a *population*. The smaller group selected for testing is called a *sample*. The sample is then used to make generalizations about the population from which it was drawn.

The degree to which the sample differs from the population is termed *error*. There are two general sources of error: sampling error and sample bias. *Sampling error* refers to chance variations among samples selected from the same population. Imagine a person who draws successive samples of 50 marbles each from a large bowl containing 1000 marbles, half black and half white. After each selection is noted, the marble is returned to the bowl. Some samples would contain a majority of black marbles and others a majority of white marbles. Ideally, if there were enough trials, the characteristics of all the samples would *average* 25 white marbles and 25 black marbles. However, any single sample of 50 marbles is likely to deviate from this average. The difference between the samples and the actual population characteristics (50 percent black and 50 percent white) is the *sampling error*. This can never be totally eliminated, but it can be estimated statistically. A common method of reducing the influence of chance variation is to draw a large sample. As the sample size approaches the population size, it becomes a more accurate representation.

Sample bias refers to error introduced by a sampling procedure that favors certain characteristics over others. In selecting the marbles from the jar, it is possible that the black marbles, by absorbing heat, are slightly

warmer than the white marbles. The blindfolded subject may unconsciously select the warmer black marbles. This source of error could be
reduced by having the blindfolded subject wear gloves. Increasing the sample size is not effective in reducing sample bias. The source of the bias must
be identified and then reduced or eliminated.

Types of Samples

Although probability sampling, described below, is necessary for generalization to the population (a matter of external validity), there are occasions
when we do not need to go through the trouble and expense of obtaining
a probability sample. For example, we might have a specific group of people in mind, or the study is a class project where learning how to interview
is more important that generalizing the findings. In such cases, *nonprobability* sampling is acceptable. The specific type will depend on the needs of
the project.

Probability Sampling

Probability samples are those in which we know the probability for the
inclusion of any given individual. Two general types of probability samples are *random samples* and *stratified samples.* Visiting a college campus
and interviewing every fourth person on the sidewalk is *not* likely to yield
a random sample of the student body, because each student will not have
an equal chance of being selected. The chances of being selected will be
affected by the location, time of day, weather, etc.

Random Sample

In random sampling, every person in the entire population being studied
has an equal likelihood of being selected. For random sampling, the
researcher must have access to each member of the population, that is,
know how many people there are and how to reach them.

Drawing names out of a hat is one way of selecting students randomly
from a class. A more formal procedure is to use a table of random numbers, such as Table A-5 in Appendix A. These are numbers that follow no
particular pattern. The researcher can start anywhere in the table and proceed in any direction.

Example

The gym teacher interested in running speed wants to select a random sample
of 20 first-grade boys and 20 first-grade girls from a school population of 71 girls
and 68 boys in the first-grade classes. The teacher obtains a combined list of all
first-grade classes. Then, using a table of random numbers, the teacher begins

anywhere on this table, assigning successive two-digit numbers to every boy and girl on the list. For this particular study, the teacher started at the line marked in the second column and proceeded down the list.

Student name	Two-digit numbers from Table A-5
Jim A.	72
Sue F.	09
Bill S.	43
Martin F.	48
Alice P.	90
Nancy M.	61
.	.
.	.
.	.
.	.

The researcher can then select the 20 boys and 20 girls with the lowest numbers for the sample. If some of these students cannot participate, additions to the sample can be made from among those with the next lowest numbers.

A simpler method for selecting a sample, but with a higher risk of bias, involves the use of every third or fourth name on the list. The use of the first 20 names should be avoided unless the list has been compiled in a fully random manner. Students who registered late may be at the end of the list; some ethnic groups will be more heavily represented in some parts of the alphabet than in others. These same considerations apply in selecting locations in which to interview people. Houses for a neighborhood survey should be chosen according to a random procedure. Allowing the interviewer to select houses may introduce sampling bias (e.g., choosing only the more attractive houses and ignoring those that are rundown or have "No Trespassing" signs). Corner locations may differ in some ways from those in the middle of the block (more traffic? higher real estate values?). The way to avoid such problems is to develop a clear procedure for randomly selecting houses rather than leaving the decision to the interviewer.

Stratified Sample

A stratified sample is a variation of the random sample. Instead of selecting each person randomly, criteria are set up to ensure representation of particular groups within the sample proportionate to their numbers in the population. For example, if the population in question is made up of 55 percent males and 45 percent females, then a stratified sample is set to have 55 percent males and 45 percent females. Similar criteria may be set for age, residence, religion, and other variables of interest. Within categories, individuals are chosen randomly. Public opinion polls rely on stratified samples. They select a relatively small number of families to represent various levels of age, income, region, ethnic status, and other variables. The use of a representative sample requires an accurate knowledge of the characteristics of the population.

Nonprobability Sampling

Samples in which the likelihood of selection is not actually known are called nonprobability samples. There are three general types: *quota samples, purposive samples,* and *accidental samples.*

Quota Sample

Sometimes the researcher does not want or need a perfectly stratified sample. Let us imagine that in the school in which the running study is being conducted, there is only a small number of Hispanic students. If the researcher draws a random or stratified sample, it will probably provide too few Hispanic students in each sex and grade level. An alternative is for the researcher to use a *quota sample* in which the selection categories are specified according to the needs of the investigator. Within those categories, individuals are chosen randomly. A quota sample of school children might include 50 percent boys and 50 percent girls, one-sixth of them at each grade level, and one-third from each major ethnic category (black, white, Hispanic). These percentages would *not* necessarily reflect the actual composition of the school. They would, however, provide enough individuals in each part of the research design to permit adequate comparisons to be made. While the number of individuals in each category of a quota sample is chosen according to the researcher's needs, the particular individuals are chosen randomly.

Purposive Sample

A *purposive sample* is one in which individuals thought to be most important or relevant to the issue studied are targeted for the research. For example, a study of city policy may require interviews with particular individuals in leadership positions. For an experiment studying the effect of two types of video terminal monitors on employee productivity, one might select the employees who will be using the system most often to be the experimental and control subjects.

A special type of purposive sample is the *snowball sample* where the researcher asks respondents for other persons to contact. This technique is useful when studying particular groups where membership may not be obvious or where access to members may be difficult, for example, political activists, members of a religious cult, or gang members.

Accidental Sample

An *accidental sample* is taking what you can get. Interviewing people on a particular day in a local shopping mall, or observing students at lunchtime on campus are examples of accidental samples. A variant is the volunteer sample—comprised of people who are willing to participate in a research project. The characteristics and behavior of volunteers may be quite different from those of nonvolunteers.

Generalizability

Generalization from the results obtained with a probability sample is limited to the population from which the samples were drawn. Elementary schools differ so much that it is risky to generalize from one school to another. The investigator can subsequently enlarge the study to include students from schools in other parts of the country or in other nations. If such studies repeatedly turn up the same sex difference, this result can reasonably be considered genuine and not simply characteristic of a single school.

If the investigator has used a nonprobability sample such as a quota plan that does not reflect the population's characteristics (randomly choosing 100 black, white, and Hispanic children when this is not the ethnic ratio among the student body), generalization can be made only within each ethnic group. It cannot be extended to the total student body unless some adjustment is made based on the proportional membership of each ethnic group in the total population.

While nonprobability samples are limited in generalizability, steps can be taken to increase their validity. Purposive or quota samples should be selected randomly within the targeted groups. Observations made at different times of day will reduce some bias. Interviews in a shopping mall can be made of every fifth person entering. Using systematic procedures that are devised ahead of time may be very effective in reducing sample bias even when a pure random sample is not obtained. The point is to try to approximate randomness in the technical sense (to provide as equal an opportunity for selection as is possible), and to devise ways of reducing or eliminating sources of error.

How Large a Sample?

Other things being equal, large samples provide more reliable and representative data than small samples. Samples of 50 marbles randomly selected from the 1000-marble bowl will show less variability in the proportion of black and white marbles than will smaller samples of 10 marbles each. While it would be unusual to select 40 black and 10 white marbles, it would be far more likely to draw a sample of 10 marbles that contained 8 black and 2 white marbles.

In deciding on sample size, there is an interesting difference between statistical logic and practicality. The reduction in sampling error that results from a large sample may not be worth the extra time and effort required to obtain the additional data. Some public opinion polling firms find that they can make accurate predictions of voting trends based on interviews with a representative sample of 2500 individuals. To increase the sample to 5000 or 10,000 would reduce sampling error but would not be worth the extra time, effort, and expense. In public opinion surveys, time is very important. The extra two days that might be required to double the sample would make the results less useful to the client.

The following factors should be considered in making a decision on sample size:

1. *Size of the population.* For a survey of library *readers,* a sample of 100 individuals would probably be sufficient. For a survey of library *employees,* this would be far too many. There may not even be 100 employees. The researcher might eventually decide upon a 50 percent sample among library desk clerks and an 80 percent sample of administrators in order to obtain enough individuals in each category.

2. *Available resources and time constraints.* Pilot testing will reveal the cost in terms of time and effort for each testing session. The *maximum* size of the sample can be determined from such constraints. The *optimal* size of the sample will depend on other factors.

3. *Strength of the effect.* When the independent variable has a strong and clear effect on the dependent variable, a smaller sample can be used. For example, only a few subjects would be needed to demonstrate the effect of five ounces of alcohol on reaction time. A much larger number of subjects would be necessary to determine the effect of one ounce of alcohol, since this produces inconsistent and often contradictory results.

4. *Number of subsets to be compared.* If the researcher wishes to compare groups within the sample by dividing it according to social class, age, ethnicity, or gender, for example, the sample must be large enough to include a sufficient number of individuals in each of the subcategories.

5. *Refusal and spoilage rates.* A sample must be increased to allow for unusable data. It may be possible to predict in advance the number of people who will be unable to follow the instructions, drop out of the experiment, or terminate the interview prematurely. A questionnaire given to and collected from a group of clerical employees is likely to have a high return rate, perhaps in excess of 80 percent. However, the same questionnaire mailed to an unselected group of individuals with a request to return by mail may have a return rate of 10 to 15 percent.

Sample size should be specified in advance. This avoids the accusation that data collection was halted as soon as the results supported the hypothesis. The completion of one study does not rule out the possibility of additional ones. It is useful to begin a study with a small sample. The investigator interested in sex differences in running speed might compare 20 boys and 20 girls in one class. If the trends are very clear, the researcher could stop testing in that grade and look for trends in other grades. However, if the original results indicated a weak trend the researcher could repeat the study with additional groups of boys and girls at the same grade level. Two independent studies represent a more powerful test of a hypothesis than a single study involving twice as many subjects.

A description of the sampling procedure should always be included in the survey report. Here is an account of the methods used in a telephone survey of consumer attitudes toward food preservatives:

> A questionnaire developed for a survey of 370 consumers from the Statistical Metropolitan Survey Area of Seattle-Everett, Washington, in 1974 was adapted for use in this survey. Structured interviews were conducted in the same district by telephone. Phone numbers were selected at random from the telephone directory; 220 households were contacted and 170 usable replies were obtained. Only persons responsible for the major food purchases for the household unit being studied were interviewed. Each interview took 5–7 minutes, and all were conducted by the same interviewer (Martinsen & McCullough, 1977).

Limitations

A sample that is perfectly representative is difficult to obtain. Census records are probably out of date, not everyone is listed in the telephone directory, and door-to-door surveys are expensive. Many investigators are willing to settle for less than a perfect sampling procedure in order to obtain samples which are accessible and cooperative.

Summary

The entire group of people in a category is called a population. The smaller group selected for testing is called a sample. The degree to which the sample differs from the population is termed error. Two general sources of error are sampling error and sample bias. *Sampling error* refers to chance variations among samples selected from the same population. It is reduced by increasing the size of the sample. *Sample bias* refers to error introduced by a sampling procedure that favors certain characteristics over others. Ways of reducing sample bias are using probability samples or eliminating the bias by good research design such as using systematic procedures where the sample cannot be truly random.

Probability samples are either random or stratified. In a *random sample,* each member of the population has an equal chance of being selected. A *stratified sample* is selected so that its characteristics are proportionate to those present in the total population.

There are three types of nonprobability samples: quota, purposive, and accidental. In a *quota sample,* the selection categories are specified according to the needs of the investigator. A *purposive sample* targets key individuals for study. An *accidental sample* uses what's available.

The generalizability of a probability sample is limited to the population from which it is drawn. Nonprobability samples have very limited generalizability (external validity).

Other things being equal, large samples provide more reliable and representative data than small samples. The decision on sample size is influenced by the size of the population, available resources and time constraints, strength of the effect, number of subsets to be compared, and expected refusal and spoilage rates.

Limitations: Sampling is often done under less than ideal conditions. An investigator may be willing to trade off some representativeness for a sample that is more accessible and willing to participate in the study.

References

Martinsen, C. S., & McCullough, J. (1977). Are consumers concerned about chemical preservatives in food? *Food Technology, 7,* 56–59.

Further Reading

Backstrom, C., & Hursh-Cesar, G. (1981). *Survey research.* New York: Wiley (see Ch. 2).
Chein, I. (1976). An introduction to sampling. In C. Selltiz, L. S. Wrightsman, & S. W. Cook (Eds.), *Research methods in social relations* (3rd ed.) (pp. 511–540). New York: Holt, Rinehart and Winston.
Sudman, S. (1983). Applied sampling. In P. H. Rossi, J. D. Wright, & A. B. Anderson (Eds.), *Handbook of survey research* (pp. 145–194). New York: Academic Press.
Sudman, S. (1976). *Applied sampling.* New York: Academic Press.

17 Descriptive Statistics

How many uses can you think of for a top hat?

"It could be a scoop, a target, a container, a musical instrument."

"You could throw snowballs at it, use it as a paperweight, a mouse might use it for a boat on the water. You could use it as a fan if you got hot."

"You could use it as a vase or keep sugar or fish in it."

These are some of the answers students have given to the top hat question, part of a test used to measure creativity. Students receive a score for every new category of uses. The student who said that a top hat could be used as a vase, a sugar bowl, and fishbowl would receive only one point, since these are all single uses of the top hat (i.e., as a container). Table 17-1 shows a set of scores for 16 college students asked the top hat question.

These figures illustrate the *raw data* for the test. The raw data consist of the firsthand test scores. Notice how difficult it is to make any sense out of all these replies. Here a knowledge of statistical technique is useful. Statistics provide a way to reduce a mass of numbers to manageable proportions. This process is neither mysterious nor frightening; in general, it follows the rules of common sense. The best way to learn statistical techniques is to apply them to a set of data. In much of this chapter, we will be using the creativity test scores presented in Table 17-1. The measure used is a continuous one. Continuous measures are scores that vary along a continuous dimension or distribution, such as age in years, months, and days; income in dollars and cents; and creativity test scores

TABLE 17-1. Number of Uses for a Top Hat Given by 16
College Students

Student	Number of uses
1	8
2	5
3	5
4	11
5	6
6	7
7	6
8	4
9	9
10	4
11	5
12	7
13	6
14	6
15	8
16	7

ranging from zero to some upper limit. The following descriptive statistics are used for *continuous measures*. They do not apply to *categorical* measures—counts of separate and distinct units. Sex, country of residence, and political party affiliation are examples of categorical measures. They do not reflect continuous dimensions. A person is scored as falling into one category or another.

Frequency Distributions

An initial step in summarizing test results is to arrange them in a frequency distribution. This is a table with two columns. The scores from highest to lowest are written in one column; the *frequencies,* or number of times each score occurred, are in the second column.

Commonly used symbols or abbreviations in a frequency distribution are:

X = raw score
f = frequency
N = number of cases

Number of uses for a top hat X	Number of people giving this number of uses f
11	1
10	0
9	1
8	2
7	3
6	4
5	3
4	2

When the scores span a wide range, they can be grouped in *intervals* of equal size. Intervals may be of any size, although multiples of five are the most common. Interval grouping works best with 10 to 20 intervals. Fewer than 10 will obscure the differences in spread, while too many intervals are likely to dilute any trends. Because there are only 16 creativity test scores and since they vary over such a limited range (4 to 11), there is no point in interval grouping. Table 17-2 uses a different set of test scores to illustrate the use of interval grouping in a frequency distribution.

Cumulative Frequencies

Cumulative frequencies are shown in Table 17-3. These are formed by beginning at the bottom of a frequency distribution and summing all the frequencies at and below each level. An advantage of a cumulative distri-

TABLE 17-2. Frequency Distribution of Arithmetic Achievement Scores for 142 Children, Ages 10 to 10½ Years

X	*Tally	f
160–169	|	1
150–159	|	1
140–149	|||	3
130–139	⊬⊦⊦ ⊬⊦⊦ ||||	14
120–129	⊬⊦⊦ ⊬⊦⊦ ⊬⊦⊦ ||||	19
110–119	⊬⊦⊦ ⊬⊦⊦ ⊬⊦⊦ ⊬⊦⊦ ⊬⊦⊦ ||	27
100–109	⊬⊦⊦ ⊬⊦⊦ ⊬⊦⊦ ⊬⊦⊦ ⊬⊦⊦ ⊬⊦⊦ ||	32
90–99	⊬⊦⊦ ⊬⊦⊦ ⊬⊦⊦ ⊬⊦⊦ |||	23
80–89	⊬⊦⊦ ⊬⊦⊦ ⊬⊦⊦	15
70–79	||||	4
60–69	||	2
50–59	|	1

*The *tally* should not be included in your presentation of results. It is shown here merely to illustrate how the frequencies are obtained.

TABLE 17-3. Arithmetic Achievement Scores for 142 Children,
Ages 10 to 10½ Years, Expressed in Cumulative
Frequencies and Percentages

Interval	f	Cumulative f	Cumulative %
160–169	1	142	100
150–159	1	141	99.2
140–149	3	140	98.6
130–139	14	137	96.4
120–129	19	123	86.7
110–119	27	104	73.2
100–109	32	77	54.2
90–99	23	45	31.7
80–89	15	$1 + 2 + 4 + 15 = 22$	15.5
70–79	4	$1 + 2 + 4 = 7$	$\dfrac{7}{142} = 4.9$
60–69	2	$1 + 2 = 3$	$\dfrac{3}{142} = 2.1$
50–59	1	1	$\dfrac{1}{142} = 0.7$

bution is that it shows the number of cases falling below each interval score. From the third column in Table 17-3, we find that 45 children scored below 100 (45 were at or below the interval of 90–99). Note that the cumulative frequency listed at each interval includes those cases within the interval as well as those below. The cumulative frequency can be transformed into a *cumulative percentage* by dividing it by the total number of cases and multiplying by 100. The 45 children scoring below 100 are 31.7 percent of the total sample (see Table 17-3, fourth column).

Figures and Graphs

Up to this point, the data have been presented in statistical tables. It is also possible to present the same data in graphs and figures. One form of presentation is the *bar graph* or *histogram* (see Figure 17-1). Here the intervals are shown along the horizontal axis (base) and the frequencies along the vertical axis.

The *frequency polygon* is another form of graphic representation. As in the bar graph, the individual scores or the intervals are listed along the horizontal axis. However, instead of bars, dots are placed on the graph at the *midpoint* of each interval to indicate the frequency of scores. Then a line is drawn connecting the points (Figure 17-2).

When comparing different-sized groups, bar graphs and frequency polygons can be based on percentages instead of frequencies. Cumulative fre-

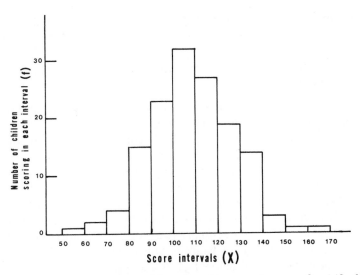

FIG. 17-1. Histogram showing arithmetic achievement scores for 142 children, ages 1 to 10½ years.

FIG. 17-2. Frequency polygon showing arithmetic achievement scores for 142 children, ages 1 to 10½ years.

209

quencies and cumulative percentages can also be presented in graphic form. Figure 17-3 shows cumulative percentages for the same data as both a bar graph and a curve.

While the rules for constructing graphs and figures are not rigid, there are some guidelines:

1. Scores are presented along the base (horizontal axis) and frequencies or percentages on the vertical axis.

2. Numbers run from left to right, beginning with the low numbers. Low numbers are placed at the bottom of the vertical axis.

3. The entire graph and everything on it should be clearly labeled. Any symbols used should be defined.

4. The overall impression conveyed by a graph is affected by the ratio of the vertical to the horizontal axis. Some writers suggest keeping the vertical axis about three-quarters as long as the horizontal axis.

5. The title of a table or figure is called the *legend*. This is generally placed above tables and below figures and graphs.

FIG. 17-3. Cumulative percentages of arithmetic achievement scores for 142 children, ages 1 to 10½ years.

This may be the time to stop momentarily. The next part of the chapter will deal with measures of central tendency. However, before going on, you may wish to review some of the earlier parts of this chapter.

Measures of Central Tendency

A further step in the analysis of continuous scores is the calculation of an average. There are three types of averages: mean, median, and mode. If you have taken a test, knowing the mean, median, and mode gives you a better idea of your performance relative to that of others who took the test. Measures of central tendency are also useful for comparing the scores from two groups of people on the same test.

Mean

The mean is the arithmetic average. There are two ways of calculating it. (1) Add up the individual scores and divide by the total number of cases.

Formula: $\overline{X} = \dfrac{\Sigma X}{N}$

Where $\overline{X}$ = mean
Σ = sum of
X = raw score
N = number of cases

Example
The mean of the creativity scores is calculated for the test scores as follows:
Sum of all scores (ΣX) = 104
Number of tests scores (N) = 16
Mean ($\overline{X}$) = $\dfrac{104}{16}$ = 6.5

When data are in a frequency distribution:

Multiply each score X by its frequency,
Sum those products,
Divide by the total number of cases.

Formula: $\overline{X} = \dfrac{\Sigma(Xf)}{N}$

Table 17-4 illustrates the calculation of the mean from the frequency distribution of creativity scores.

The mean is the most frequently used measure of central tendency. It is usually the most reliable of the three measures since it varies less among samples drawn from the same population.

TABLE 17-4. Calculation of the Mean from the Frequency
Distribution of Creativity Scores

Number of uses for a top hat X	Number of people giving this number of uses f	(X multiplied by f) Xf
11	1	11
10	0	0
9	1	9
8	2	16
7	3	21
6	4	24
5	3	15
4	2	8
	$N = 16$	$\Sigma(Xf) = 104$

$$\text{Mean } (\overline{X}) = \frac{\Sigma(Xf)}{N} = \frac{104}{16} = 6.5$$

Median

The median is the midpoint of the distribution when all the scores are arranged from highest to lowest. Half of the scores fall above the median and half below. The advantages of the median over the mean are that it is quickly calculated from a frequency distribution, and it is a better indicator of central tendency when there are a few extremely high or extremely low scores. The mean is much more influenced by extremes than is the median.

To calculate the median from a frequency distribution, arrange the scores from highest to lowest. The median is the middle score, or the point between the middle two scores if there is an even number of scores. The left-hand column of Table 17-5 shows the calculation of the median for the creativity test. Since there were 16 scores, the median is halfway between the eighth score (6) and the ninth score, which is also 6.

The median can also be computed from a frequency distribution. (This is useful when there are too many scores to list individually.) The total number of cases in the *f* column is divided by 2. Counting either from the top or bottom of the distribution of the *f* column, the middle score is found, or halfway between the two middle scores if there is an even number of cases. This halfway point is the median. Calculation of the median from a frequency distribution is shown in the right-hand column of Table 17-5.

Mode

The *mode* is the single score that occurs most often in a distribution. Of the three measures of central tendency, it is the easiest to compute but often the least informative, since it provides only a rough estimate of cen-

TABLE 17-5. Calculation of the Median Number of Uses for a Top Hat

Rank all scores from highest to lowest and find the middle score	Find the score (X) of the middle case in the frequency distribution	
Creativity score (X)	X	f
11 ⎤	11	1
9	10	0
8	9	1 8th and 9th
8 N = 16	8	2 (middle) cases
7 8 scores (50%	7	3 fall here.
7 of all scores)	6	4 ← Median = 6
7 above	5	3
6 ⎦	4	2

Median = 6 $N = 16$

6 ⎤	One-half of 16 is 8. Find the 8th and 9th	
6	cases in the frequency distribution,	
6	counting either from the top or bottom.	
5 8 scores (50%	The median is the score lying between	
5 of all scores)	them.	
5 below		
4		
4 ⎦		

tral tendency. Table 17-5 indicates that four people gave six uses for a top hat—more than gave any other single number of uses. The *mode* of this distribution is therefore 6. It is not unusual for a distribution to have more than one mode. When there are two modes, the distribution is called *bimodal*.

Measures of Variability

Measures of variability indicate the amount of spread or dispersion within the distribution of scores. In some studies, the scores show very little spread, clustering around the indicators of central tendency. In other studies, scores are greatly spread out. This information is important in the interpretation of research findings. It can show, for example, whether or not the group average has been unduly influenced by a few extreme scores. The most commonly used measures of variability are the *range* and the *standard deviation*. The range provides a quick and easy assessment of spread. To compute the range, simply subtract the lowest score from the highest. On the creativity test, the highest score was 11 and the lowest was 4. The range is $11 - 4 = 7$.

The standard deviation is a much more complicated statistic, but it is also more informative and useful than the range, since it is included in many other statistical tests. The larger the standard deviation, the greater the spread of scores within the range. The standard deviation takes into account the distance of each score from the mean of the distribution.

A small standard deviation indicates that most scores are grouped around the mean. A larger standard deviation indicates greater variability of the scores from the mean (see Figure 17-4).

A formula for computing the standard deviation is:

$$\text{S.D.} = \sqrt{\frac{\Sigma X^2 - \frac{(\Sigma X)^2}{N}}{N}}$$

Where

S.D.   = Standard Deviation
ΣX^2 = each score squared and then summed
$(\Sigma X)^2$ = all scores summed and then squared
N = number of cases

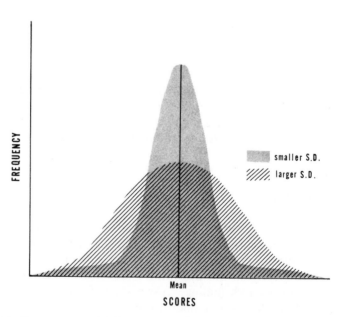

FIG. 17-4. Two curves with identical means and ranges but different standard deviations.

Do not be surprised if you find other formulas for calculating the standard deviation. They vary among statistics texts. Table 17-6 shows the calculation of the standard deviation for the results of the creativity study. In calculating a standard deviation, it is not necessary to list the scores from highest to lowest. They can be written in any order. They are presented in order here to follow the previous example.

What is the purpose of this procedure? First, the standard deviation provides an indication of variability. Second, it is also used in many other statistical tests.

The reader may welcome a brief illustration of the practical significance of a standard deviation. If half the children in the arithmetic example used earlier had scored very high on the test and the other half had scored very low, the mean (average score) would have meant little. It would tell us nothing about the typical performance, because none of the children would have received an average score. Such a distribution (with cases spread far away from the mean) would show a high standard deviation. When pre-

TABLE 17-6. Calculation of the Standard Deviation for the
Creativity Scores

Number of uses for a top hat X	X^2	
11	121	$\text{S.D.} = \sqrt{\dfrac{\Sigma X^2 - \dfrac{(\Sigma X)^2}{N}}{N}}$
9	81	
8	64	
8	64	$= \sqrt{\dfrac{728 - \dfrac{10{,}816}{16}}{16}}$
7	49	
7	49	
7	49	
6	36	$= \sqrt{\dfrac{728 - 676}{16}}$
6	36	
6	36	
6	36	$= \sqrt{\dfrac{52}{16}}$
5	25	
5	25	$= \sqrt{3.25}$
5	25	
4	16	$\text{S.D.} = 1.80$
4	16	

$\Sigma X = 104 \quad \Sigma X^2 = 728 \quad N = 16$
$(\Sigma X)^2 = (104)^2 = 10{,}816$

senting research results, it is helpful to the reader to include, besides the mean, an index of variability such as the standard deviation.

Categorical Measures

As mentioned earlier, the descriptive statistics mentioned thus far apply primarily to continuous measures. However, frequencies and the mode are appropriate to calculate for categorical measures. For example, if a sample of voters are asked whom they prefer as president, the number of people preferring each candidate constitutes a frequency, and the most frequently made selection is the mode. It would be impossible to calculate a mean, median, or standard deviation.

Graphic presentation of categorical data is best made with bar graphs. Frequency curves should *not* be used with categorical data. They are misleading because the connecting lines suggest the existence of intermediate points which do not occur with distinct categories.

Further Reading

Bruning, J. L., & Kintz, B. L. (1977). *Computational handbook of statistics* (2nd ed.). Glenview, IL: Scott, Foresman.
Guilford, J. P., & Fruchter, B. (1978). *Fundamental statistics in psychology and education* (6th ed.) New York: McGraw-Hill.
Runyon, R. P., & Haber, A. (1984). *Fundamentals of behavioral statistics* (5th ed.). Reading, MA: Addison-Wesley.

Sample Problems

1. Here is the frequency distribution of running speed scores from several sixth-grade classes.

Time (in seconds)	Frequency
40–44	1
45–49	6
50–54	10
55–59	22
60–64	25
65–69	16
70–74	8
75–79	4
80–84	2

Use these scores to construct a bar graph or histogram. Be sure to label both the vertical and horizontal axes properly.

Calculate the cumulative frequencies percentage at each interval.

2. Here are the scores from 10 sixth-grade boys who participated in a study of running speed.

Name	Time in Seconds
John H.	52
Henry B.	62
Alan C.	47
Henry C.	59
Tom R.	50
Jerry W.	72
Matt S.	50
Andy F.	71
Ken P.	48
Eric A.	50

Compute each of the following descriptive statistics for the above scores: mean*, median, range, standard deviation.*

*Use of a calculator will be helpful.

Answers to Problems

1. Cumulative frequencies: 2, 6, 14, 30, 55, 77, 87, 93, 94
   Cumulative percent: 2.1, 6.4, 14.9, 31.9, 58.5, 81.9, 92.6, 98.9, 100

2. Mean = 56.1
   Median = 51 (midpoint between 50 and 52)
   Range = 72 − 47 = 25
   Standard Deviation = 8.916*

*Some calculators use a slightly different formula, employing $N - 1$ rather than N in the denominator. In that case, the standard deviation is 9.398.

18 Inferential Statistics

"Smoke Gets in Your Eyes" is a very romantic song but not a very pleasant experience for many people. Kathryn Anthony (1977) wanted to find out whether people stood farther away from smokers than from nonsmokers. She recruited student volunteers from psychology classes. When they arrived at the designated room, each volunteer was introduced to the research associate (a person working with Ms. Anthony) and asked to "choose the distance most comfortable for conversation between you and this person, assuming you had just met." Once the student had created a comfortable conversational distance, a tape measure was used to calculate it in centimeters. During approximately half of the 76 sessions, the research associate was smoking a lit cigarette. During the other sessions, the associate did not smoke.

Anthony found that students stood a mean distance of 62.5 cm from the nonsmoking associate. When the associate was smoking, the distance was 80.3 cm.

From these average distances, it appeared that the cigarette had an effect on conversational distance. However, there may have been a large overlap in the scores, and perhaps only one or two extreme scores was responsible for these differences. A single student who, for example, remained 4 m away from a smoking person might have been responsible for this entire difference. The problem involves deciding when a difference is reliable and when it is due to chance fluctuations, perhaps the result of a few extreme scores in one group. One solution is to repeat the study and see if similar differences are obtained. Another approach is to test the reliability of differences between groups using an *inferential* test. *Inferential statistics* permits generalization from samples to populations.

Chapter 16 on sampling described the process of generalizing from a *sample* to a *population,* making inferences from a subset to the whole. There were two problems that arose in doing this. One was *sampling error,* chance fluctuation that is inevitable when taking small samples from large populations. The second problem was *sample bias,* which comes from faulty sample selection resulting in a subset that does not accurately represent the population. Statistical techniques are used to take care of the problem of *sampling error,* the chance fluctuation one must expect. Statistical manipulation *cannot* solve problems of inadequate or biased sampling. That is a research design problem. Statistics cannot salvage an inadequately designed or poorly conducted piece of research. To repeat, statistics are used to deal with sampling error, to estimate the role of chance in the findings.

Note to the reader: If you have not taken a course in statistics, this chapter will seem more difficult than others because of the many new terms and formulas. It is probably best to read this chapter for understanding rather than to attempt to grasp all the details of each statistical test. Do not be concerned if you cannot understand immediately how these tests can be applied. This will come in time as you work with actual data.

Testing the Null Hypothesis

The idea that any differences are due to chance fluctuations and that the independent variable has no effect on the dependent variable is called the *null hypothesis.* This is a conservative way of phrasing the research question; the investigator predicts that there will be no reliable difference between groups.

Following a statistical test of the null hypothesis, it is either accepted (no difference) or rejected (there is a reliable difference). If we find the differences could be attributed to chance, then we believe (accept) the null hypothesis. When the null hypothesis is accepted, the researcher concludes that the independent variable had no effect on the outcome. If the null hypothesis is *rejected* (the difference was *not* due to chance), then the conclusion is that there was an effect. Acceptance or rejection of the null hypothesis can be done quickly and easily when you know the techniques. Formulas and tables necessary for interpreting the results have been worked out by statisticians.

Alternative Hypothesis

The working hypothesis is stated in positive terms—that there *is* a difference between groups or that the independent variable will have a significant effect on the dependent variable. This is called the *alternative hypothesis* because it is an alternative to the null hypothesis.

Testing the null hypothesis feels odd because you are usually more interested in confirming your working (alternative) hypothesis. This is probably what you were interested in initially. Nevertheless, statistical practice requires that the fate of the alternative hypothesis actually rests on acceptance or rejection of the null hypothesis.

Probability Levels

In using inferential statistics, it is the null hypothesis that is tested. Whether or not your own hypothesis can be accepted depends on whether you are able to reject the null hypothesis that no reliable difference exists. Rejecting the null hypothesis is a gamble. The *probability level* of a statistic indicates the odds. If the probability of the difference occurring by chance alone is less than 5 in 100, most researchers are willing to gamble that the outcome is *not* one of these five cases, and will therefore reject the null hypothesis and accept the research hypothesis that a genuine difference exists.

A common practice in the social sciences is to use this .05 probability level for testing the null hypothesis. This is also called the *.05 level of significance* and is abbreviated as $p < .05$. When the odds of a difference being due to chance are less than 5 in 100 ($p < .05$), the null hypothesis will be rejected. When the likelihood of a difference being due to chance is more than 5 in 100, then the null hypothesis—that the difference is probably due to chance—can be accepted. Some researchers prefer the .01 level of significance ($p < .01$), rejecting the null hypothesis only if the odds of a difference being due to random fluctuation are less than 1 in 100. The .01 probability level reduces the likelihood of mistaking a chance difference for a genuine difference.

Do not confuse statistical significance with practical importance. To say that a difference is "statistically significant" means only that it is not due to chance. With very large samples, even a tiny difference can be statistically significant even though it probably will not have much practical relevance.

Statistical Tests for Continuous Data

The two most common tests for continuous data are the *t* test and analysis of variance. The *t test* is used for comparing two groups. *Analysis of variance* is used for comparing differences among two or more groups. These tests take into account the amount of overlap in the distribution of scores in order to make a judgment about the significance of the *difference between means*. Before either test can be employed, there is an important condition that must be met: The distribution of scores in the population from which scores were drawn should approximately follow the normal curve. A perfect normal curve is the symmetrical bell-shaped curve shown in Figure 18-1. Characteristics measured in nature among large populations often produce this kind of frequency curve. If we measure the length of tigers' tails, the age at which children lose their milk teeth, or the production of fruit during the growing season, we would get a heavy concentration of scores in the middle with scores diminishing in frequency to the two ends of the curve. In a perfectly normal distribution, the mean, median, and mode are identical.

Most distributions of behavioral data do not perfectly match a bell-shaped curve but rather approximate it, as in Figure 18-2. This is acceptable for employing one of the tests for continuous data.

Sometimes a distribution of scores deviates markedly from a normal curve. This happens when there are many extreme scores at the upper or lower ends of the distribution, as in Figure 18-3. Such distributions are said to be *skewed*. It is necessary to know whether data approximate a normal curve or instead are skewed in order to select the best statistical technique for describing them and testing any differences between groups. When the data are continuous and the frequency distribution is close to normal (it will rarely be a perfectly normal curve), then a *t* test or analysis of variance can be employed. If your results are skewed, but you think the characteristic being measured is probably normally distributed in the population, then you can still use a *t* test or analysis of variance. If you think the population data do not approximate a normal curve, then a statistical test for categorical data described later in this chapter should be used.

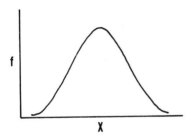

f

X

FIG. 18-1. Normal curve.

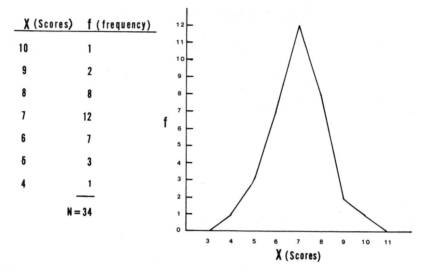

X (Scores)	f (frequency)
10	1
9	2
8	8
7	12
6	7
5	3
4	1
	N = 34

FIG. 18-2. Normally distributed data and frequency polygon.

How to Do a t Test

The *t* test assesses the significance of the difference between the means of two groups of scores. The numerical result of this test is called a *t ratio.* There are two formulas for a *t* test. One is used when the two groups are independent; the other is used when the two groups compared have been matched on some characteristic or the same people have been tested before and after an experimental treatment. The latter are called *matched scores* or *correlated measures.*

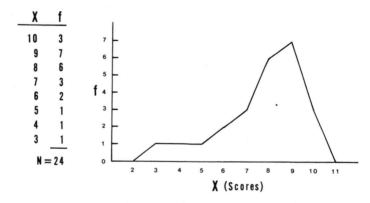

X	f
10	3
9	7
8	6
7	3
6	2
5	1
4	1
3	1
	N = 24

FIG. 18-3. Skewed data and frequency polygon.

The formula for a *t* test for independent groups and an example of its use are shown in Box 18-1.

BOX 18-1. Calculation of a *t* test for Two Independent Groups

Two groups of employees are given a test. One group contains five people, the other six. Do the employees in Group 1 score significantly higher than the employees in Group 2, or is the difference between them the results of random fluctuation?

Scores on Test	
Group 1 (X)	Group 2 (Y)
4	4
5	9
5	2
3	3
3	3
	4

The formula for a *t* test for independent groups is

$$t = \frac{\bar{x} - \bar{y}}{\sqrt{\left[\frac{\left(\Sigma X^2 - \frac{(\Sigma x)^2}{N_x}\right) + \left(\Sigma Y^2 - \frac{(\Sigma y)^2}{N_y}\right)}{N_x + N_y - 2}\right] \cdot \left[\frac{1}{N_x} + \frac{1}{N_y}\right]}}$$

X = score in Group 1
Y = score in Group 2
N_x = number of scores in Group 1
N_y = number of scores in Group 2

Computation
Step 1. Add up scores in Group 1: $\Sigma X = 20$.
    2. Square total for all scores in Group 1: $(\Sigma X)^2 = 400$.
    3. Square *each score* in Group 1. Add together $\Sigma X^2 = 84$.
    4. Find number of scores in Group 1: $N_x = 5$.
    5. Compute mean for Group 1: $\bar{X} = \frac{\Sigma X}{N} = 4.0$.

(Steps 6–10. Repeat steps for Group 2)
    6. $\Sigma Y = 25$.
    7. $(\Sigma Y)^2 = 625$.
    8. $\Sigma Y^2 = 135$.
    9. $N_y = 6$.
    10. $\bar{Y} = 4.17$.

---

11. Enter these figures in the formula for the t test for independent groups.

$$t = \cfrac{4.0 - 4.17}{\sqrt{\left[\cfrac{\left(84 - \cfrac{400}{5}\right) + \left(135 - \cfrac{625}{6}\right)}{5 + 6 - 2}\right] \cdot \left[\cfrac{1}{5} + \cfrac{1}{6}\right]}} =$$

$$\cfrac{-.17}{\sqrt{\left(\cfrac{4 + 30.83}{9}\right)(.20 + .17)}} = \cfrac{-.17}{\sqrt{(3.87)(.37)}} =$$

$$\cfrac{-.17}{\sqrt{1.43}} = \cfrac{-.17}{1.20} = -.14$$

12. Compute degrees of freedom $df = (N_x - 1) + (N_y - 1) = 4 + 5 = 9$ Check Table A - 1 in Appendix A. Look at 9 degrees of freedom. Table A-1 shows that a t ratio of 2.26 or greater is required for significance at the .05 level with 9 degrees of freedom. Since $t = .14$ (the minus sign can be ignored), this difference is *not* significant.

The t *Test for Matched Scores*

When two sets of scores have been matched in some way, such as the same individuals tested before and after an experimental treatment, the t test for matched scores is used.

BOX 18-2. Calculation of a t Test for Matched Scores

A group of workers is given a hand steadiness test before and after taking a drug. Does the drug have a significant effect on their performance?

Score on Hand Steadiness Test

Employee name	Before	After	d	d²
Bill	72	70	+2	4
John	81	78	+3	9
Mary	75	74	+1	1
Sue	77	78	−1	1
Al	84	80	+4	16
Sam	72	72	0	0

Step 1. Compute the difference (d) between each person's scores before and after taking the drug. Subtract each *after* score from each *before* score. Pay close attention to the sign (plus or minus) of each difference (d).
  2. Square each difference (d^2).
  3. Compute $\Sigma d = 9$.
     Note: Pay close attention to plus and minus signs.
  4. Compute $(\Sigma d)^2 = 81$.
  5. Compute $\Sigma d^2 = 31$.
     Note: All numbers here are positive since they have been squared.
  6. $N = 6$.
  7. Enter figures into formula. The formula for a t test for matched scores is:

$$t = \frac{\dfrac{\Sigma d}{N}}{\sqrt{\dfrac{\Sigma d^2 - \dfrac{(\Sigma d)^2}{N}}{N(N-1)}}}$$

d = difference between the matched scores
N = number of *pairs* of scores

Computation

$$t = \frac{\dfrac{\Sigma d}{N}}{\sqrt{\dfrac{\Sigma d^2 - \dfrac{(\Sigma d)^2}{N}}{N(N-1)}}} = \frac{\dfrac{9}{6}}{\sqrt{\dfrac{31 - \dfrac{81}{6}}{6(6-1)}}} =$$

$$\frac{1.5}{\sqrt{\dfrac{31 - 13.5}{30}}} = \frac{1.5}{\sqrt{.58}} = \frac{1.5}{.76} = 1.97$$

  8. Compute degrees of freedom. For related scores, $df = N - 1 = 6 - 1 = 5$.
  9. Check Table A-1 in Appendix A. The critical value for t to be significant at the .05 level for 5 degrees of freedom is 2.57 or greater. Since this t ratio is only 1.97, it is *not* significant.

Interpreting the t *Ratio*

Having computed the t ratio according to one of the formulas shown in the boxes, the next step is to determine the *degrees of freedom (df)*. This is a fairly complicated concept to understand. Fortunately, it is very easy to compute. For a t test with independent scores, the degrees of freedom are the total number of scores less one for each group. For a t test for matched scores, the degrees of freedom are the number of matched pairs less one.
     The final step in interpretation is to consult Table A-1 in Appendix A.

The table is used to decide whether an obtained t ratio is due to chance. Using the .05 level of statistical significance, a probability of *less than* 5 in 100 that an obtained difference is due to chance calls for *rejection* of the null hypothesis (i.e., concluding that the obtained difference is reliable). When the probability that an obtained difference is due to chance is *more than* 5 in 100, the null hypothesis (no reliable difference) is *accepted*. If the investigator wants to be very certain of the results, a probability level of 1 in 100 (.01) may be used.

To find the significance of a t ratio in Table A-1, first consult the left column and find the degrees of freedom closest to those in your study.

Example: In the cigarette study there were two unrelated groups of 39 and 37 subjects. This produced 74 degrees of freedom $(39 - 1 + 37 - 1)$. Since this table does not show $df = 74$, the nearest degrees of freedom (100) are used. Now move to the right of $df = 100$ to find the appropriate t ratios for the .05 and .01 probability levels. These are 1.98 and 2.63, respectively. Since the obtained t ratio between the groups (3.36) is larger than either of these figures, we conclude that the difference is reliable at the .01 level of significance, and the null hypothesis can be rejected.

Analysis of Variance (ANOVA)

Analysis of variance, sometimes abbreviated ANOVA, can be used when there are more than two sets of continuous scores. The principles of interpreting differences are similar to those for the t test. Like the t test, ANOVA is used to judge the reliability of differences between means. Its advantage is that it can be used for more than two means at a time or it can be used in place of t for two means. An additional benefit is that ANOVA can also be used to assess the effects of more than one independent variable at a time. However, our example will involve an experiment with only one independent variable.

One-way ANOVA

An Air Force researcher is interested in the effect of sleep deprivation on information processing by air traffic controllers. The independent variable is sleep deprivation measured at three levels: none, slight, and moderate deprivation. The dependent variable is the number of mistakes made on the task. Four subjects are randomly assigned to each group, giving a total of 12 individuals in the study. The results are in Table 18-1.

The question to be answered by the statistical analysis is whether or not the means of these three groups differ significantly from one another (i.e., more than to be expected by chance). We are concerned with the differences *between* groups, but we gauge the chance variation by looking at the variability of scores *within* each group. In this example we will get a mea-

TABLE 18-1. Sleep Deprivation Data

Group 1		Group 2		Group 3	
No deprivation	Number of mistakes	Slight deprivation	Number of mistakes	Moderate deprivation	Number of mistakes
Subject 1	1	Subject 5	3	Subject 9	2
Subject 2	2	Subject 6	2	Subject 10	3
Subject 3	0	Subject 7	3	Subject 11	4
Subject 4	2	Subject 8	4	Subject 12	4
Means	1.25		3.0		3.25

sure of the differences between the groups, with respect to the number of mistakes, and judge that against the distribution or spread of mistakes within each group. The between group differences must be significantly greater than those within groups in order for the differences between means to reach statistical significance.

Looking at the means in this example, it appears that the sleep deprivation leads to more errors, but the differences between them are not large and could reasonably be attributed to chance. The ANOVA will allow us to decide the odds of that being the case. The statistical calculation requires computing *sums of squares (SS)*, which take into account the spread of scores within the sample. The calculations are entered into an ANOVA table, which is shown at the end of Box 18-3. Going through the necessary steps, the F ratio is generated. It is a ratio of the average between-group to the average within-group variability. Its statistical significance is evaluated using Table A-6 in the Appendix.

Additional tests called *mean comparisons* can be made to find exactly

---

BOX 18-3. Calculation of a One-Way Analysis of Variance (ANOVA)

Step 1. Arrange the scores by groups.

Group 1		Group 2		Group 3	
No deprivation	Number of mistakes	Slight deprivation	Number of mistakes	Moderate deprivation	Number of mistakes
Subject 1	1	Subject 5	3	Subject 9	2
Subject 2	2	Subject 6	2	Subject 10	3
Subject 3	0	Subject 7	3	Subject 11	4
Subject 4	2	Subject 8	4	Subject 12	4

The results of each set of steps are entered on an ANOVA table:

ANOVA Table

Source	SS	df	MS	F
Total	SS_{tot} ———			
Treatment (deprivation groups)	SS_{bet} ———			
Error	SS_{within} ———			

A. Calculation of the total sum of squares (SS_{tot}).

NOTE: If you are using a calculator with a X^2 key, you can do steps 2 and 3 at the same time.

Step 2. Add the scores in *each* group. This is the *sum* for each group.

	Group 1	Group 2	Group 3
	1	3	2
	2	2	3
	0	3	4
Sum	2	4	4
	5	12	13

Step 3. Square each individual score and add these squared values together.

$1^2 + 2^2 + 0^2 + 2^2 + 3^2 + 2^2 + 3^2 + 4^2 + 2^2 + 3^2 + 4^2 + 4^2$
$= 1 + 4 + 0 + 4 + 9 + 4 + 9 + 16 + 4 + 9 + 16 + 16$
$= 92$ This is ΣX^2

Step 4. Add all the groups sums (in step 2) together to get the sum for all scores, the grand total.

$5 + 12 + 13 = \Sigma X_{tot} = 30$

Step 5. Square the grand total (step 4).

$(\Sigma X_{tot})^2 = (30)^2 = 900$

Step 6. Divide the result of step 5 by N, the total number of cases.

$N = 4 + 4 + 4 = 12$

$\dfrac{(\Sigma X_{tot})^2}{N} = \dfrac{900}{12} = 75$

This is called the *correction factor*.

Step 7. Subtract the *correction factor* (step 6) from the result of step 3, the sum of the squared values.

$\Sigma X^2 - (\text{correction factor}) = 92 - 75 = 17.0$

This is the *total sum of squares* (SS_{tot}).

Enter it in the ANOVA table (see model table in Section H).

B. Calculation of the between group sum of squares (SS_{bet}).

Step 8. For *each* group, square the sum (step 2) and divide by the number of scores in the group.

$\dfrac{5^2}{4} + \dfrac{12^2}{4} + \dfrac{13^2}{4} = 84.5$

Step 9. Subtract the correction factor (step 6) from the value in step 8.

$84.5 - 75 = 9.5$

This is the between groups sum of squares (SS_{bet}).

Enter this value in the ANOVA table.

C. Calculation of the within group sum of squares (SS_{within}).

Step 10. Subtract the between group sum of squares (step 9) from the total sum of squares (step 7)

$$17 - 9.5 = 7.5$$

This gives the within group sum of squares (SS_{within}) Enter in the ANOVA table.

D. Calculate degree of freedom (df) and enter on the ANOVA table.

Step 11. For SS_{tot} df_{tot} = (total number of cases) − 1

$$df_{tot} = 12 - 1 = 11$$

For SS_{bet} df_{bet} = (number of groups) − 1

$$df_{bet} = 3 - 1 = 2$$

For SS_{within} $df_{within} = df_{tot} - df_{bet}$

$$df_{within} = 11 - 2 = 9$$

E. Calculate mean squares (MS) for the *between* and *within* group measures.

Step 12. The mean squares (MS) are computed as SS/df (Note: MS_{tot} is not needed)

$$MS_{bet} = \frac{SS_{bet}}{df_{bet}} = \frac{9.5}{2} = 4.75$$

$$MS_{within} = \frac{SS_{within}}{df_{within}} = \frac{7.5}{9} = .83$$

Enter these in the ANOVA table.

F. Calculate the F ratio.

Step 13. $$F = \frac{MS_{bet}}{MS_{within}} = \frac{4.75}{.83} = 5.72$$

Enter the value on the ANOVA table.

G. Statistical significance.

Step 14. See Table A-6 in Appendix A to find the probability associated with the F ratio.

There were 2 degrees of freedom *(df)* in the numerator of the F ratio, and 9 *df* in the denominator. Using Table A-6, first go across the columns until you reach 2 *df* for the numerator, then proceed down this column until you reach 9 *df* for the denominator. This shows that for the differences among the means to be significant at the .05 level, the obtained F ratio must equal or exceed 4.26, and to be significant at the .01 level, must equal or exceed 8.02.

Because the obtained statistic, 5.72, exceeds to critical value at the .05 level, we can reject the null hypothesis at the .05 level, and conclude that sleep deprivation has a negative impact on task performance. See the notation, $p < .05$, on the ANOVA table.

H. Model ANOVA Table.

Source	SS		df	MS	F
Total	SS_{tot}	17.0	11		
Treatment (deprivation groups)	SS_{bet}	9.5	2	4.75	5.72 $p < .05$
Error	SS_{within}	7.5	9	0.83	

where the significant difference lies. In our example, the difference between groups 1 and 2, and between 2 and 3 was significant, while the difference between groups 2 and 3 was not.

There are many more variations of the ANOVA technique that extend its range of applications.

ANOVA for Groups of Unequal Size

In natural experiments or observational studies, it is common to have unequal numbers of subjects at various levels of the independent variable. When this occurs, the calculations must be adjusted to take into account the unequal numbers. The underlying assumptions of ANOVA are such that it is preferable to have equal numbers in each group whenever possible. For this reason, some researchers will use a random number procedure to eliminate scores from the larger groups to bring all groups to an equal size. There are formulas available in statistics books for ANOVA with groups of unequal size.

Factorial Design

The example in Box 18-3 illustrates the steps for doing a one-way ANOVA. It is called one-way because it involves only one independent variable or factor. When more than one factor or independent variable is introduced, the design is termed *factorial* (i.e., two-factor or two-way ANOVA, three-factor or three-way ANOVA, etc.). When additional factors are introduced, interpretation of the ANOVA becomes more complex.

The research design for the sleep deprivation study could be modified by introducing three levels of job experience as an additional factor: less than 1 year experience, 1 to 5 years experience, and more than 5 years experience. Such a design would allow for (1) assessment of the effects of sleep deprivation, (2) assessment of the effects of job experience, and (3) an assessment of a possible *interaction* between the two. For example, sleep deprivation may be of less importance for experienced than for beginning air controllers. The potential for judging interactions makes the factorial design a very useful one.

Repeated Measures Design

This design is used when the same subjects are studied at different times or under different conditions. In the air controller example, it would have been possible to study the same subjects under the different conditions of sleep deprivation.

The repeated measures design is very powerful or sensitive as it permits the removal of individual differences in gauging the effects of the independent variable. In the statistical calculation, subjects becomes a second factor and subject-by-treatment interaction serves as the error term for assessing chance variability.

Analysis of Covariance

This technique takes into account scores on some other variable believed to effect the action of the independent variable. Instead of introducing amount of experience as a second factor (independent variable) in our treatment of the groups, we could statistically control for it by adding years of experience for each subject into our calculations. It would not be manipulated as an independent variable, but its effect could be taken into account. Analysis of covariance in this example would tell us the effects of sleep deprivation, after making an adjustment for job experience.

Multivariate Designs

In ANOVA, only one dependent variable is used per analysis. There are also *multivariate* procedures in which the relationship between two or more dependent variables enters into the statistical calculation. These are complex and generally done by computer. While relatively easy to generate because the computer does the work, their interpretation requires a well-grounded understanding of statistical concepts and inference.

These are only a few of the important variations of the ANOVA technique. They are beyond the scope of an introductory course in research methods. Many colleges and universities teach advanced statistics courses devoted entirely to analysis of variance. Additional information on ANOVA can be found in the books listed at the conclusion of this chapter.

A Statistical Test for Categorical Data: Chi-Square

A university class in research methods undertook a series of observational studies. One study was designed to see whether men or women bicyclists were more likely to ignore a stop sign at a major intersection when leaving the college campus. The researchers thought that there might be a sex difference, but were not sure which direction it would take. They made 30-minute observations during weekday afternoons over a 2-week period. The observations produced categorical data. Each cyclist was classified as having stopped or not stopped at the sign. Since the *t* test could not be used with categorical data like these, the researchers chose to use a Chi-square test. (Chi (χ) is a Greek letter pronounced *ki*, as in *kite*.)

The Chi-square statistic is used to test whether the actual results (such as the bicycle observations) differ reliably from what could be expected by chance. The two key sets of figures in this test are the *obtained values* (O) and the *expected values* (E). The *obtained values* (O) are the raw data arranged in the appropriate cells of a *contingency table* with the totals in the margins (see Box 18-4). This arrangement is called a contingency table because being in cell A is contingent in this case on being male and having stopped at the sign.

The *expected values* (E) are those that would occur due to chance alone. The marginal totals, the characteristics of the sample as a whole, are used to calculate the E values for each cell in the contingency table. For example, in the bicycle study, out of the entire sample of people, 192 stopped at the sign, which represents 192/301 of the sample. Furthermore, 91 of the people in the sample were male. Therefore, based on the characteristics of the entire sample, if no other factors were influencing behavior, we would expect 192/301 of the 91 males to have stopped at the sign. This gives us our E value of 58.05. This is the rationale for the calculation of the expected values. Box 18-4 shows a more simple procedure for calculating the E values.

After the E values are calculated, the Chi-square statistic is computed. The formula for the Chi-square and a computational example using the bicycle observations are shown in Box 18-4.

Interpretation of the Chi-square follows the same general principles as were used in the *t* test. Table A-2 in Appendix A is used to determine whether the Chi-square is statistically significant at the .05 or .01 level. When the computed value is larger than the figures shown in the table under the appropriate degrees of freedom, we can conclude that the difference is reliable.

The Chi-square test may be used for any number of rows and columns. However, when there are more than four rows or four columns, interpretation of the results becomes awkward. However, there is no need to have the same number of rows and columns.

> Example: The Chi-square can be used with categorical data in each of the following forms.

Contingency table patterns.

BOX 18-4. Calculation of Chi-square for Bicycle Observations

Step 1. Arrange the obtained data in the form of a *contingency table*. For the bicycle study, this is a table with two columns and two rows (2 × 2 table). Each cell shows the number of individuals meeting the conditions described in the margins—i.e., 66 males stopped at the sign. As a convention, the individual cells of the table are lettered.

Step 2. Add up the totals for each row (A + B, C + D) and for each column (A + C, B + D). Note: rows are horizontal, columns vertical.

	Response to stop sign		
	Stop	*No stop*	
Male	A 66	B 25	91 = 66 + 25
Sex			
Female	C 126	D 84	210
	66 + 126 = 192	109	301 = 91 + 210
			check: 192 + 109 = 301

Step 3. Compute the expected frequencies (E). This is done by multiplying each column total by each row total and dividing by the grand total (301).

Cell A $\dfrac{192 \times 91}{301} = 58.05$

Cell B $\dfrac{109 \times 91}{301} = 32.95$

Cell C $\dfrac{192 \times 210}{301} = 133.95$

Cell D $\dfrac{109 \times 210}{301} = 76.05$

As a check, the value of E must also add up to the marginal totals.

Step 4. For each cell, subtract the expected value (E) from the observed value (O), square this figure, and divide by E. Sum the resulting numbers.

Formula: $\chi^2 = \Sigma \dfrac{(O - E)^2}{E}$

Cell A $\dfrac{(66 - 58.05)^2}{58.05} = \dfrac{(7.95)^2}{58.05} = 1.09$

Cell B $\dfrac{(25 - 32.95)^2}{32.95} = \dfrac{(7.95)^2}{32.95} = 1.92$

Cell C $\dfrac{(126 - 133.95)^2}{133.95} = \dfrac{(7.95)^2}{133.95} = .47$

Cell D $\dfrac{(84 - 76.05)^2}{76.05} = \dfrac{(7.95)^2}{76.05} = .83$

$\chi^2 = 1.09 + 1.92 + .47 + .83 = 4.31$

Step 5. Compute the degrees of freedom for the contingency table. Formula for degrees of freedom for the Chi-square:

df = (number of rows − 1) (number of columns − 1)

$df = (2 - 1)(2 - 1) = 1$

Step 6. To find the significance of the Chi-square, consult Table A-2 in Appendix A. Check the left-hand column under the appropriate degrees of freedom ($df = 1$) and then move to the right to the appropriate probability level. Table A-2 shows that with one degree of freedom, a Chi-square of 3.84 or greater is required to reject the null hypothesis at the .05 level. Since the Chi-square for the bicycle observations is larger than this, we can conclude that there was a reliable sex difference in stopping at this intersection. The direction of the difference can be seen in the contingency table used in Step 2 above. This shows that a higher percentage of men than women respected the stop sign at this intersection.

The Chi-square becomes unreliable when the *expected* frequencies (*E*) are very small (i.e., less than 5). It should never be used when an expected frequency is 0. Note that this applies only to *E* rather than to the observed frequencies (*O*), which can be any size, including zero.

Note to the reader: This is another good place to stop and review this material.

Correlation

The statistical tests mentioned thus far have dealt with differences between groups either by testing differences between means (*t* test and ANOVA), or by comparing observed with expected frequencies of occurrence (Chi-square). Another issue of concern to the researcher is *correlation*. This refers to an association between two sets of scores. For example, is there a relationship between years in college and a person's income at middle age? One way to answer this question is to plot the data on a graph in the form of a scattergram. The vertical axis in Figure 18-4 shows income and the horizontal axis shows years in college.

The data from a group of 20 individuals have been plotted on this graph. The pattern of dots shows a fairly clear trend for income to rise with years in college. This is a *positive relationship,* since an increase in one variable is accompanied by an increase in the other. It is also possible for

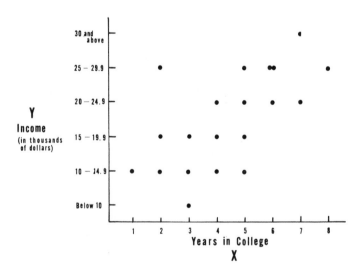

FIG. 18-4. Scattergram of the relationship between years in college and income in middle age (*N* = 20).

two variables to be *negatively correlated;* that is, as one variable increases, the other variable decreases. This is also called an *inverse relationship.* An example of a negative correlation would be that between midsummer temperature and physical activity. As the days become more hot, activity declines. Figure 18-5 shows scattergrams for a positive relationship, a negative relationship, and no relationship between two variables.

A scattergram provides an instant visual picture of the association between two variables. For many purposes, a more precise indication of the degree of relationship is necessary. This calls for the use of a *correlation coefficient.* A correlation coefficient of +1.0 indicates a perfect positive relationship like that shown in the first scattergram in Figure 18-5. A perfect negative relationship, such as that shown in the second scattergram, produces a correlation coefficient of −1.0. The absence of any relationship, such as in the third scattergram, produces a correlation coefficient of 0. The higher the correlation coefficient, either in a positive or a negative direction, the stronger the association between two variables.

Correlation does not prove causation. The fact that two variables are correlated does not mean that one causes the other. In the example of college education and income, it is tempting to assume that going to college produced the higher income during middle age. However, it is likely that people who attended college for several years came from wealthier families in the first place. It is possible that some factor *other* than the two variables being measured may be the cause of the relationship.

The Correlation of Continuous Data: Pearson Product-Moment Coefficient (r)

When both sets of scores to be correlated are continuous, a Pearson product-moment coefficient (*r*) is a widely used statistic. The null hypothesis for a correlation states that there is no relationship between two sets of

FIG. 18-5. Scattergrams produced by positive, negative, and absence of correlation.

scores. If the probability level of the coefficient is less than .05 (or .01, to be more conservative), we can reject the null hypothesis and conclude that the two variables are correlated. The formula and a computational example for r are shown in Box 18-5.

Student	Arithmetic score X	Spelling score Y	X^2	Y^2	XY
Jeanine	8	13	64	169	104
Howard	6	8	36	64	48
Tamara	5	7	25	49	35
Blossom	10	14	100	196	140
Hugh	7	12	49	144	84
Bradford	9	15	81	225	135
Clayton	2	3	4	9	6
Lorraine	3	3	9	9	9

$N = 8$ $\Sigma X = 50$ $\Sigma Y = 75$ $\Sigma X^2 = 368$ $\Sigma Y^2 = 865$ $\Sigma XY = 561$

$(\Sigma X)^2 = (50)^2 = 2500$

$(\Sigma Y)^2 = (75)^2 = 5625$

Computation

Step 1. Sum X scores: $\Sigma X = 50$.

Step 2. Square ΣX: $(\Sigma X)^2 = 2500$.

Step 3. Square each X score. Add together $\Sigma X^2 = 368$.

(Steps 4–6 repeat with Y scores)

Step 4. $\Sigma Y = 75$.

Step 5. $(\Sigma Y)^2 = 5625$.

Step 6. $\Sigma Y^2 = 865$.

Step 7. Multiply each X score by its corresponding Y score. Sum all XY products. $\Sigma XY = 561$.

Step 8. Find number of pairs: $N = 8$.

Step 9. Insert these figures into the formula for r:

$$r = \frac{N\Sigma XY - (\Sigma X)(\Sigma Y)}{\sqrt{[N\Sigma X^2 - (\Sigma X)^2][N\Sigma Y^2 - (\Sigma Y)^2]}}$$

$$r = \frac{8(561) - (50)(75)}{\sqrt{[8(368) - 2500][8(865) - 5625]}} =$$

$$\frac{4488 - 3750}{\sqrt{(2944 - 2500)(6920 - 5625)}} = \frac{738}{\sqrt{(444)(1295)}} =$$

$$\frac{738}{\sqrt{574,980}} = \frac{738}{758.27} = .97$$

Step 10. Compute the degrees of freedom. The formula for degrees of freedom for r is: $df = N - 2$, where N is the number of pairs. $df = 8 - 2 = 6$.

Step 11. Interpreting the significance of r. Consult Table A-3 in Appendix A. First, look down the vertical column to $df = 6$; then move to the right, to the column indicating the .05 level of confidence. This table indicates that when $df = 6$, a coefficient must be at least .707 to be statistically significant at the .05 level. Incidentally, this value of .707 holds for both positive and negative coefficients. The sign of the coefficient is unimportant in testing whether or not it is statistically significant. The sign *is* important in determining the direction of the relationship. Since the obtained coefficient in this example is .97, the relationship is reliable and the null hypothesis can be rejected. The sign of the coefficient (+) indicates that there is a positive association between the two variables; that is, as one increases, the other also increases.

BOX 18-5. Computation of the Pearson Product-Moment
              Coefficient (*r*)

A researcher tested the relationship between arithmetic and spelling test scores among a group of sixth graders. The hypothesis tested was that students who do well in arithmetic are also good spellers (a positive correlation). The highest possible arithmetic score was 10, and the highest possible spelling score was 20.

Correlating Ranked Data: Spearman Rank-order Coefficient (rho)

The Pearson coefficient (*r*) is strongly influenced by extreme scores. If one person in the previous example had an income of $1 million a year, perhaps from a trust fund, this would have seriously distorted the correlation in the direction of that single case. When the data are not normally distributed, one possiblity is to use ranks instead of actual scores. The person with the highest income receives a rank of 1, the person with the next highest income receives a 2, and so on. This automatically reduces the influence of extreme scores. Two people with the same income would receive tied ranks. To rank tied scores, add together the ranks that would be occupied by these individuals and divide by the number of individuals obtaining the score.

Example

Income	Rank
$50,000	1
$48,000	2
$46,000	3.5
$46,000	3.5
$45,000	5
$41,000	7
$41,000	7
$41,000	7
$40,000	9
. . . .	. .

The two individuals earning $46,000 occupied the third and fourth positions. Their ranks are computed by summing $3 + 4 = 7$ and dividing by 2 (number of individuals tied for that rank) = the tied rank score of 3.5. Remember that when you assign tied ranks to two individuals, you use up two ranks in the series. In the example above, the two individuals earning $46,000 both received ranks of 3.5, and the next person in the series receives a rank of 5. The three individuals earning $41,000 are tied for the sixth, seventh, and eighth places, respectively. To compute their tied rank scores, add all three ranks together and divide by the number of individuals ($6 + 7 + 8 = 21 \div 3 = 7$). Each of the three individuals earning $41,000 receives a tied rank score of 7 (a combination of ranks 6, 7, and 8). Therefore, the next individual receives a rank of 9.

When individuals are assigned a rank on each of the two measures, a Spearman rank-order coefficient *(rho)* is used to compute the correlation. The formula and computation of *(rho)* are shown in Box 18-6. The *(rho)* coefficient is most useful when there is a small number of cases. It would be very time consuming to rank more than 30 scores.

Correlating a Continuous Variable with a Ranked Variable

If one of the variables is continuous and the other is ranked, it is easy to transform the continuous scores into ranks and use *rho*. Simply rank the continuous scores from highest to lowest and then use the ranks to compute *rho*.

Other Measures of Correlation

Still other correlation coefficients are useful under special circumstances. When one variable has been artificially split into two categories (e.g., between people of age 30 and over and those under 30) and the other is in the form of a continuous distribution (e.g., a score on an attitude scale), the Biserial coefficient (r_b) may be used. When both variables have been artificially split into two categories, the Tetrachoric coefficient (r_t) or the Contingency coefficient (C) can be used. Formulas and methods for computing these coefficients can be found in most statistical textbooks. However, while these coefficients are appropriate under special circumstances, the Pearson r is the most stable and reliable measure of correlation and should be used wherever possible.

Limitations of This Chapter

This chapter is intended only as an introduction to a few basic techniques. Of necessity, many other useful statistical tests have been omitted. The

---

BOX 18-6. Computation of the Spearman Rank-order Coefficient (rho): Rankings by the Team Coach of the Running Skill of Team Members Correlated with their Performance in a Track Meet

Runner	Coach's ranking before race X	Order of finish in race Y	d	d^2
MacClean	1	4	3	9
Smolenski	2	6	4	16
Jones	3.5	7	3.5	12.25
Jackson	3.5	1	2.5	6.25
Heinz	5	2	3	9
Baker	6	5	1	1
Harris	7	3	4	16

$$\Sigma d^2 = 69.50$$

Before beginning the computation, check to see that all ranking has been done correctly.

Computation

Step 1. Compute the difference (d) between the coach's rankings and the actual performance for each individual. You do not need to pay attention to plus or minus signs, since the numbers will be squared.

Step 2. Square each difference and sum them: $\Sigma d^2 = 69.50$.

Step 3. Find number of pairs: $N = 7$.

Step 4. Enter these figures in the formula: $rho = 1 - \dfrac{6\Sigma d^2}{N(N^2 - 1)}$

$$rho = 1 - \frac{6(69.50)}{7(49 - 1)} = 1 - \frac{417}{336} = 1 - 1.24 = -.24$$

Step 5. Evaluting *rho*. Table A-4 in Appendix A shows the significance levels for *rho*. First, look in the left-hand column under N. Note that this column uses the number of pairs (N) rather than degrees of freedom. This table shows that with an N of 7, a *rho* of .714 or greater (+ or −) is required for significance at the .05 level. Because the obtained coefficient in this example was −.24, we can accept the null hypothesis and conclude that there was no reliable relationship between the coach's ranking and the runner's performance in the race.

---

student who would like to know more about statistical analysis should consult a textbook in the area. There are books available for the beginner as well as for advanced students.

At this point, we will repeat something said at the beginning of this chapter: Do not be concerned if you have not understood everything about inferential statistics. The origin of many statistical tests goes far beyond what is needed to use them in practice. Once you start working with actual data, the meaning of the tests, as well as their limitations, will become more clear.

BOX 18-7. Common Statistical Notations

X	An individual score.
Y	An individual score (used for a second set of scores).
N	Number of scores.
Σ	Sum of the term that follows.
ΣX	Sum of all the individual scores.
ΣX^2	Sum of squares. Each score is individually squared and then all the squared scores are added together.
$(\Sigma X)^2$	Sum squared. First, the individual scores are added together; then, this total is squared.
$\overline{X}$	Arithmetic average (mean) of the X scores.
$\overline{Y}$	Arithmetic average (mean) of the Y scores.
SD	Standard deviation, a measure of variability or dispersion, often noted as σ.
t	Test for the difference between two sets of scores with continuous distributions.
ANOVA	Analysis of Variance
χ^2	Test for determining the difference between two sets of categorical scores.
ρ	Probability that the results of a statistical test are due to chance.
$>$	Greater than.
$<$	Less than.
df	degrees of freedom.
r	Pearson product-moment coefficient; a measure of correlation for continuous data.
rho	Spearman rank-order coefficient; a measure of correlation for ranked data.
r_b	Biserial coefficient.
r_t	Tetrachoric coefficient.
C	Contingency coefficient.

BOX 18-8. Steps in the Selection of Appropriate Statistical Tests Mentioned in Text

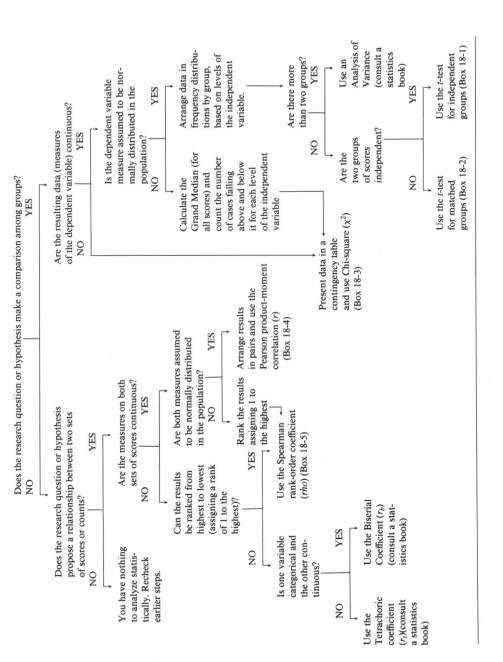

241

Summary

A *t* test or ANOVA is used when for testing the significance of differences between means. If you are looking at differences between groups where the measures are categorical, such as observed frequencies or counts, use Chi square.

Correlation answers a different type of question. It indicates the *degree* of a relationship between two sets of scores. A correlation may be either positive or negative.

Box 18-7 lists all of the statistical notations and definitions used in these chapters. Box 18-8 can be used as a guide in selecting an appropriate statistical test for your data.

Reference

Anthony K. (1977). On cigarette smoking—Where do you stand? *GASP Educational Foundation News, 11,* p. 3.

Further Reading

Bruning, J. L., & Kintz, B. L. (1977). *Computational handbook of statistics* (2nd ed.). Glenview, IL: Scott, Foresman.

Guilford, J. P., & Fruchter, B. (1978). *Fundamental statistics in psychology and education* (6th ed.). New York: McGraw-Hill.

Lovejoy, E. P. (1975). *Statistics for math haters.* New York: Harper & Row.

Runyon, R. P., & Haber, A. (1984). *Fundamentals of behavioral statistics* (5th ed.). Reading, MA: Addison-Wesley.

Sample Problems

1. Describe in words the meaning of each of the following statistical expressions.

$t = 2.53$

$N = 20$

$\sigma = 1.9$

$r = .41\ (p < .01)$

$r = .30\ (p < .05)$

$r = .15\ (p > .10)$

$t = 2.53,\ df = 18,\ p < .05$

2. A college instructor wants to see if there is a difference in the final grade between students who participate frequently in class and those who never say a word. In a class of 26 students, the instructor identified 6 participants and 7 nonparticipants. Below is a list of the final grades of these students (A = 4, F = 0). Apply a *t* test for independent measures to see if there is a significant difference between the final grades of high and low participants.

Final Grade (A = 4, F = 0)

High Participants N = 6	Non-participators N = 7
4	4
4	3
3	3
3	2
3	2
1	1
	1

3. Use a *t* test for *dependent measures* to see if subjects in an attitude change experiment became more favorable to space exploration after seeing a NASA film.

| | Attitude scale score | |
	Before film	After film
Eva B.	62	64
Matt B.	71	75
Gretchen H.	68	67
Cindy H.	51	52
Roger M.	58	61
Margy S.	84	85

4. Is there a correlation between age and speed on a running test? First compute a Spearman rank-order coefficient for the following data using the formula in Box 18-6 and then compute a Pearson product-moment coefficient using the formula in Box 18-5. After you have done this, check the appropriate significance tables in Appendix A to find out whether these coefficients are statistically significant.

Age (years)	Running speed (in seconds)
12	20
13	18
13	19
14	14
15	17
16	16
16	13
16	15

Answers to Problems

2. $t = 1.16$, $df = 11$, not significant
3. $t = 2.33$, $df = 5$, not significant
4. Spearman *rho* $= -.744$, $df = 7$, significant at the .05 level (but not at .01)
   Pearson $r = -.785$, $df = 6$, significant at the .05 level (but not at .01)

19 Calculators and Computers

Calculators

Many makes and models of hand calculators are available. Some are as expensive as a microcomputer and can do almost as much. Others are inexpensive models that can perform simple arithmetic operations but not much else. In between are many low- and moderate-priced calculators that will perform most of the major operations needed for statistical tests. The size of a keyboard doesn't necessarily reflect its potential utility. For most behavioral problems, there will be no need to transform gallons into liters or compute the reciprocals of cosines. Logarithms can more efficiently be looked up in statistical textbooks on those rare occasions when they are needed in behavioral research than retrieved on a calculator. We have not found programmable calculators to be especially useful to beginning researchers. At the point when students are ready to write programs, they might be better served by a computer that will open many more avenues for analysis than are available with a hand calculator.

Some features increase the usefulness of a hand calculator. These features are identified by symbols or terms found on particular keys or just above. When a symbol is written above rather than on a key, a separate function button (F) must be pressed first. Symbols vary among different makes or models even when the operations they perform are similar.

Box 19-1 lists useful keys that reflect our experiences with the computational needs of beginning researchers. For those whose work becomes highly specialized, certain keys such as mean ($\bar{x}$) or percentage (%) may

244

BOX 19-1. Helpful Features in Calculators

STO or M	Memory storage. Used for placing items into memory to make them available in subsequent calculation. Several memories are better than one. Essential.
RCL	Memory recall—recalls items placed into memory. Essential.
x^2	Squares each number. Essential.
$\sqrt{x}$	Square root key. Essential.
SS, Σx^2, or $\Sigma+$	Sum of squares. Key used for squaring numbers individually and then summing them. Very useful.
σ, s, or S.DEV	Standard deviation. Very useful.
r or corr	Correlation coefficient or Pearson r. Very useful.
t or t_{ind}	t ratio for independent scores. Very useful.
t_{dep}	t ratio for dependent (correlated) scores. Occasionally useful.
χ^2	Chi-square. Occasionally useful.
F	F ratio—used in analysis of variance. Occasionally useful.
Var or s^2	Variance or square of the standard deviation. Occasionally useful.

increase efficiency, even though these operations can be performed using other keys with little extra effort. The keyboard symbols may vary slightly according to make or model.

Computers

The rapid pace of development in computer technology and software (programs) makes it impossible to provide an up-to-date survey of available aids. However, we can offer a few general guidelines for computer use.

Finding a Computer

Nearly all universities and colleges, and many other institutions and organizations, such as school districts and corporations, own or have access to a *mainframe computer*. These are large computers (e.g., IBM, Burroughs, Siemans, Vax) that can process extensive quantities of data in a very short period of time. Instead of a mainframe, your organization may provide access to *microcomputers*—smaller desktop versions such as the Apple, IBM/PC, TRS-80, and other personal computers. The microcomputer cannot handle as much data as the main frame, but is often sufficient for a small research project. If you are doing survey research with hundreds of respondents, you will probably need to use a mainframe computer for data analysis.

If you are considering the purchase of a personal computer, read through some of the inexpensive paperback books that offer useful and helpful hints *before* you spend your money. Also talk with friends about their computers. Beware of fancy packaging. The best-looking computer may not be the one you need. Think through as clearly as possible how you will be using it. For example, there are two types of printers (the typewriter aspect)—letter quality and dot matrix. Letter-quality print is similar to that of a typewriter. A dot-matrix printer constructs the letters out of tiny dots. A letter-quality printer gives text that is more readable and pleasing to the eye than dot matrix. However, dot-matrix printers tend to be less expensive, and you can print graphics—pictures. Also, the print styles (the shape and size of letters) is practically infinite. If you intend to use a letter-quality printer because you will be working with written text, it will be of no value to buy a computer for which there are marvelous graphics programs—because you won't be able to print any of them. The point is that it is a good idea to think through as clearly as possible what you want to do with your computer. See what programs are available for your purposes. Then select the computer that will run the desirable programs.

A major consideration in purchasing a computer is the availability of support, that is, having someone to contact whose job it is to help you learn how to use your computer. Try to purchase your computer close to home so your daily telephone calls for assistance will not result in an astronomical bill. No matter how "user friendly" your computer is, or how well-written the user's manual, you will need advice and occasional encouragement while getting used to your machine. Additional sources of information and support are specialized magazines and user groups. In many communities, there are informal organizations of computer owners. When you are considering purchase, ask the salesperson for names of people involved in the local users group, and don't hesitate to contact them. Members of these groups are generally very willing to share experiences and offer advice.

Finding a Program for Data Analysis

For a Mainframe Computer

Organizations that invest in mainframe computers are likely to have consultants available to assist potential users. Take full advantage of resource people and materials, such as introductory training packages or published guides, in educating yourself about available programs. There are special programs available for statistical analysis. You will not need to write your own computer programs. Some commonly used programs for analyzing behavioral data are SPSS-X (Statistical Package for the Social Sciences), Minitab, BMDP, and SAS (Statistical Analysis System). Each of these has a published manual describing what the program does and how to use it Minitab even has a tutorial in the computer program itself.

For Microcomputers

If you have access to a personal computer, you will be faced with a multitude of programs. Look for the key term, *statistical analysis* in the program title. Database management and spreadsheet programs might help you organize information, but will be limited with regard to the degree of statistical analysis available. These programs have been designed for business purposes. Instead, look for statistical packages available for your brand of computer. A much easier way to approach the problem is to find other behavioral researchers who have used your computer and ask them what programs are available. Also, salespeople in computer software stores might be able to help you.

Analyzing Your Data

Now that you have access to a computer and have a program to do your analysis, the first step is to read through the program and be certain you understand all the terms used. You will need to decide on short names for all of your variables. After you have a general picture of how the program works, run a dummy study. Make up some data with easy numbers for a few cases, and then run it. It won't cost much if you are using the mainframe, and it is good way to check yourself out, and to find out exactly what the program will do with your data. A trial run on either the mainframe or a microcomputer will save you great amounts of time and effort in avoiding problems that will be more difficult to trace in your actual data. You will be anxious to plunge ahead with the real thing, but DON'T DO IT. First run your dummy study. Otherwise you may end up correlating the responses to question 14 with the item numbers. Unless you know exactly what each number on the computer output means, you run a terrible risk of producing uninterpretable results and drawing incorrect conclusions.

Another reason for running a dummy study is that it will assist you in designing your data collection to facilitate computer analysis. You will then be able to design your study in such a way as to make it easier to code the information and enter it into the computer record.

Avoid Blind Analysis

The computer has greatly extended the range of statistical techniques available to researchers. The computer can perform operations in a matter of seconds or minutes that would take hours or days to analyze with a hand calculator. The positive effect of this has been to broaden the range of methods of data analysis available, but the new freedom of choice brings the risk of asking the computer to perform analyses that the researcher does not understand. It is unwise to take a complicated printout of data to a statistical consultant in the hope that he or she can make sense of it. The consultant may be familiar with the statistical tests but not the nature or limitations of the data being analyzed.

As a general rule, a researcher should not travel too far beyond the bound of personal understanding in doing a statistical analysis. The problem was less serious with hand calculation where a researcher could gain familiarity with a technique in the course of doing the computations. Today, a computer does everything so quickly that there is little time for understanding to develop. You should read about a statistical method before asking the computer to perform it. This doesn't mean that you have to understand the derivation of all the formulas in order to apply a statistical test. What is needed is a general understanding of the nature of the test and the assumptions behind it, what it can and cannot do, and the meaning of key concepts and terms. This understanding can be gained from reading some of the statistical textbooks listed in Further Readings at the conclusion of Chapter 18.

Summary

For data analysis, select a calculator that has some memory capacity and keys for calculating square roots and for squaring numbers. Having the capacity to accumulate the sums of the squares is very useful.

Two general types of computers are mainframe and microcomputers. If your institution has a mainframe computer, it is likely that consultants are available to help you. Commonly used data analysis programs are SPSS-X, Minitab, BMDP, and SAS.

Desktop microcomputers are useful for analyzing data from small- to moderate-size studies. If you decide to purchase a computer, consult other users and read books to familiarize yourself with what is available. Carefully think through your research needs. Find out what programs exist to meet those needs, and then buy the computer that will run them. Letter-quality printers are preferable for written work, but dot-matrix printers may be acceptable, are generally less expensive, and have graphic capabilities.

Run a small dummy set of data in order to understand exactly how a program works. A trial run will assist you in setting up your data collection and coding to facilitate computer analysis.

Avoid blind analysis. Be knowledgeable about the specific statistical techniques you are using.

Further Reading

Bear, J. (1983). *Computer wimp,* Berkeley, CA: Ten Speed Press.
Kahn, E., & Seiter, C. (1985). *The skeptical consumer's guide to used computers.* Berkeley, CA: Ten Speed Press.
Norusis, M. J. (1983). *SPSS^x Introductory statistics guide.* New York: McGraw-Hill.

20   Writing the Report

Set aside a special time for writing and editing. Don't expect to complete the analysis of your data and hand in the final report a few days later. Several drafts will probably be required. It is important to get feedback from other people. Early drafts should be labeled as preliminary and dated.

There are two general classes of reports. One is an article for a scientific journal and the other is a technical report written for a specific client or audience. The journal format is easier to use for hypothesis-testing studies. Opinion or attitude surveys and evaluation studies are more easily written in technical report form. The rules for the form of a scientific article are quite precise. Technical reports can be much more varied in style and order of presentation. The decision regarding the form of data presentation will depend on the type of dissemination you want. If you desire to write articles for ohter researchers, you will have to learn journal style.

Article for a Scientific Journal

Many scientific periodicals require that contributors follow a specific style. This is usually mentioned in the inside front cover under the heading "Instructions to contributors." When you write for a specific journal, be sure to check these instructions before beginning the report. Another way to find out what a periodical wants is to glance through recent issues. If you follow the style used by present contributors, you will probably be correct. The American Psychological Association (APA) publishes a style manual for its journals. This manual can be ordered directly from the American Psychological Association, 1200 17th Street N.W., Washington, D.C. 20036. An example of an article written according to APA style is presented in Appendix B. This style is also used in related fields, such as education. However, journals in sociology and anthropology follow a different format.

The typical layout of a journal article includes the following sections: abstract, introduction, method, results, discussion, and references. Box 20-1 contains a checklist of items for a scientific article.

Abstract

Because this is all of the report that most people are likely to read, it is very important that the abstract be clear, concise, and accurate. Its length will depend on the publication or distribution. The abstract of an article for a scientific journal should not exceed 150 words. Someone reading an abstract should be able to see at a glance the area covered by the study and the main findings. The reader who wants more information should consult the body of the report. In practice, the abstract is written after the rest of the report is completed.

Introduction

The introduction begins with a statement of the problem, its theoretical and practical significance, and its place in a larger body of knowledge. The introduction includes a review of related studies and a list of specific hypotheses or predictions.

Method

This section describes specifically what was done. The interested reader should be able to repeat your study from the account provided here. Included should be a description of the apparatus, tests, or observation sheets, the subjects and how they were selected, the interviewers and their training, a description of the physical setting in which the data were collected, instructions to the subjects, and mention of any special problems that arose. Describe any pilot tests or reliability checks made on the procedure or equipment.

Results

This is the place for factual information about what was found. Opinions and interpretations are reserved for the discussion. Begin the section with the findings most relevant to the hypothesis or problem. Then present secondary or related findings. The order of presenting results should follow the order of the hypotheses in the introduction. Don't skip from hypothesis 1 to 4 and then back to 2. Let the reader see how each hypothesis fared before going on to the next.

Do not overwhelm the reader with raw data, particularly if you are also presenting summary statistics such as percentages, averages, and probabilities. Generally, you will be able to present the necessary summary data in the text or in tables.

Tables and Figures

If they are needed, most tables and figures will be presented in the Results section. *Tables* refer to tabular information that can be typeset, such as lists of terms or columns of numbers or percentages. *Figures* are charts, graphs, drawings, photographs, or any other type of pictorial information. Figures are more time-consuming and expensive to prepare and reproduce than either text or tables. Each table and figure must have a numbered descriptive title, for example, "Figure 1. Creativity Scores by Respondent Age." The sample report in Appendix B contains an example of a table. Figures (and tables) do not speak for themselves. Many readers automatically skip them. Therefore, it is essential to provide a written description as well.

If you are considering tables and figures, use the following questions adapted from the Publication Manual of the American Psychological Association (1983).

Is the table necessary?
Does every column have a column heading?
Is it simple, clean, and free of extraneous detail?
Is it easy to understand—is its purpose readily apparent?
Are the titles brief but explanatory?
Is the table or figure referred to in the text?
Does the text include an indication of placement for each table and figure?

Figures submitted for publication need to be photographed on a glossy print, identified on the back lightly in pencil, and accompanied by the numbered caption typed on a separate page.

Discussion

This is your opportunity to interpret the findings, discuss their significance, and suggest directions for future research. There is no need to repeat everything that was said in the results. Instead, describe how your findings fit existing theories and other research in the field. What general conclusions can you draw? Based on what you have learned, what issues should be investigated next? What are some of the flaws and limitations of the study? If you were to repeat the study, what would you change?

References

This is a list of materials cited in the body of the report. It does *not* include relevant work not specifically mentioned. A long list of references is no mark of scholarship if they have come from secondary sources (accounts about other people's work) and you have not read the original articles. Reference lists should be triple checked. It is frustrating to try to locate an article that is supposed to be in Volume 12 and find that it is in Volume 21, or that a book author's name is Hemminski rather than Chemminski. The specific form for the references will be determined by the periodical or audience for whom you are writing. The American Psychological Association (APA) style manual requires the following form for citing articles.

Example of an article citation:

Smith, R. S., & Jones, D. A. (1984). Children's response to colored glasses. *Journal of Child Development, 30,* 14–26.

Example of a book citation:

Brown, O. (1979). *Organizational behavior.* New York: Smith Publications.

The American Sociological Association (ASA) requires a different reference style for its major research journal, the *American Sociological Review.*

Example of ASA style for an article citation:

Robinson, R. A. and Philip Agisism
  1951 "Making mail surveys more reliable," Journal of Marketing 15:415–24.

For a book citation:

Ornstein, M. D.
  1976 Entry into the American Labor Force. New York: Academic Press.

BOX 20-1. Checklist for Writing a Scientific Article

Title page
  Title summarizes the main idea of paper.
  Name and institutional affiliation of author(s).
  Running head—abbreviated title no more than 50 characters.
  Acknowledgments of assistance and research support.

Abstract
  Specify subject characteristics (number, age, sex, etc.).
  One or two sentences describing the problem, the method, and findings.

Introduction
   Opening paragraph tells what study is about, and introduces the problem.
   Subsequent paragraphs describe background material and previous studies.
   Specify hypotheses or questions underlying the research, and present rationale
      for each.

Method
   Subjects
      Number and method of selection, characteristics (age, sex, etc.), procedures for
         handling refusals, or nonreturns.
   Apparatus (or *materials*)
      Description of observation sheets, tests, scales, or measuring devices.
      Methods of development if novel instruments were employed.
      Coding and scoring procedures.
   Procedure
      Experimenters/observers/interviewers—relevant characteristics, training.
      Reliability of procedures and instruments.
      Setting—location and relevant environmental characteristics (lighting, sound,
         temperature, etc.)
      Instructions to subjects/respondents.
      Duration and number of sessions
      Control features such as randomization or counterbalancing.

Results
   Begin with most relevant findings.
   Describe results in quantitative way (numerical) and provide necessary descrip-
      tive statistics (means, standard deviations, contingency tables, etc.) along with
      the inferential statistics.
   Make a summary statement about these results.
   Properly label all tables and figures.
   Tell the reader what to look for in tables or figures.
   Describe qualitative findings that are pertinent and important.

Discussion
   State whether hypotheses were supported or rejected, or address questions raised
      in the introduction.
   Discuss similarities and differences between current findings and earlier ones.
   Describe the implications of the findings.
   Describe ways of improving the research, unanswered questions, new questions
      raised, and directions for future research.

References
   List all citations that appear in the text.

Technical Reports

Often a study is written for a specific client, such as an organization, firm,
or public agency that sponsored the study. It may depart from the scientific

journal format. Some clients want everything included, others want only brief accounts of the major findings. Don't hesitate to check the form, style, and length used by others who have written similar reports. Consider this part of the literature review. You won't need to follow the style used by others exactly, but it is important to known how they have presented their work. Two widely used style manuals are *The Chicago Manual of Style* (University of Chicago, 1982) and *The U.S. Government Printing Office Style Manual.* An example of a technical report can be found in Appendix C.

The length of the report depends largely on the wishes of the sponsor and the projected audience. The decision involves a compromise between presenting sufficient information so that the findings and basis for the recommendations are clear but not given in so much detail that people will be discouraged from reading the document. A frequently used way of getting the point across, while providing sufficient backup information, is to begin with an *executive summary*. An executive summary is as brief as possible, but covers all of the necessary information—the problem, method, results, and conclusions.

Photographs and drawings can be used to liven up a technical report. A study of housing needs of the elderly might include pictures of senior citizens and various housing options. Large organizations such as government agencies or corporations that commission numerous printed docu-

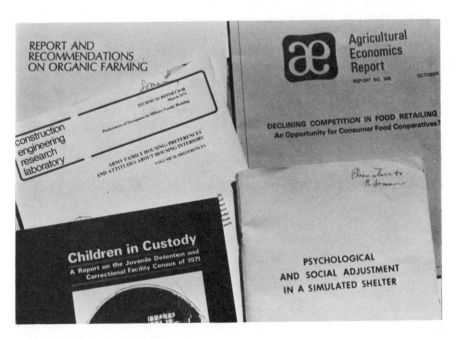

Some examples of technical reports.

ments may require a specific format and style for all technical reports. The report may use a standard cover displaying the corporate logo and a statement of endorsement by an executive officer. Advance approval may be necessary before a report is officially released. Prior to writing a technical report for a sponsor, check in advance about approval policies.

Appendix

A technical report is likely to conclude with an appendix section. This is the place for all supplementary materials not included in the main body of the report. Appendices are arranged in sequence with letters (e.g., Appendix A, Appendix B, etc.). The appendix contains material that is not essential for understanding the report. It will be used most often by readers with a special interest in the topic who want detailed information. Typical items considered for inclusion in the appendix are:

1. Score sheets, questionnaires, or observational sheets used in the study. An exception would be instruments that are commonly used and widely available. These can be omitted.
2. Detailed tables and charts primarily for reference purposes. Tables and figures necessary for the reader's understanding should be placed in the results section.
3. Lists of technical terms. For a general audience, technical terms should also be defined as they occur in the text.
4. Other relevant documents not essential to the reader's comprehension of the report. These might include the sign-up sheet for recruiting subjects, interviewer instructions, instructions for coding interview data, the follow-up letter to respondents who did not reply, etc.

Helpful Hints

Avoid plagiarism. Place quotation marks around any material that is quoted verbatim. Omit quotation marks with material that is paraphrased (expressed in your own words rather than the author's), but be sure to mention the author's name.

Avoid footnotes wherever possible. Footnotes break the continuity of a passage, and many readers will ignore them. Long footnotes that contain detailed explanations are rarely appropriate. The information should be included in the body of the report or omitted.

Double check all the tables for misprints. See that the percentage columns add up to 100. Check that the graphs and figures are titled and inserted in their correct locations. Also, check to see that the vertical and horizontal axes of graphs are labeled correctly. Double check the names of people cited in the literature review and triple check the reference list at the end of the report.

Be sure to show a draft of your report to other people before the final version is typed. Discussing it with people not directly involved with the issue may provide fresh ideas.

Further Reading

American Psychological Association. (1983). *Publication manual of the American Psychological Association* (3rd ed.). Washington, DC: Author.

Day, R. (1983). *How to write and publish a scientific paper* (2nd ed.) Philadelphia: ISI Press.

Houp, K. W., & Pearsall, T. E. (1980) *Reporting technical information* (4th ed.). New York: Macmillan.

Lannon, J. (1985). *Technical writing* (3rd ed.). Boston: Little Brown,.

Silverman, R. J. (1982). *Getting published in education journals.* Springfield, IL: Charles C. Thomas.

University of Chicago Press. (1982). *The Chicago manual of style* (13th ed., rev.). Chicago: Author.

Zeisel, H. (1968). *Say it with figures* (3rd ed., rev.) New York: Harper & Row.

21 After the Report

Jason Tyburczy, an undergraduate psychology major, studied human-animal interaction in a veterinary hospital waiting room. It was an interesting setting where humans, dogs, cats, birds, and occasional rodents and snakes coexisted in very close quarters. Tyburczy observed pet owners and interviewed them about their level of satisfaction with the visiting area. Having completed the study, he was faced with the question of what to do with the findings. He mailed a copy of the report to the hospital director. No response came back. This lack of spontaneous feedback is fairly typical among recipients of survey results.

Tyburczy next considered various publication outlets. He went to the university library and consulted a reference librarian. He described the study and his ideas about who might be interested in the results. The librarian suggested a number of periodicals. Tyburczy looked at copies to find out which were the most suitable. After some deliberation, the choice narrowed to either a national or a state veterinary journal. The chances of publication seemed better in the state journal so this was the outlet selected.

The report was rewritten in a style appropriate for the periodical and submitted. A few months later, a favorable review was received along with a request for revision. The revised paper was eventually accepted by the journal and appeared in print seven months later (Sommer & Tyburczy, 1978). A copy of the published article was sent to the hospital director and this time a formal letter of thanks was received. Apparently the published article was more impressive than the typed draft report. A year later, the director asked the researcher for a copy of the findings to be used in a proposed renovation of the waiting area. Several additional requests for reprints and further information about the study were also received.

258

Further Research

A good study will probably raise more questions than it answers. What begins as a small investigation can easily mushroom into a larger research program requiring a major commitment of time and effort. Procedures developed in one study may be extended to new classes of problems or people. Or the original sample can be retested using different procedures.

Beginning researchers tend to think in terms of single studies. Experienced researchers think in terms of larger programs in which several related studies are linked together. A research program is economical in time and effort since later studies build on earlier work. A follow-up study is also the opportunity to correct the mistakes of an earlier investigation. There is an old saying among researchers that a first study is *always* flawed. Beginning researchers may not realize this if they read only published articles in which everything seems correct. Many published papers are not first studies but third or fourth attempts to wrestle with a difficult and complex problem. The final version looks methodologically correct because the studies were repeated several times and the manuscript underwent numerous revisions prior to publication.

Journal Review

The review of papers by scientific journals is a time-consuming process. A typical sequence of events is shown in Figure 21-1. For a paper submitted to a behavioral science journal, it is likely that editorial review will take

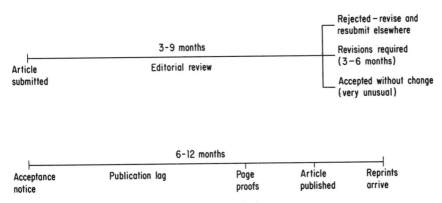

FIG. 21-1. Timetable for publication in a scientific journal.

three to nine months, not including needed revisions, or rejection and resubmission to another journal, which involve extra time. If a paper is accepted, there is likely to be a 12-month delay before it is finally published. This may seem a long wait but it is typical of science. Experienced researchers deal with the numerous delays by conducting several studies that overlap in time. While one study is being reviewed, the researcher is working on others which are in various stages of completion. There are also less time-consuming types of dissemination, such as presenting the results at a professional meeting.

Choosing a Journal

Discuss possible publication outlets with those experienced in the specialty area. Also see where related articles have been published. Then visit a university library and look over the most likely prospects. In some fields there is a wide choice among publication outlets. There are more than a dozen English language journals that carry papers on social psychological topics. The same is true of journals in animal behavior. However, in some specialty areas, such as program evaluation or psycholinguistics, the choice among potential outlets is more limited. Check the table of contents and the editoral policy statement of a journal before considering a submission. Journal titles can be misleading, as in the case of *Psychological Bulletin,* which carries lengthy reviews, while the *Psychological Review* publishes mainly theoretical articles, and *Contemporary Psychology* publishes book reviews, only on request from the editors. Often a beginning researcher is wise to choose a less prestigious journal with a lower rejection rate than a top journal that rejects 9 out of 10 papers.

Some journals have submission fees; others charge authors of accepted papers according to article length. For some journals, these charges may be waived for students and others without support funds, and other journals charge no fees. This information is available in the Instructions to Authors section of the journal, which is often found on an inside cover.

Drafts

It is standard practice to circulate preliminary versions of papers to colleagues for their comments. Their input will be invaluable in preparing the final draft for submission. Date the cover page of a preliminary draft and write at the top "Draft copy—for comments only" or "Draft copy—not to be cited." This will indicate to the recipient that the contents are subject to revision before the final draft is submitted.

Dealing with Rejection

The rejection rate among major behavioral science journals is high. For some journals it can reach 80 to 90 percent of all submitted papers. When a paper has been rejected, it can be revised on the basis of reviewer comments and sent to a second journal for consideration. It is inappropriate to submit an article to more than a single journal at a time. It is worthwhile developing back-up plans for a second or third journal in case the first choice rejects the paper.

Preprints

When an article has been accepted for publication, this can be noted on the cover page of the final version with the notation "In press, Journal of ————." It is legitimate to send copies of an accepted final version (this is called a *preprint*) to interested colleagues who would otherwise wait many months to see it published. Recipients of an "in press" article will be able to cite the article in their own writings. An article formally accepted for publication has virtually the same status and legitimacy as a published article. Note that an article "in press" has been formally accepted for publication, while one "in preparation" is still in the process of review or revision.

Page Proofs

A journal editor may make minor editoral changes on an article accepted for publication. Any changes will be indicated on the page proofs sent to the senior author. This will be the last opportunity to correct typographical or other errors. This is *not* the time to add new material to an article that has already been accepted. Editors discourage this practice and the journal may charge a stiff fee for each line of page proof altered by the author.

Reprints

Most journals do not require an author to purchase reprints. This is an optional matter and depends on the resources available, cost, potential demand, etc. Some journals supply a small number of free reprints to authors. Other journals charge for all reprints. They may also allow authors to photocopy their own articles and distribute photocopies in lieu of buying reprints. Other journals do not allow this practice. Check the policies of the journal in regard to authors' rights to photocopy their own papers. Ordering reprints is generally done on a separate form that accompanies the page proofs.

Application

The goal of a study may not be further research but application, such as using the information to change policies and practices in an organization. When application is the researcher's goal, a scientific article by itself may be insufficient for changing long-established attitudes and procedures. Consider writing an article for a periodical directed specifically to practitioners. Most occupations, professions, and specialties have periodicals concerned with applied issues. Your reference librarian can help you locate appropriate outlets for applied studies. Such outlets will require a more lively writing style and format than is customary for a scientific journal. However, even in an applied article, busy administrators may not see the potential usefulness of the findings. A common response among administrators to research findings is that they are interesting but not directly relevant. There are always reasons why things should be left unchanged. The researcher may have to convince busy administrators of the value and relevance of the findings through personal discussion.

Application is also an opportunity to learn the limitations and shortcomings of a study. The researcher becomes aware of questions that should have been included on the survey but were omitted, or questions that yielded ambiguous answers. This may demonstrate the need for further studies on the topic to pinpoint problems and develop solutions.

Research can be a valuable tool in the change process but by itself will probably not be sufficient to alter long established attitudes and practices. The action research approach pioneered by Kurt Lewin (1946) described in Chapter 1 called for a combination of research and technical assistance in which the clients (potential users of the information) are intimately involved in all stages of gathering, analyzing, and disseminating the information. When people have been personally engaged in a study, they are more likely to understand the methods used in gathering the information and the implications of the findings. However, there is no sure and easy road to applying behavioral science findings. Changing organizations is as difficult (perhaps more so) as changing individuals. Several specialty areas such as organizational development and program evaluation have developed around the issue of organizational change.

News Releases

In addition to reaching other researchers through a scientific article, practitioners through a trade publication, and a client through a technical report, a researcher may also want to bring the findings to the attention of a wider audience, such as readers of local newspapers or the audience of local TV stations. This requires a different format and style than is appropriate for a journal article or technical report. Place the maximum emphasis on the findings and their implications for action, and eliminate any jargon. Even a modest study by a student researcher may rate a column in the local press if the issue is newsworthy. Such articles need not be a dull presentation of the results, boring the reader with endless statistics. A lively writing style can help maintain reader interest in the study without unduly distorting the findings.

Talks at Meetings

Communication intended to be heard rather than read requires a different style. Assuming that you have already done a written report, you should prepare a separate outline for a talk. It is boring to hear someone read a written manuscript word for word. Since a major goal of presenting a talk to a live audience is to obtain feedback, be sure to leave time for questions. A few points well made will be more productive than trying to cram all of your study into a 15-minuted session. Practice your talk on friends or colleagues beforehand. This will enable you to keep within the time limit and find out which statements are unclear.

Audiovisual aids

Use visual aids wherever possible. Showing an audience what the experimental room or observational sheet looked like will have more impact than a verbal description. Things that people can see are likely to be remembered better than things merely talked about. Be sure that your displays or slides are visible and intelligible from all parts of the room. Know how to operate the audiovisual system prior to the session.

Frequent problems at talks include the following: previous session runs over and your talk starts late, faulty or incomplete introduction, microphone improperly adjusted or not working (e.g., emits high-pitched whistles), difficulty in locating proper switches for dimming lights, a slide in wrong order or upside down, other slides under- or overexposed making them took dark or too light, talk exceeds time limit). The best solution to these and other problems is to stage a dress rehearsal before a sympathetic audience. If possible, do it in the actual room where you will be speaking. If this is impossible, arrive early to familiarize yourself with the room and to check out the audiovisual equipment.

Summary

A single study points the way to other studies, leading to a research program involving several linked investigations. The review of papers by scientific journals is a time-consuming process. Potential authors need to exercise care in choosing from among available journals and have back-up plans available in case the first journal rejects the paper. A manuscript is likely to go through several revisions (drafts) before it is finally accepted for publication.

A study may also have implications for practice. Practitioners can be reached through articles in occupational or trade periodicals. Action research stimulates change by involving the potential users of the information in the research process.

News releases and talks at meetings provide additional ways of getting your information to an audience. Keep such presentations lively and to the point using audiovisual aids when feasible. Practice your presentation ahead of time.

References

Lewin, K. (1946). Action research and minority problems. *Journal of Social Issues, 2,* 34–46.
Sommer, R., & Tyburczy, J. (1978, March). Waiting rooms: A study in user perception. *California Veterinarian, 32,* 21–23.

Further Reading

Day, R. (1983). *How to write and publish a scientific paper* (2nd ed.). Philadelphia: ISI Press.
Foster, M. (1972). An introduction to the theory and practice of action research in work organizations. *Human Relations, 25,* 529–556.
Mullins, C. J. (1982). *A guide to writing and publishing in the social and behavioral sciences.* New York: Wiley.
Schlosberg, H. (1965). Hints on presenting a paper at an APA convention. *American Psychologist, 20,* 606–607.
Stone, Janet, & Bachner, J. (1977). *Speaking up: A book for every woman who wants to speak effectively.* New York: McGraw-Hill.
The *Journal of Applied Behavioral Science* and *Human Relations* emphasize articles on organizational change and the application of social science methods and findings.

22 Concluding Notes

This book began with an introduction to the multimethod approach. This was followed by a discussion of reviewing the literature and research ethics. We then moved to specific methods. First came observational methods, experimental design, interviews and questionnaires, followed by the less common techniques of content analysis, and the case study. We also described the data sources provided by personal documents and archives, as well as apparatus, standardized tests, calculators, and computers. Discussing each technique in a separate chapter may have undermined the notion of a multimethod approach. However, it seemed necessary to discuss each method separately, since the principles involved in running an experiment, for example, are different from those of doing an interview or analyzing personal documents. Having many techniques at your disposal is like being a skilled worker with a kit full of tools. In all likelihood, several tools rather than one will be needed on a specific job. Training and experience will aid you in their selection and use.

The statistical tests described in Chapters 17 and 18 are likely to seem abstract and difficult until you try to use them with your own data. When the questionnaires and observations have a personal significance because you yourself have collected them, the application of statistical tests will be more satisfying and meaningful than when you are using arbitrary numbers from a textbook example. Knowing the origins of statistical tests is not necesary in order to use them. Descriptive statistics are tools for reducing a mass of numbers to a few informative figures such as means, medians, and standard deviations. Inferential statistics are ways of analyzing data that allow you to choose among alternative explanations.

The chapters on reports attempted to place the research process within the larger context of science and practice. The study described was not earthshaking; few studies are. This one was undertaken by a graduate student under the supervision of one of the authors. Portions of it were published—which indicates, among other things, that a study need not be profound in order to be published. As a beginning behavioral scientist, you should aim at doing good research—nothing more. A small, concise study properly done is a better learning experience for the beginner than a massive work that is never completed, analyzed, or written.

Before closing, we would like to offer a few additional suggestions to the beginning researcher. Some of these apply to specific techniques, others to behavioral research in general.

Helpful Hints

Always check reliability. No matter how simple and straightforward the behavior being observed, it is still necessary to check observer reliability. Remember the adaptation of Murphy's law—if something can be misinterpreted, it will be. The number of people in a room should be easy to record reliably. Not so—people come and go and move about. Even a count of billboards, road signs, or some other tangible items is likely to produce discrepancies between observers. Questions arise as to whether store signs along the road count as billboards, whether a sign divided into two parts is considered two signs or one, and so on. A scoring system considered reliable in earlier studies may be interpreted differently by a new observer.

Replication is useful. Don't worry if halfway through your research, you discover that someone has done a similar study. Science depends on repeated observations. If you come up with the same results, you have done a good job. If your results differ, this indicates a problem that must be resolved either through a finer-grained analysis or additional research.

Don't include too much in a single study. For a beginning researcher, there is a great temptation to keep on adding experimental conditions or test questions in the hope of positive results. There is the feeling of foreboding that the study will end inconclusively. Attempting to "cover yourself" by adding more conditions may create even further trouble. Every new variable increases the likelihood of finding relationships due to chance. If you compare enough things enough times, relationships will be found. Do not deceive yourself that such findings are meaningful. With unpredicted findings in a multivariable study, it is necessary to repeat the study at least one more time before there is any assurance that the obtained difference is not a random fluctuation.

Be careful about data collected by others. A tired interviewer may not be strongly motivated to do a good job. Occasionally interviewers have interviewed themselves and written the replies as if they came from other people. Pollster Albert Sindlinger declares, "If you hire somebody with any intelligence, after the tenth interview they are going to sit down and make up the other twenty-five" (Crouse, 1977). This view may seem a bit cynical, but it illustrates the need to check that field interviewers and observers are actually doing their job.

Specify in advance the characteristics for including subjects in the study as clearly and explicitly as possible (e.g., a good command of English, good eyesight and hearing with corrective devices, over age 18 and under 60, and so on). List in advance, if possible, the ways to identify nonserious answers. One possibility is to discard replies that show a fixed or illogical pattern. There is reason to question a person who checks "strongly agree" to every statement, including those for and against an issue. Some researchers automatically discard any questionnaire that shows a stereotyped pattern of responses. Another way of determining nonserious answers is to ask the same questions several times in slightly different form. The person who strongly agrees with one form of the statement but disagrees with another is not a reliable respondent. It is useful to consult with colleagues, other researchers, or fellow students before discarding data. Occasionally, a response that looks unusual will make sense if you know the respondent's particular situation. Obtaining a second opinion will help answer the criticism that replies were rejected because they did not fit the hypothesis.

Double check information. Always check what you are told by those in authority. Seemingly factual statements such as "The park closes at 6:30 P.M." or "All the dormitory residents occupy double rooms" may be incorrect. It is surprising how often administrators are out of touch with what is going on in their own departments. The custodian is likely to know more about people's working habits than the company president. Don't be offensively distrustful of what people say or challenge their statements. Quietly check the facts and figures to see if they are accurate, complete, and current. Numerous horror stories could be recited of people who based their research projects on what authorities told them. A woman studying litter in city parking garages was told that the garages were swept every morning. Not so, she found, during several preliminary vists. The floors were cleaned once every 2 days at most. Had she not inspected the garages, her estimates of litter would have been grossly inflated.

Double check any maps or floor plans that are being used in an observational study. A faulty floor plan can invalidate otherwise good observations. In one study, observers recorded classroom participation in several lecture halls. It was later found that one observer had included an extra row of chairs and another had not indicated clearly the front of the room and occasionally reversed front and back locations. Neither of these errors was detected until after the study was completed. All their data had to be discarded.

Don't overanalyze the data. Only so much can be learned from a single study. Once the totals and averages have been computed, the major trends should be apparent. Overanalysis is a common error among beginning researchers, who are so eager to fully interpret the data that they tend to inflate the results. The amount of "noise" in behavioral research requires caution in interpreting trends that are not obvious. If 69 percent of the managers and 62 percent of the clerical employees are satisfied with working conditions, the difference between them is probably not worth underscoring. The similarity between the two groups seems more significant than the difference.

When the major findings have been extracted from the data, you should seriously consider (1) stopping because you have learned what you wanted, or (2) undertaking another study. Either of these options is likely to be more sensible than spending the next 6 months attempting to squeeze the last bit of information out of the data. People become attached to their findings. This is quite normal; it is good to feel positive toward your findings. However, you should look upon each study as an attempt to answer certain questions. When this has been done, it is time to develop the implications of the findings and answer new questions that have arisen during the study. The danger of becoming bogged down in the data is particularly serious if your results have been analyzed by computer, creating a tremendous stack of printouts. You should accept the fact that most of the comparisions are probably not worth understanding or analyzing. Including them in the report will probably overwhelm the reader and detract attention from the major findings.

Not every study need be earthshaking. Science is a cumulative enterprise. Breakthrough discoveries occasionally occur, but most scientific investigation consists of small studies that shed light on one particular aspect of a topic.

Don't be concerned about the possibility that your methods or findings will be stolen. It is not necessary to copyright your term paper or class project. Sharing your findings with colleagues and fellow students can yield valuable feedback and ideas.

Don't be overly concerned about novelty. Doing good research does not mean demolishing all previous studies in the field. Behavioral science is based on a steady accumulation of solid studies that improves our understanding of human behavior. This includes small and large studies, minor and major adaptations of previous studies, new studies, and replications.

Avoid jargon in talking with outsiders. Scientific terms are intended for communication within the scientific community. A technical vocabulary is essential for keeping terms distinct and meaningful. Nonetheless, the same terminology that is helpful in communicating with other scientists may be a source of confusion and resentment when used with outsiders. Behavioral research is increasingly a collaborative effort, requiring communication with technical people from related fields and with lay people.

Be a responsible critic. Don't seize upon the limitations of a study in order to dismiss the entire project. Every study has its flaws. A responsible critic is obliged not only to indicate the nature of any limitations but how they operate to distort the data. Most of the landmark studies in behavioral research, including the classic investigations of Sigmund Freud, Jean Piaget, and Margaret Mead, were severely flawed in their methodology. The person who blazes a trail into a forest should not be criticized for not building a four-lane highway.

Be especially tolerant of the work of beginning researchers. They are the future of science. Try to specify what is good as well as what is missing in their studies.

Reference

Crouse, T. (1977, April). Washington column. *Esquire*, p. 16.

Appendixes

Appendix A

TABLE A-1. Critical Values for *t* Test[1]

Degrees of freedom (df)	Probability level[2] .05	.01
5	2.57	4.03
6	2.45	3.71
7	2.36	3.50
8	2.31	3.36
9	2.26	3.25
10	2.23	3.17
11	2.20	3.11
12	2.18	3.06
13	2.16	3.01
14	2.14	2.98
15	2.13	2.95
16	2.12	2.92
17	2.11	2.90
18	2.10	2.88
19	2.09	2.86
20	2.09	2.84
25	2.06	2.79
30	2.04	2.75
40	2.02	2.70
50	2.01	2.68
100	1.98	2.63
∞	1.96	2.58

[1]Abridged from Fisher and Yates, *Statistical tables for biological, agricultural, and medical research* (London: Longmans Group, Ltd.), 6th ed., 1974. (Previously published by Oliver and Boyd, Edinburgh.) Used with permission of the authors and publishers.

[2]These are *two-tailed* probability levels. They are used when the investigator has made no specific prediction about the direction of the difference. A *one-tailed* test is used when the investigator has predicted the direction of the difference. The probability levels for a one-tailed test are half those of a two-tailed test. Since two-tailed tests are more conservative, it is good practice to use them routinely.

TABLE A-2. Critical Values for Chi-square Test[1]

Degrees of freedom (df)	Probability level	
	.05	.01
1	3.84	6.63
2	5.99	9.21
3	7.81	11.34
4	9.49	13.28
5	11.07	15.09
6	12.59	16.81
7	14.07	18.48
8	15.51	20.09
9	16.92	21.67
10	18.31	23.21
11	19.68	24.73
12	21.03	26.22
13	22.36	27.69
14	23.68	29.14
15	25.00	30.58
20	31.41	37.57
30	43.77	50.89

[1]See footnotes for Table A-1.

TABLE A-3. Critical Values for Pearson Product-moment Correlation Coefficient (r)[1]

Degrees of freedom (df)	Probability level	
	.05	.01
5	.754	.874
6	.707	.834
7	.666	.798
8	.632	.765
9	.602	.735
10	.576	.708
11	.553	.684
12	.532	.661
13	.514	.641
14	.497	.623
15	.482	.606
16	.468	.590
17	.456	.575
18	.444	.561
19	.433	.549
20	.423	.537
25	.381	.487
30	.349	.449
40	.304	.393
50	.273	.354
60	.250	.325
80	.217	.283
100	.195	.254

[1]See footnotes for Table A-1.

TABLE A-4. Critical Values for Spearman Rank-order Coefficient *(rho)*[1]

Number of pairs N	Probability level[2]	
	.05	.01
5	.900	1.000
6	.829	.943
7	.714	.893
8	.643	.833
9	.600	.783
10	.564	.746
12	.506	.712
14	.456	.645
16	.425	.601
18	.399	.564
20	.377	.534
22	.359	.508
24	.343	.485
26	.329	.465
28	.317	.448
30	.306	.432

[1]Reprinted with permission from E. G. Olds, Distributions of sums of squares of rank differences for small numbers of individuals. *Annals of Mathematical Statistics,* 1938, 133–148.

[2]Unlike the earlier tables, which contain two-tailed probability levels, the levels for *rho* are one-tailed levels. They assume that the researcher has predicted the direction of the relationship as positive or negative. If no prediction has been made, the researcher can use the more conservative .01 probability levels.

TABLE A-5. Abridged Table of Random Numbers

73	17	86	15	27	10	42	72
64	46	07	88	76	45	61	55
19	09	22	09	35	99	76	34
08	72	60	22	84	17	81	39
90	09	97	61	90	37	23	52
34	43	09	17	30	20	59	61
02	48	34	21	18	03	99	61
45	90	33	88	89	70	04	80
03	61	05	61	77	70	17	47
05	56	83	78	26	48	35	06
15	86	60	14	49	10	51	17
38	07	45	88	06	06	29	92
60	22	86	92	52	31	00	47
81	94	25	53	73	89	42	62
87	97	01	09	03	40	86	12
17	35	11	60	12	23	83	26
71	27	96	45	07	60	71	82
66	38	80	72	74	42	21	53
94	84	69	37	69	35	59	32
03	26	07	66	93	88	48	54

TABLE A-6. Critical Values of F

The F ratio is statistically significant when it exceeds or equals the values below. The .05 level is shown in light type; the .01 level in bold type.

Degrees of freedom in numerator

	1	2	3	4	5	6	7	8	9	10	20	50	100	∞
1	161 **4052**	200 **5000**	216 **5402**	225 **5625**	230 **5764**	234 **5859**	237 **5928**	239 **5980**	241 **6022**	242 **6056**	248 **6208**	252 **6302**	253 **6334**	254 **6366**
2	18.51 **98.50**	19.00 **99.00**	19.16 **99.17**	19.25 **99.25**	19.30 **99.30**	19.33 **99.33**	19.36 **99.34**	19.37 **99.36**	19.38 **99.38**	19.39 **99.40**	19.44 **99.45**	19.47 **99.48**	19.49 **99.49**	19.50 **99.50**
3	10.13 **34.12**	9.55 **30.81**	9.28 **29.46**	9.12 **28.71**	9.01 **28.24**	8.94 **27.91**	8.88 **27.67**	8.84 **27.49**	8.81 **27.34**	8.78 **27.23**	8.66 **26.69**	8.58 **26.30**	8.56 **26.23**	8.53 **26.12**
4	7.71 **21.20**	6.94 **18.00**	6.59 **16.69**	6.39 **15.98**	6.26 **15.52**	6.16 **15.21**	6.09 **14.98**	6.04 **14.80**	6.00 **14.66**	5.96 **14.54**	5.80 **14.02**	5.70 **13.69**	5.66 **13.57**	5.63 **13.46**
5	6.61 **16.26**	5.79 **13.27**	5.41 **12.06**	5.19 **11.39**	5.05 **10.97**	4.95 **10.67**	4.88 **10.45**	4.82 **10.27**	4.78 **10.15**	4.74 **10.05**	4.56 **9.55**	4.44 **9.24**	4.40 **9.13**	4.36 **9.02**
6	5.99 **13.74**	5.14 **10.92**	4.76 **9.78**	4.53 **9.15**	4.39 **8.75**	4.28 **8.47**	4.21 **8.26**	4.15 **8.10**	4.10 **7.98**	4.06 **7.87**	3.87 **7.39**	3.75 **7.09**	3.71 **6.99**	3.67 **6.88**
7	5.59 **12.25**	4.74 **9.55**	4.35 **8.45**	4.12 **7.85**	3.97 **7.46**	3.87 **7.19**	3.79 **7.00**	3.73 **6.84**	3.68 **6.71**	3.63 **6.62**	3.44 **6.15**	3.32 **5.85**	3.28 **5.75**	3.23 **5.65**
8	5.32 **11.26**	4.46 **8.65**	4.07 **7.59**	3.84 **7.01**	3.69 **6.63**	3.58 **6.37**	3.50 **6.19**	3.44 **6.03**	3.39 **5.91**	3.34 **5.82**	3.15 **5.36**	3.03 **5.06**	2.98 **4.96**	2.93 **4.86**
9	5.12 **10.56**	4.26 **8.02**	3.86 **6.99**	3.63 **6.42**	3.48 **6.06**	3.37 **5.80**	3.29 **5.62**	3.23 **5.47**	3.18 **5.35**	3.13 **5.26**	2.93 **4.80**	2.80 **4.51**	2.76 **4.41**	2.71 **4.31**
10	4.96 **10.04**	4.10 **7.56**	3.71 **6.55**	3.48 **5.99**	3.33 **5.64**	3.22 **5.39**	3.14 **5.21**	3.07 **5.06**	3.02 **4.95**	2.97 **4.85**	2.77 **4.41**	2.64 **4.12**	2.59 **4.01**	2.54 **3.91**
11	4.84 **9.56**	3.98 **7.20**	3.59 **6.22**	3.36 **5.67**	3.20 **5.32**	3.09 **5.07**	3.01 **4.88**	2.95 **4.74**	2.90 **4.63**	2.86 **4.54**	2.65 **4.10**	2.50 **3.80**	2.45 **3.70**	2.40 **3.60**
12	4.75 **9.33**	3.88 **6.93**	3.49 **5.95**	3.26 **5.41**	3.11 **5.06**	3.00 **4.82**	2.92 **4.65**	2.85 **4.50**	2.80 **4.39**	2.76 **4.30**	2.54 **3.86**	2.40 **3.56**	2.35 **3.46**	2.30 **3.36**
13	4.67 **9.07**	3.80 **6.70**	3.41 **5.74**	3.18 **5.20**	3.02 **4.86**	2.92 **4.62**	2.84 **4.44**	2.77 **4.30**	2.72 **4.19**	2.67 **4.10**	2.46 **3.67**	2.32 **3.37**	2.26 **3.27**	2.21 **3.16**

df													
14	4.60 **8.86**	3.74 **6.51**	3.34 **5.56**	3.11 **5.03**	2.96 **4.69**	2.85 **4.46**	2.77 **4.28**	2.70 **4.14**	2.65 **4.03**	2.60 **3.94**	2.39 **3.51**	2.24 **3.21**	2.19 **3.11**	2.13 **3.00**
15	4.54 **8.68**	3.68 **6.36**	3.29 **5.42**	3.06 **4.89**	2.90 **4.56**	2.79 **4.32**	2.70 **4.14**	2.64 **4.00**	2.59 **3.89**	2.55 **3.80**	2.33 **3.36**	2.18 **3.07**	2.12 **2.97**	2.07 **2.87**
16	4.49 **8.53**	3.63 **6.23**	3.24 **5.29**	3.01 **4.77**	2.85 **4.44**	2.74 **4.20**	2.66 **4.03**	2.59 **3.89**	2.54 **3.78**	2.49 **3.69**	2.28 **3.25**	2.13 **2.96**	2.07 **2.86**	2.01 **2.75**
17	4.45 **8.40**	3.59 **6.11**	3.20 **5.18**	2.96 **4.67**	2.81 **4.34**	2.70 **4.10**	2.62 **3.93**	2.55 **3.79**	2.50 **3.68**	2.45 **3.59**	2.23 **3.16**	2.08 **2.86**	2.02 **2.76**	1.96 **2.65**
18	4.41 **8.28**	3.55 **6.01**	3.16 **5.09**	2.93 **4.58**	2.77 **4.25**	2.66 **4.01**	2.58 **3.85**	2.51 **3.71**	2.46 **3.60**	2.41 **3.51**	2.19 **3.07**	2.04 **2.78**	1.98 **2.68**	1.92 **2.57**
19	4.38 **8.18**	3.52 **5.93**	3.13 **5.01**	2.90 **4.50**	2.74 **4.17**	2.63 **3.94**	2.55 **3.77**	2.48 **3.63**	2.43 **3.52**	2.38 **3.43**	2.15 **3.00**	2.00 **2.70**	1.94 **2.60**	1.88 **2.49**
20	4.35 **8.10**	3.49 **5.85**	3.10 **4.94**	2.87 **4.43**	2.71 **4.10**	2.60 **3.87**	2.52 **3.71**	2.45 **3.56**	2.40 **3.45**	2.35 **3.37**	2.12 **2.94**	1.96 **2.63**	1.90 **2.53**	1.84 **2.42**
25	4.24 **7.77**	3.38 **5.57**	2.99 **4.68**	2.76 **4.18**	2.60 **3.86**	2.49 **3.63**	2.41 **3.46**	2.34 **3.32**	2.28 **3.21**	2.24 **3.13**	2.00 **2.70**	1.84 **2.40**	1.77 **2.29**	1.71 **2.17**
30	4.17 **7.56**	3.32 **5.39**	2.92 **4.51**	2.69 **4.02**	2.53 **3.70**	2.42 **3.47**	2.34 **3.30**	2.27 **3.17**	2.21 **3.06**	2.16 **2.98**	1.93 **2.55**	1.76 **2.24**	1.69 **2.13**	1.62 **2.01**
40	4.08 **7.31**	3.23 **5.18**	2.84 **4.31**	2.61 **3.83**	2.45 **3.51**	2.34 **3.29**	2.25 **3.12**	2.18 **2.99**	2.12 **2.88**	2.07 **2.80**	1.84 **2.37**	1.66 **2.05**	1.59 **1.94**	1.51 **1.81**
50	4.03 **7.17**	3.18 **5.06**	2.79 **4.20**	2.56 **3.72**	2.40 **3.41**	2.29 **3.18**	2.20 **3.02**	2.13 **2.88**	2.07 **2.78**	2.02 **2.70**	1.78 **2.26**	1.60 **1.94**	1.52 **1.82**	1.44 **1.68**
100	3.94 **6.90**	3.09 **4.82**	2.70 **3.98**	2.46 **3.51**	2.30 **3.20**	2.19 **2.99**	2.10 **2.82**	2.03 **2.69**	1.97 **2.59**	1.92 **2.51**	1.68 **2.06**	1.48 **1.73**	1.39 **1.59**	1.28 **1.43**
200	3.89 **6.76**	3.04 **4.71**	2.65 **3.88**	2.41 **3.41**	2.26 **3.11**	2.14 **2.90**	2.05 **2.73**	1.98 **2.60**	1.92 **2.50**	1.87 **2.41**	1.62 **1.97**	1.42 **1.62**	1.32 **1.48**	1.19 **1.28**
∞	3.84 **6.64**	3.00 **4.61**	2.60 **3.78**	2.37 **3.32**	2.21 **3.02**	2.10 **2.80**	2.01 **2.64**	1.94 **2.51**	1.88 **2.41**	1.83 **2.32**	1.57 **1.87**	1.35 **1.52**	1.24 **1.36**	1.00 **1.00**

Degrees of freedom in denominator

Appendix B. Example of an Article Written According to the Style Manual of the American Psychological Association

Chapter 2 contained the research approval form for a study by Kathryn Anthony on the topic of personal space and smoking. The data from this study were also used in the illustration of the t test, found in Chapter 18. Now we will use the study to illustrate the form and layout of a journal article. The presentation follows the style manual of the American Psychological Association. Had the same article been written for a public health journal, which would also have been an appropriate outlet, a different style would have been required. When you write an article for a specific periodical, it is necessary to consult either the style manual issued by the publisher or a recent issue of the journal. If you are writing a research report not intended for publication, check the style used by others who have written similar reports.

SMOKING, PERSONAL SPACE, AND PERSON PERCEPTION
Kathryn H. Anthony
University of California, Berkeley

Abstract

Seventy-six college students were asked to converse with another person and rate the other person afterward. During approximately half the sessions, the other person was smoking; the rest of the time, the other person was not. Both conversational distance and negative trait impressions increased when the other person was smoking. In a waiting room situation, students changed places more often when seated next to a lit cigarette in an ashtray than when they were next to a soda cup. The implications of these findings for public areas that accommodate both smokers and nonsmokers were discussed.

There is considerable concern about the need for separating smokers from nonsmokers in public areas. Little objective research has been done on the spatial distance that nonsmokers remain from smokers under natural conditions. Hostility of many nonsmokers toward smokers is shown in a study by Bleda and Sandman (1977). The researchers invited 75 male soldiers to participate in a task with another man who either didn't smoke, smoked in a courteous manner, or blew smoke toward the subject. Afterward each subject rated his task mate in terms of politeness, likability, consider-ateness, and desirability as a partner, and rated his own feelings during the experience. Nonsmokers considered smokers, regardless of whether they smoked courteously or blew smoke right at them, to be less considerate, less polite, and less personally attractive than were subjects who did not smoke.

Weir (1967) showed 347 male high school students a matched series of photographs that were identical, except that sometimes the person in the photograph was smoking and sometimes not. Subjects were asked to describe each person in the photograph using an adjective checklist. The smoking models were perceived as being more adventurous and immature and had narrow interests, while nonsmoking models were perceived as more mature, frank, and having broader interests.

People's use of space provides many clues to their motives and feelings (Hall, 1959; Mehrebian, 1974; Sommer, 1969). The present study was designed to find out whether smoking would affect conversational distance. It was hypothesized that subjects in a conversation would stand farther away from someone who was smoking than from someone who wasn't smoking. It was further predicted that subjects would assign more negative ratings to the personality of the smoker than of the nonsmoker.

Experiment 1
Method

A total of 76 undergraduates (42 males and 34 females) served as subjects for the experiment. They were volunteers from an introductory psychology class who received small amounts of extra credit for their participation. Most (71) were nonsmokers, while 5 were current smokers. The experiment was conducted in a large office, which was carpeted, had two large windows, and was well ventilated. Subjects were asked to enter the office one at a time and were introduced to a decoy, who was a confederate of the experimenter. Both male and female decoys were used in each of the experimental conditions.

Then 37 such subjects were introduced to a nonsmoking decoy and 39 to a decoy who was smoking. Subjects were asked to "choose the distance most comfortable for conversation between you and _____,

assuming you had just met." Once the student had assumed this distance, this phase of the experiment was essentially complete. A tape measure was placed by the experimenter from the tip of the subject's foot to the tip of the decoy's foot, and the distance was measured in centimeters. Following this, the subjects were asked to complete a questionnaire about the decoy. The questionnaire contained 18 pairs of attributes, half negative and half positive. Subjects were asked to check one item from each pair to describe their immediate impressions of the other person. Subjects were also asked, "Would you choose this person as your friend?" Subjects were asked if they had any further comments about the experiment before being told the purposes of the experiment by the researcher.

TABLE 1. Mean Distance from Smoking and Nonsmoking Decoy

Experimental condition	Av. distance from decoy (cm)	Standard deviation (σ)	t ratio (t)	Probability level (p)
Smoking decoy N = 39	80.3	24.1		
			3.36	.01
Nonsmoking decoy N = 37	62.5	21.4		

Results

Subjects were found to stand an average fo 62.5 cm from the nonsmoking decoy and 80.3 cm from the smoking decoy. A t test showed that this difference was statistically reliable ($t = 3.36$, $df = 74$, $p < .01$).

A finding that had not been expected was that subjects stood farther away from male decoys than from female decoys. The mean distance from male decoys was 78.1 cm, whereas the mean distance from female decoys was 63.5 cm ($t = 2.70$, $df = 74$, $p <$

.01). While the sex of the decoy made a difference in how far away people stood, the sex of the subject did not make a difference.

Following the personal space experiment, the subjects were asked to complete a personality questionnaire about the decoy. The average number of negative traits assigned to the smoking decoy was 6.4 compared to 2.2 for the nonsmoking decoy. This difference was analyzed through a nonparametric Kruskal-Wallis test.[1] Results showed that

[1] This statistical test is useful when continuous data are not normally distributed. Like most other special-purpose statistical tests, it is beyond the scope of this chapter. It is mentioned here because it was used in the actual study by Anthony and to remind the reader that there are many useful special-purpose statistical tests. Further information about this and other tests appropriate for data that are not normally distributed can be found in most statistics books under the chapter heading "Nonparametric Statistics."

the number of negative attributes assigned to the smoking decoy was significantly greater than those assigned to the nonsmoking decoy.

Because only 5 of the subjects were smokers and these were spread over the two treatment conditions, no statistical comparison of their results was possible. We did not choose to recruit subjects on the basis of their smoking habits, as this might have biased our results.

Experiment 2

Subjects scheduled for the experiment spent several minutes waiting outside the office door before the session. This presented an opportunity to conduct a brief observational study to see if the presence of a lit cigarette in an ashtray would alter the subject's choice of seats. Specifically, it was predicted that subjects would sit farther away from a lit cigarette in an ashtray than they would from another object of similar size.

Method

For the last 27 subjects, a row of 5 identical chairs was lined up directly outside the experimental room. Subjects were scheduled for the experiment at 10-minute intervals and asked to have a seat outside the office while waiting. When two people arrived simultaneously, one was sent away and asked to return shortly. For 13 subjects, a styrofoam cup half full of soda containing a straw was placed on the first of 5 chairs, directly adjacent to the office door. In that location, 14 subjects were confronted with a lit cigarette in an ashtray.

Results

The two groups of subjects displayed radically different behaviors. Subjects who selected a chair near the soda remained there throughout their waiting time. However, those sitting close to the lit cigarette underwent a number of behavioral adaptations. Some stood up, some moved to another seat, one moved the ashtray to the floor, and one subject extinguished the cigarette.

Discussion

These results coincide with those of other researchers, who found that positive relationships are reflected by closer spatial distances. Subjects rated the personality of the smoking decoy negatively and also stood farther away from the smoking decoy. That the sex of the decoy affected interpersonal distance is also coincident with other research. Several studies have shown that subjects are more likely to sit and stand closer to females than to males (Leibman, 1970; Little, 1968). However, another factor may produce these results. Height of the decoys may influence the subject's distance from them. Generally speaking, the male decoys were taller than the female decoys. Conversing with a tall person may force one to move farther back so as not to strain one's neck. The relationship of height differences to personal space is an area which needs to be explored.

That subjects attributed more negative judgments to the smoking decoy supports the finding of Weir (1967), who examined people's perceptions of smokers and nonsmokers. He found, as we did, that smoking made the subject's evaluation of another person more negative.

These results raise some interesting questions about the motives of smokers. The present study has documented that people leave more distance between themselves and others who are smoking. It is an interesting hypothesis that smokers may use their smoking to obtain greater distance from other people, to increase their privacy in the same way that a teenager uses a transistor radio to create a curtain of sound.

References

Bleda, P. R., & Sandman, P. H. (1977). In smoke's way. *Journal of Applied Psychology, 62,* 452–458.

Hall, E. T. (1959). *The silent language.* Garden City, NY: Doubleday.

Leibman, M. (1970). The effects of sex and race norms on personal space. *Environment and Behavior, 2,* 208–246.

Little, K. B. (1968). Cultural variations in social schemata. *Journal of Personality and Social Psychology, 10,* 1–7.

Mehrebian, A. (1974). *Nonverbal communication.* Chicago: Aldine.

Sommer, R. (1969). *Personal Space.* Englewood Cliffs, NJ: Prentice-Hall.

Weir, J. M. (1967). Male student perceptions of smokers. In S. V. Zagora (Ed.), *Studies and issues in smoking behavior.* Tucson: University of Arizona Press.

Appendix C. Example of Style Used for a Technical Report

The following report was produced in England by a research laboratory affiliated with a government agency. It is a good example of a brief, focused, and well-written technical report. The problem, methods, findings, and conclusions are clearly stated. The limitations of the study, in terms of artificiality of the experimental roadway and the experienced volunteer subjects, are mentioned. The full document consisted of a blue-and-white cover of a style used by the research laboratory, 4 pages of introductory material, 17 pages of text, and 12 pages of appendices. Because the report is used in this section to illustrate style, some of the details are abridged or omitted. The report is presented through the courtesy of the Transport and Road Research Laboratory, Berkshire, England.

TRANSPORT AND ROAD RESEARCH LABORATORY
Department of the Environment
Department of Transport
SUPPLEMENTARY REPORT 357
ATTITUDES OF A SAMPLE OF CYCLISTS TO USING SINGLE-LANE ROADS
F. J. Nicholson

Any views expressed in this report are not necessarily those of the Department of the Environment or of the Department of Transport.

1978
Table of Contents

ATTITUDES OF A SAMPLE OF CYCLISTS TO USING SINGLE-LANE ROADS
Abstract

This Report describes an experiment to determine the attitudes of 25 cyclists to sharing single-lane roads with motor vehicles. Three widths of road (2.75 m, 3.00 m and 3.25 m) were examined and, on each width of road, all cyclists both passed a car traveling in the opposite direction and were overtaken by a car.

Objective measurements and the responses given by the cyclists to questionnaires are presented and compared. Variations in results according to road width, age of cyclist and manoeuvre undertaken are discussed.

Generally, no significant difference was found between results for the two age groups of cyclists (under sixteen and sixteen or over) or for the two manoeuvres. Cyclists stated that they felt unsafe in 22 of the 50 runs on the 2.75 m wide road, in 10 of the 49 runs on the 3.00 m wide road and in 0 of the 49 runs on the 3.25 m wide road. Whilst there was a diversity of opinion amongst the cyclists over whether single-lane roads are a good concept, a width of 3.00 m for such roads was found to be acceptable to many subjects and 3.25 m to virtually all.

No attempt is made in this report to predict the likely safety record of such single-lane roads.

1. Introduction

The Housing Development Directorate (HDD) of the Department of Environment has proposed that single-lane access roads up to 4.00 m in width could be used on housing estates. Guidelines on the design of such roads have been published recently as a Design Bulletin. The Laboratory has cooperated with HDD in investigating various aspects of this proposal. One investigation was concerned with the use of such single-lane roads by cyclists. This Report describes an experiment conducted at TRRL in August 1976 to determine the attitudes of a number of cyclists towards sharing single-lane roads with motor vehicles. No attempt is made to predict the likely safety record of such single-lane roads.

Recommendations are given on the minimum width required for single-lane roads if cyclists are to find them acceptable.

2. Experimental Method

2.1 Experimental Layout

. . . In planning the cycling experiment, it was decided that it was necessary to determine the attitude of cyclists to the "worst" conditions that they would be likely to encounter regularly on the access roads. It was therefore decided to investigate the attitudes of the cyclists to two manoeuvres that they would have to execute on single-lane roads. The manoeuvres were (a) to meet and pass a motor vehicle at a point between two passing bays, and (b) to be overtaken by a motor vehicle at a point between two passing bays . . .

2.2 Experimental Procedure

Two tests per cyclist were carried out for each of the three experimental widths . . .

2.3 Selection of Cyclists for the Experiment

Cyclist subjects were obtained by placing advertisements in local papers, asking for volunteer cyclists aged 16 and over, and by issuing a circular within the laboratory asking for volunteers aged under 16 from among children of staff . . . The overall division of the subjects by sex and by eligibility to hold a motor vehicle license corresponded with the distribution of an earlier travel survey . . .

2.4 Selection of Drivers and Vehicles for the Experiment

As school children were involved in the experiment, vehicles had to be driven by (drivers associated with the laboratory). Four drivers took part in the experiment. Careful consideration was given to the type of motor vehicle to be used . . .

2.5 Method of Analysis

The analysis of the experiment fell into three sections (a) analysis of the time-lapse film, (b) analysis of the questionnaire responses, and (c) comparison of the result of the film and questionnaire analyses . . .

3. Results

(This section contained 11 pages, including nine tables with descriptive text.)

4. Conclusions

1. The conditions for the experiment and the experience and physical stability of the 25 cyclists taking part were, on the average, better than might be expected in reality . . .

2. The results of the experiment did not, in general, differ according to either the age group of the subjects or the type of manoeuvres carried out (meeting, passing, or overtaking).

3. Cyclists said they felt unsafe in 22 of the 50 runs simulating a road 2.57 meters wide, in 10 of the 49 runs on a 3.00 meter road, and on none of the 49 runs on a 3.25 meter road . . .

4. Thirteen of the 25 subjects at some time thought that other cyclists would have felt less safe. . . . The main reasons given by the subjects for feeling safer were that they considered themselves to be more experienced and more physically stable than other cyclists and that the experimental conditions were artificially safe.

5. Observations from film of the experiment showed that the incidence of motorists driving off the road decreased as the width of the road increased. . . .

6. Cyclists generally failed to report significant events such as their slowing down or motorists driving off the road. They were also poor judges of whether the motorist had left as much clearance as possible. . . .

7. There was a diversity of opinion among the cyclists over whether the sharing of single-lane roads with motor vehicles is a good idea.

8. Given the limitations of conclusions

1-7 above, an actual road width of 3 meters is acceptable to a substantial number of the subjects and an actual road width of 3.25 meters is acceptable to virtually all subjects.

9. The results of this experiment show clearly the attitudes of a small number of cyclists to the shared use of single lanes but cannot give any guide to the likely safety record of such facilities.

5. Acknowledgments

(Statement of thanks to cooperating agencies.)

6. References

(Presented in numerical order as they appeared in text.)

7. Appendix

(Copies of questionnaires, diagrams and photograph of experimental roadway, and bar graphs showing results.)

Glossary

Accidental Sample A nonprobability sample comprised of those individuals available for study. Sometimes called a convenience sample.

Accretion The buildup of a residue or product of an interaction; something added to the situation.

Action Research Combines the testing of theory with application. Approach pioneered by Kurt Lewin.

Aggregate Data Analysis Studying the characteristics of groups using census data or other social statistics.

Alternative Hypothesis Although the null hypothesis is stated in negative terms (that there will be no effect), the working or alternative hypothesis is stated in positive terms (i.e., that there will be an effect).

Analysis of Covariance An adaptation of analysis of variance that takes into account scores on an additional variable believed to affect the independent variable.

Analysis of Variance or ANOVA Statistical technique for comparing differences between means. See Chapter 18 for computational procedures.

Anonymity Refers to a situation in behavioral science research in which the researcher does not know the identity of the participants in the study (i.e., observing people at a street corner or bus station).

ANOVA See *Analysis of Variance*.

Applied Research Uses systematic procedures to provide answers to pressing questions. Motivated primarily by the need to solve an immediate problem.

Archives Public records and documents.

Attitude Scale A type of questionnaire designed to produce scores indicating the overall degree of favorability of a person's attitude on a topic.

Average A generic term referring to various measures of central tendency—the mean, median, and mode.

Balance In survey research, balance refers to the neutrality of questions and providing sufficient items so that those leaning toward one view are balanced by an equal number leaning toward the other view.

Bar Graph Graph made up of bars showing frequency of occurrence of scores or category levels. Also called a histogram.

Basic Research Investigation designed to answer general long-range questions. Motivated primarily by curiosity.

Behavioral Map A chart of peoples' locations in space. Maps can be place centered or person centered.

Behavior Setting Geographic location linked to customary patterns of behavior.

Blind Testing In sensory evaluation or drug research, blind testing indicates that the subject is not aware of the identity of the stimulus. If the experimenter is also unaware of the identity of the stimulus, this is called a *double blind procedure*.

Case Study In-depth investigation of a single instance. The unit can be as small as an individual or as large as an entire community.

Casual Observation Observation without prearranged categories or scoring system. Eyeball inspection of what is happening.

Categorical Variable Variable with mutually exclusive categories, whose levels are more qualitative than quantitative. Gender and place of residence are generally categorical variables.

Chi-square A statistical test used with categorical data to test whether an obtained distribution of scores differs reliably from what would be expected by chance.

Closed Questions Respondents are asked to choose among fixed alternative answers; also known as multiple-choice questions.

Coding The transformation or reduction of raw data into a set of standard categories for statistical analysis. Frequently used in scoring responses to open-ended interview questions and in content analysis of mass media.

Cognitive Map A cognitive representation of the location of objects in space.

Confidentiality Participant or respondent identity is known to researcher but is not publicly revealed. Frequently achieved by removing identifying information from published reports.

Confounding Confusion of the effects of variables, resulting in an inability to determine which variable is the cause of an observed effect.

Connotative Meaning The subjective or personal meaning of something, as distinct from its physical characteristics.

Content Subject matter; in content analysis, refers to specific topics or themes, in contrast with format that refers to form or structure.

Content Analysis A technique for systematically describing the form and content of written or spoken material. Frequently used for quantitative study of mass media.

Continuous Variable Variable with a continuous distribution of scores, such as age or income.

Control Group A subject group that resembles the experimental group in every respect except that it is not exposed to the independent variable. Used to control for the effects of extraneous variables on the dependent variable.

Converging Operations Using several procedures rather than one in conducting research on a topic.

Correlation The association between two sets of scores. Often expressed in terms of a *correlation coefficient,* which is a numerical indication of the degree of relationship between two sets of scores.

Counterbalancing Reversing the order of presentation of variables.

Cumulative Scores Accumulation of frequencies from the bottom to the top of a frequency distribution, formed by starting at the bottom of a frequency distribution and summing all the frequencies at and below each level. Can be transferred into a *cumulative percentage* by dividing each score by the total number of cases and multiplying by 100.

Degrees of Freedom The number of values that are free to vary after certain restrictions have been placed on the data. Used to evaluate the results of various statistical tests.

Dependent Variable Assumed to be influenced by or dependent on the independent variable. If you study the effects of alcohol on speed of response, then speed of response is the dependent variable in this experiment.

Depth Interview A form of unstructured interview in which the interviewer follows the respondent's answers with a request for more information at an increasing level of depth.

Descriptive Statistics Techniques to organize and summarize data. Numerical values describing the characteristics of or within a sample.

Double Blind Procedure A research design in which neither the experimenter nor subject is aware of which treatment condition to which the subject has been assigned.

Equivalent Forms Two different, but comparable forms of a scale; used for assessing reliability or to avoid practice effects.

Erosion The deterioration or wear that provides an index of usage patterns; something is worn down or removed.

Ethnography A type of qualitative research involving the description and study of specific peoples and places.

Experimental Group A subject group exposed to the independent variable; sometimes called the treatment group.

External Validity The generalizability of research findings.

Extraneous Variable A source of error, other than the independent variable, which might influence the dependent variable.

Face Validity The appearance of being a valid measure of something; a measure that "looks right" to an outside observer.

Factor The independent variable or treatment. A study investigating the effects of age and education on attitude would be a two-factor study. If additional factors, such as gender were added, this would become a multifactorial study.

Factorial Design Involves more than a single factor or independent variable in a study.

Field Experiment Experiment in which the independent variable is manipulated in a natural setting rather than in a laboratory.

Format Structure; pertains to the appearance, order, and wording of items in a questionnaire or interview; in contrast to content, which refers to meaning.

Frequency Number of times a score or category level occurs.

Frequency Distribution Arrangement of scores from highest to lowest, together with the frequency of each score (i.e., the number of times each score occurs).

Frequency Polygon or Curve A type of graph representing a frequency distribution, in which a continuous line is used to indicate the frequency of the corresponding scores.

Graphic Rating Scale The respondent places a mark along a continuous line.

Halo Effect The tendency to make rating of specific abilities on the basis of an overall impression.

Histogram Similar to a bar graph.

Horizontal Axis The straight line at the base of a graph.

Hypothesis A research question phrased in the form of a statement; a testable proposition.

Independent Variable The variable that is systematically manipulated by the researcher. Also known as the experimental variable.

Inferential Statistics Statistical techniques used to make generalizations from samples to populations.

Instrumental Research Undertaken as an academic, vocational, or professional requirement. Goal is to demonstrate competence in research.

Internal Validity   The degree to which the instruments or procedures in a study measure what they are supposed to measure.

Latent Content   The less obvious and hidden information, the underlying meaning of a response as distinct from the manifest content, which is on the surface and obvious.

Legend   Title and brief description accompanying a table, figure, or graph.

Level   The amount or value of a variable; dimensions along which a single variable differs. Using hair color as a variable, the levels are blond, brunette, etc.

Life History   Biographical technique useful in qualitative research.

Likert Scale   A type of attitude scale containing statements that are clearly favorable or clearly unfavorable. The respondent indicates degree of agreement.

Mainframe Computers   Computers capable of manipulating large data sets, generally available only at large institutions.

Manifest Content   That portion of an interview or response that is obvious and contained in the spoken or written information. Can be contrasted to latent content that is less obvious.

Matched Groups   Assigning subjects so that the experimental and control groups are as similar as possible. A means of controlling extraneous variables.

Mean   Arithmetic average; sum of scores divided by the number of cases.

Median   Midpoint of the distribution when all the scores are arranged from highest to lowest. Half the scores fall above the median and half below.

Microcomputers   Small, desk-size personal computers.

Mode   The single score that occurs most often in a distribution. If there are two modes, the distribution is called *bimodal.*

Multivariate Analysis   Analysis of the interrelationships among several variables at the same time. For example, in an opinion survey, the effects of age, education, and income could be analyzed simultaneously through the use of multivariate analysis.

Natural Experiment   A study which uses a naturally occurring event or policy change as the independent variable. Not a true experiment because the researcher does not directly manipulate or control the independent variable, and/or the subjects are not randomly assigned to treatment conditions.

Networking   A strategy of gaining information by using the references in recent articles to find other related articles or information.

Nonprobability Samples   The likelihood of selection is not actually known to the researcher. Three general types are quota, purposive, and accidental samples.

Normal Curve   A symetrical bell-shaped curve which often approximates the frequency of occurrence of events in nature.

Null Hypothesis   A conservative way of phrasing the research questions, to state that the independent variable has no effect on the dependent variable.

Open-ended Questions   Respondents fill in their own answers.

Operational Definition   Defining a variable by the means used to measure it. Intelligence can be operationally defined as a score on an IQ test.

Panel Study   Frequently used in public opinion research, in which the same sample of respondents is interviewed on repeated occasions.

Participant Observation   The observer becomes part of the event being studied and uses this position to make observations.

Pearson Product-moment Correlation (r)   A widely used statistic for measuring the relationship between two sets of scores that are assumed to be continuously distributed.

Person-centered Map   A diagram showing people's movements and activities over a specified period of time.

Place-centered Map   A diagram showing how people arrange themselves within a particular location.

Population   The entire group of people, objects, or events in a category.

Probability Level   When used in statistics, it indicates the likelihood that an obtained difference on a statistical test is due to chance alone. A common practice in behavioral research is to use the .05 probability level (also called the .05 level of significance).

Probability Sample   A sample that is drawn in such a way that the probability for the inclusion of any given individual can be estimated. Two general types of probability samples are *random samples* and *stratified samples.*

Probe   A question or comment during an interview designed to keep the person talking or obtain clarification.

Program Evaluation   Systematic procedures used to determine the effectiveness of a program.

Projective Test   An instrument used in clinical testing and research that relies on questions or stimuli that are deliberately vague or incomplete.

Psychophysics   The connection between the physical qualities of objects and their sensory attributes; very important in sensory evaluation.

Purposive Sample   A type of nonprobability sample in which the individuals considered most relevant to the issue studied are selected for inclusion.

Quantification   Expressing information in numbers.

Quasi-Experiment   Also known as a natural experiment or ex post facto experiment. An experiment in which the independent variable occurs naturally and is not under the direct control of the experimenter.

Questionnaire   A series of written questions on a topic about which the respondents' opinions are sought.

Quota Sample   A type of nonprobability sampling in which quotas are assigned to characteristics according to the needs of the investigator, and then sampling is done to achieve these quotas.

r   See Pearson product-moment coefficient.

Random Assignment   Subjects in an experiment are randomly placed in treatment and control groups. A means of controlling extraneous variables.

Random Sample   Every individual in the entire population being studied has an equal chance of being selected.

Range   A measure of dispersion or variability, computed by subtracting the lowest from the highest score.

Raw Data   Firsthand scores or measures. The actual measurements or data collected before they have been reduced, coded, or analyzed.

Regression   Pertains to correlation; the relationships between sets of scores.

Reliability   Consistency in measurement; the repeatability or replicability of findings.

Repeated Measures Design   Research design involving the same subjects studied at different times or under different conditions.

Replication   To repeat an earlier study to see if its findings can be duplicated. Important in increasing the confidence in research results.

Rho   See Spearman rank-order coefficient.

Salience   Refers to the importance of an issue in people's minds.

Sample   The group of individuals selected for testing from a population is called a sample. The sample is used to make generalizations about the population from which it was drawn.

Sampling Bias   The error introduced by a sampling procedure that favors certain characteristics over others.

Sampling Error   Chance variation among samples selected from the same population.

Scale   A series of ordered steps at fixed intervals used as a standard of measurement.

Semantic Differential   A rating scale developed by Charles Osgood for measuring the meaning of concepts.

Simulation   Deliberate creation of an artificial reality. Depends less on literal resemblance than on functional resemblance.

Skewed Distribution   A distribution of scores that deviates markedly from a normal curve.

Snowball Sample   A type of purposive (nonprobability) sample in which the researcher asks respondents for other people who should be contacted.

Spearman Rank-order Coefficient (rho)   Correlation coefficient used with ranked data. Used in place of the Pearson product-moment correlation coefficient when a distribution contains extreme scores.

Split-Half Method   A means of determining reliability by comparing two halves of a scale.

Standard Deviation   A measure of dispersion or variability; sometimes abbreviated S.D. or σ. See Chapter 17 for method of computation.

Step Scale   On a questionnaire the respondent is required to select one of a graded series of intervals.

Stimulus-Response(S-R) Learning   The development of associations between specific stimuli and specific responses. Theory developed by C. Hull.

Stratified Sample   A type of probability sampling in which the characteristics of the sample are selected to be proportionate to those present in the total population.

Structured Interview   Questions are formulated beforehand and asked in a set manner in a specified order. Often called a *standardized interview*.

Subjects   Research participants or respondents.

Survey Research   The systematic gathering of information about peoples' beliefs, attitudes, values, and behavior.

Systematic Observation   Employs a scoring system and prearranged categories that are applied consistently.

t Test   Statistical technique used for comparing two groups. See Chapter 18.

Test   A systematic procedure for comparing people's performance, feelings, attitudes, or values.

Test-Retest Method   A means of determining reliability by administering a scale twice to the same people and comparing scores.

Thurstone Scale   A type of attitude scale in which people check only those statements with which they agree. A respondent's score is computed by adding up the average rating of all statements checked, and dividing by the number of statements checked.

Time Sampling Procedure   Specific times are selected according to a sampling plan for recording observed activities.

Trace Measures   Physical remains of interaction after the individuals have departed. Two types of physical traces useful in behavioral research are accretion and erosion.

Transcription Putting interview or questionnaire responses into clear form for data analysis.

Treatment Condition Refers to the presence of the independent variable, as opposed to the control condition in which the independent (experimental) variable is absent.

Unstructured Interview Although the interviewer has a general topic in mind, there is no predetermined order or specified wording to the questions.

Validity An indication that the measure accurately reflects what it is supposed to measure.

Value In research design, value refers to the amount of a variable (e.g., on a test of motor coordination with scores that can range from 1 to 20, the individual scores will represent values of the variable of motor coordination). Value has numerous other meanings in economics, philosophy, etc.

Variability The amount of spread or dispersion within a distribution of scores. The more commonly used measures of variability are the range and the standard deviation.

Variable Any characteristic or quality that differs in degree or kind. Variables have values or levels and may either be continuous or categorical.

Vertical Axis The perpendicular line showing the graph boundary. Often used to indicate frequency.

Name Index

Subject Index

Accidental sample, 200, 201, 204, 283
Accretion, 55, 57, 283
Action research, 5, 283
Aggregate data analysis, 167, 283
Alternative hypothesis, 220, 283
Analysis of variance, 221, 226–31, 242, 283
  calculation, 227–30
  table of critical values, 274–75
  groups of unequal size, 230
  one way, 226
Analysis of covariance, 231, 283
Anonymity, 13, 283
ANOVA. *See* Analysis of variance
Anthropologists' code of ethics, 17–18
Apparatus supply firms, 178
Appendix in report, 256
Applied research, 4–5, 283
Archives, 165, 168, 283
Attitude scales, 131–36, 145, 283
  comparison of Thurstone and Likert
    scales, 135
  prediction of behavior, 146
  validity, 136
Attitudes toward marijuana, 133
Audio recorders, 182
Audiovisual aids, 263–64
Autobiographies, 162, 163, 164, 168
Average, 197, 283

Bar graph, 208, 210, 216, 283
Basic research, 4–5, 283
Behavioral map, 44, 283
Behavior setting, 43, 283
Bias, in published statistics, 166
Bimodal distribution, 213
Biography, 163
Biserial coefficient, 228
Blind testing, 145, 146, 283

Cafeteria ratings, 126–27
Calculators, 244–45
Cartoons, 155
Case study, 284
  conversion to quasi-experiment, 171
  generalization from, 174
Casual observation, 30–33, 41, 108, 284
Categorical measures, 206, 216, 231
  variables, 64–65, 284
Census figures, 167
Central tendency, measures, 211
Chi-square, 231–34, 242, 284
  table of critical values, 270

Closed questions, 109, 128–29, 284
Coding, 102–3, 152–3, 284
Cognitive map, 61, 284
Comparative rating scales, 131, 145
Composite map, 47, 49
Computers, 245–47
Confidentiality, 13, 284
Confounding, 65
Connotative meaning, 136, 146, 284
Consumer rating scales, 141–42, 146
Content, 284
  in content analysis, 152
  of a questionnaire, 107–8
Contingency coefficient, 238
Contingency table, 232
Continuous measures, 205–6, 221
Continuous variable, 64, 284
Control group, 67, 284
Converging operations, 7, 284
Correlated measures, 222
Correlation, 234–38, 284
  of continuous and ranked variables, 238
  and causation, 235
Counterbalancing, 72–73, 138, 284
Covariance, analysis of, 231
Cross verification, in case study, 173
Cumulative scores, 284
  frequencies, 207–8
  percentage, 208, 210
Curve, 210

Data analysis, computer programs, 246–47
Degrees of freedom, 225, 226, 284
Dependent variable, 65, 67, 72, 74, 75, 284
Depth interview, 89, 285
Descriptive statistics, 205, 285
Diaries, 159
Direct consultation, 24
Dissemination, 260
Dot-matrix printers, 246
Double blind procedure, 145, 146, 285
Drug advertising, 151

Equivalent forms, 135, 136, 146, 285
Erosion, 55, 57, 285
Error, 192
Ethical code
  anthropology, 17–18
  psychology, 15–17
  sociology, 18
Ethnography, 35–36, 285
Executive summary, 255